Modern Urban Housing
in China
1840–2000

Modern Urban Housing in China 1840–2000

Edited by
Lü Junhua, Peter G. Rowe and Zhang Jie

Prestel
Munich · London · New York

© Prestel Verlag, Munich · London · New York, 2001
© All illustrations courtesy of Lü Junhua and Zhang Jie, by prior arrangement
with the respective copyright holders where applicable.

Prestel Verlag
Mandlstrasse 26, D-80802 Munich, Germany
Tel.: +49 (89) 381709-0, Fax: +49 (89) 381709-35

4 Bloomsbury Place, London WC1A2QA
Tel.: +44 (0)20 7323-5004, Fax: +44(0)20 7636-8004

175 Fifth Avenue, Suite 402, New York, NY, 10010
Tel.: +1 (212) 995-2720, Fax: +1 (212) 995-2733
www.prestel.com

Prestel books are available worldwide.
Please contact your nearest bookseller or write to any of the above addresses
for information concerning your local distributor.

Library of Congress Card Number: 2001086375
Die Deutsche Bibliothek – CIP Einheitsaufnahme
Cataloging data is available

Line drawings by Qu Lei
Copyedited by Bruce Murphy
Designed by Ulrike Schmidt
Lithograph by Reproteam Siefert, Ulm
Printed and bound by Passavia, Passau

Printed in Germany on acid-free paper

ISBN 3-7913-2507-8

Table of Contents

Acknowledgements

This book was the result of ongoing collaboration between the School of Architecture at Tsinghua University and the Graduate School of Design at Harvard University in the form of a joint research project, generously sponsored, in part, by David Lie and other participants in the Harvard-Tsinghua Architecture and Urban Studies Fund.

The authors would like to thank the institutions and personnel who have provided generous support and assistance for this research work. Special thanks are due to Tsinghua School of Architecture for its strong support of this project, especially to Prof. Wu Liangyong, Prof. Qin Youguo, Prof. Zuochuan and Prof. Hu Shaoxue. A similar sentiment is expressed to Prof. Krieger, John Driscoll, Huang Lei and Wang Bing at Harvard for their timely contributions along the way. Also the Reference Library of the Tsinghua School of Architecture has provided important assistance to the research work, including its generous permission to reproduce some of its collections of historic photos. Similarly, the Second Municipal Historic Archive of Nanjing City kindly opened their relevant material on research topics.

Also, many experts in China have given valuable advice on this book, including Prof. Yu Minfei, Prof. Luo Baotian, Prof. Kai Yan, Prof. Lü Zhenying, Prof. Zhao Guanqian, Prof. Jin Liming, Prof. Lü Junmin and Prof. Lü Guofu.

The authors would also like to thank John Nilson, Liu Lifeng and Ding Jian for their assistance during data collection for this book, as well as Maria Moran and Maggie Zong for their assistance in manuscript preparation.

Translator's Note

In the translation of the Chinese portions of this text into English, an attempt has been made to preserve the way in which the story was told. This includes retention of what might seem like a certain amount of repetition in argument, persistent references backwards and forwards in the historical narrative to milestone events, the habit of using slogans for underlying principles of action and the use, at times, of relatively arcane terminology.

Preface

by Wu Liangyong

China, like many other nations in the world, has its own splendid culture, including architecture, of which housing is an important part. Given its vast lands, long history and great ethnic diversity, China has enjoyed a rich residential culture and tradition since ancient times. Subsequently, after the 1920s and 1930s, residential architecture began to draw increasing academic interest. Furthermore, the great housing needs soon after the founding of the People's Republic of China in the 1950s encouraged fruitful research into traditional housing in different regions. After the low period of the 1960s and 1970s, housing issues in China have once again regained the attention of scholars from both home and abroad. Reports and publications have come out and this activity has helped to deepen housing research in China.

Academic interest in modern urban housing in China, however, has only increased recently. Despite the significance of this period of housing development and its valuable lessons, the focus of previous work was usually given to isolated topics, and a systematic treatment of the topic remained to be done. Consequently, confusion existed about some questions, and this confusion sometimes still affects thinking in the field today.

Quantitatively, China has achieved remarkable success in housing development, especially over the last twenty years. But, from the point of view of design, there has been a considerable shortage of knowledge and practice about housing types and systems, partially resulting from the lack of professional dedication by architects to become involved in housing design and research. Consequently, we see very few examples of housing projects that reflect the future direction of modern architecture with, for instance, consideration of local climate, culture, community, economics and technological conditions. Reviewing the development of housing in China, I feel strongly that many fields need to be explored and a great deal of work still needs to be done. Opportunities are opening up now for housing studies and for deepening housing reforms, as well as for responding to the increasing housing needs of China's urban population. Fortunately, today we can anticipate more achievements and developments in these regards.

With an understanding of this situation and at the suggestion of Professor Peter Rowe, the School of Architecture at Tsinghua University and the Graduate School of Design at Harvard University started a joint research project on the history of modern urban housing in China, which finally gave birth to this book after years of intensive and successful collaboration. To my knowledge, this book is the first systematic work, either in China or abroad, on modern urban housing in China and the following are some of its characteristics. First, the book divides the 160 years of modern housing history into three periods (i.e. 1840 to 1949, 1949 to 1978, and 1979 to 2000), considering both the stages of social history and the changes of urban housing types in China. This division not only depicts accurately the historical development of the modern period in housing development but also provides a clear outline for the whole work.

Second, the authors did not limit themselves to the conventional architectural history when examining the changes of urban housing types. Instead, they perceived those changes through the complicated structure of underlying political, economic, social, technological and cultural forces. It is true that changes in urban housing definitely reflect the status of people's living conditions, as well as the building environment of cities in general. Nevertheless, the reverse is also true. With this in mind, the authors have successfully provided readers with a complete picture of the history of modern urban housing in China, based on an extensive literature review, as well as numerous field surveys.

Third, understanding the past can help us predict the future. China has already moved on to a fast track with regard to urbanization, and urban housing development is an important part of the country's construction program. In addition to the development of a market economy, continuing population growth and the increasing constraint of available land resources has caused endless debates in China over the number of storeys and standards to which ordinary urban housing should be built to meet the housing needs of urban dwellers, while also considering regional differences in both economic and cultural terms. The answers to these questions, however, which still puzzle Chinese architects and planners, may not be limited to only one direction. Contradictions exist despite our attempts to resolve them, and society will also continue to develop. In due course, new thinking will be needed and, undoubtedly, comprehensive research in housing history and the present state of its development will help us understand our achievements and shortcomings, and encourage us to explore future possibilities.

Of the editors, Prof. Lü Junhua, from the School of Architecture of Tsinghua University, started to work on housing in the early 1950s, and never gave up in either research or practice. Professor Peter Rowe, the author of *Modernity and Housing*, has established a close working relationship with Tsinghua School of Architecture beginning in the early 1990s, and has shown an impressive enthusiasm for working on architecture and cities in China. Professor Zhang Jie has worked on urban conservation in China since he returned from Britain in the early 1990s, and now works in the housing field. With these key members, the constitution of the research team for this international collaboration provides a strong new model. The book is being published both in English abroad and in Chinese at home. It will not only help international understanding of housing development in China, but will also facilitate Chinese professionals in their search for direction.

Finally, I am very pleased to see this book accomplished and am happy to write a preface for it. I also would like to take this opportunity to congratulate the authors on their success.

Introduction

by Lü Junhua

The city can be likened to a history written in stone, with housing as its foundation, and the study of modern housing development in Chinese cities over the past one and a half centuries seems to unfold like a picture scroll of modern Chinese history. During the three years of writing this book, a historical review was conducted in order to get to the very root and source of this development. The changing political regimes, the transformation of institutional structures, the ups and downs of the economy and other changes in society all directly or indirectly affect the development of housing. These findings were, indeed, an eye-opener, and this study quickly ceased to be confined to housing as a technical field focusing on physical aspects like site planning, dwelling unit design and architectural engineering. Instead, it turned outwards to explore the social, political and economic circumstances behind modern Chinese housing.

The book is organized chronologically although, instead of following the conventional pattern of dividing history into periods popular in historical circles,[1] its chronology takes into consideration political and economic factors, as well as the development of housing itself. The term "modern" in this book is intended as the opposite of "traditional" and is used in a sense similar to "modernization."[2]

Essentially, the book divides the 160-year period from 1840 to 2000 into three parts. Part one spans from 1840 to 1949, when modern urban housing in China was associated with a semifeudal and semicolonial society. It started with the defeat of the Qing Dynasty in the Opium War (1840–42), when China was forced to open its doors and some trading cities arose, and lasted through the Westernization Movement, the Reform Movement of 1898 and the Revolution of 1911, when capitalist industry and commerce began to prosper in China, directly prompting the rapid development of trading cities and inland industrial and commercial cities, as well as promoting changes in China's social structure. The period ended with the War of Resistance against Japan (1937–45) and the War of Liberation (1945–49), a time of relative stagnation in urban construction. During the intervening 100-plus years, urban housing in the modern sense emerged, resulting in changes in living patterns, construction systems and housing styles.

Part two spans from 1949 to 1978, the first thirty years after the founding of the People's Republic of China (New China), a period when publicly owned housing prevailed under a socialist planned economy. It encompasses the influence of the former Soviet Union, the Great Leap Forward and the Cultural Revolution. During this period, housing policy kept changing with the political turbulence and economic fluctuations. On the one hand, the state shouldered the heavy burden of providing housing that was distributed as part of social welfare, and on the other, it was helpless in checking the deteriorating living conditions of urban residents.

Part three spans from 1979 to 2000, or roughly the twenty years after China adopted its reform and open-door policies. This was a period featuring swift economic growth and deepening housing reform focused on an emerging market orientation, during which housing development in Chinese cities was strongly promoted. In the 1990s, as the state promulgated the slogan of making housing a new consumption good and component of economic growth, modernization of the housing industry was put on the national agenda. With changes in the social and economic structure, as well as a corresponding stratification of urban dwellers and a diversification of demands, housing began to change its unvarying existing form as a ration article, and became geared to meet market demands. To be sure, future housing development in Chinese cities is an issue of common concern, although it is difficult to decide, at this stage anyway, which of the many contradictory views about it is correct.

A historical review of the past 160 years of urban development reveals two major changes in Chinese housing types. The first change was from the single-storey compound occupied by one family to diversified forms of housing, dominated by clustered multistorey residential buildings, and took place initially in the trading cities before spreading gradually to other centers. The change proceeded slowly for more than fifty years and did not really take on its emergent form until the early twentieth century. In spite of this, however, the change was far-reaching in its effects upon subsequent urban housing in China.

The second change took place after the founding of New China. Along with the implementation of the First Five-Year Plan (1956–1960), standardized multi-floor residential buildings sprang up in large, medium-sized and small cities and even in the residential districts of mining areas. At the end of the 1970s, high-rise housing was constructed in batches in big cities, such as Shanghai and Beijing. This change was both rapid and influential, continuing well into the contemporary period and, although the national drive towards reform and opening-up promoted a diversification of housing types, multi-storey and high-rise housing remained the main form of construction.

By examining changes in both social life and political-economic systems, the conclusion can be reached that these two trajectories played a decisive role in the changes of housing types, which, in turn, further transformed people's patterns of living and the appearance of urban areas. From a macro point of view, this was a development process largely independent of the individual's will. For decision-makers, developers, or residents, it was and still is an inevitable choice in a specific place at a specific time. Moreover, from a more personal point of view, the two major transformations of housing type, either slow or fast, appear to have been carried out quite smoothly through constant adjustments and adaptations.

Social modernization, and particularly the rise of the real estate industry, was the reason directly accounting for the first change. At that time, industrial and commercial proprietors, as well as country gentry, went to seek development opportunities or refuge in the trading cities, while farmers and laborers streamed into urban areas to find a different way of life. Dramatic urban development and population concentration produced an objective demand for the real estate business, and realty developers developed different kinds of clustered housing to meet this demand. Whether the new type of housing evolved from the traditional residential compound, or was introduced from Western clustered models, it reflected the economic, technical and cultural conditions at that time and was finally accepted by the Chinese people. Today, as a consequence, the *linong* housing has become the tradition in cities like Shanghai and Tianjin.

The change of the political system and particularly the transfer of housing to public ownership was the reason directly accounting for the second transformation of housing type. Although there existed compounds occupied by many poor households and linong housing that was jokingly purported to house "seventy-two tenants" prior to the founding of the People's Republic of China, compounds with courtyards, or the linong housing, were originally designed for a single household. With the founding of New China, the state gave top priority to solving the housing problem of workers and, in the 1950s and 1960s, housing areas newly constructed in a place like suburban Shanghai were named "worker's new villages." Moreover, considering the alternatives, a factory worker was only too glad to be assigned such a small unit of publicly owned housing. Furthermore, during this period, old courtyard compounds in Beijing were first occupied by citizens who had no basic accommodation, and gradually became crowded as more families moved in. Consequently, inhabitants of such overcrowded compounds never hesitated to move into an apartment assigned to them by their work unit.

Due to ideological reasons, housing construction in urban areas, shortly after the founding of the People's Republic of China, inevitably imitated practices in the former Soviet Union. Housing was designed and constructed in line with a standard model and according to state standards and rules. Aided by this standardization, housing construction unfolded on a massive scale. Indeed, industrialization seemed to be the best way to solve the problem of housing shortage.

What will be the next change after housing is commercialized under the socialist market economy of China? In addition to political and economic factors, other important features, with special Chinese characteristics, must also be taken into consideration.

1. Population

China, with the largest population in the world, is a major agricultural country. In the feudal period, despite the existence of capital cities with populations of one million or more, urbanization was at an extremely low level of around 6 percent in the late nineteenth century.[3] Some progress was made in the twentieth century, but the level of urbanization had only reached 11.2 percent by 1949. Furthermore, the economic system and the rigorous household registration system in communist China resulted in sharply contrasting housing layouts in urban and rural areas. In the thirty years following the founding of the People's Republic of China, little progress was made in urbanization, which kept lingering at 17 to 18 percent,[4] and the pressure of population growth on urban housing during this period was primarily a result of natural population growth. The reform and open-door policies, initiated in the 1980s, accelerated the process of urbanization, which rose to 29.7 percent in 1998 (Table 1), and it is predicted that by 2030 China's total population will reach 1.6 billion and the level of urbanization will increase to 55 percent. By then, China's urban population will amount to 880 million people, more than double the present 370 million, with a net increase of some 500 million people. Besides permanent residents, there are several millions of floating population in big cities, like Beijing and Shanghai, whose housing awaits proper solution. Consequently, as urbanization speeds up, the urban population expansion will impose great pressure on housing production, even

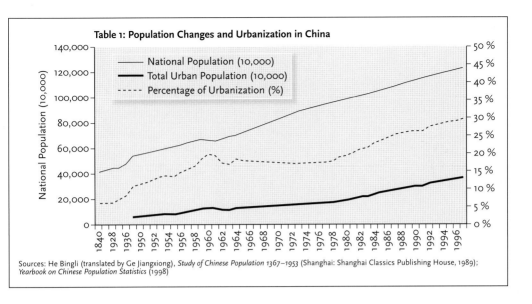

Table 1: Population Changes and Urbanization in China

Legend:
— National Population (10,000)
— Total Urban Population (10,000)
---- Percentage of Urbanization (%)

Sources: He Bingli (translated by Ge Jiangxiong), *Study of Chinese Population 1367–1953* (Shanghai: Shanghai Classics Publishing House, 1989); *Yearbook on Chinese Population Statistics* (1998)

though China remains the world's leader in the overall speed of housing construction.

2. Land

By contrast with its huge population, China has a serious shortage of land resources. The country's population density averages 135 people per square kilometer. Yet the distribution of population varies greatly between the east and the west, with a much higher density in the eastern region. The density in urban areas across the country averages close to 1,000 people per square kilometer, and, although the government is determined to enhance development in the west, it will take time to ease population pressure in the east.

Since the founding of the People's Republic of China, the per-capita proportion of cultivated land has kept diminishing with construction activity. At the end of the 1990s, the per-capita cultivated land was only 0.08 hectare (Table 2), and there is limited potential for new cultivated land. Consequently, economical use of land has become a pressing governmental issue. However, the consumption of land for urban construction is not the major reason for its diminution, as urbanization can, in fact, facilitate more intensive land use. Primarily, the per-capita land use in Chinese cities and the per-capita land use in residential areas has been diminishing in response to sheer housing inadequacy. It was not until the 1980s, when consideration of urban environmental and living quality drew more attention to this problem, that the per-capita land for con-

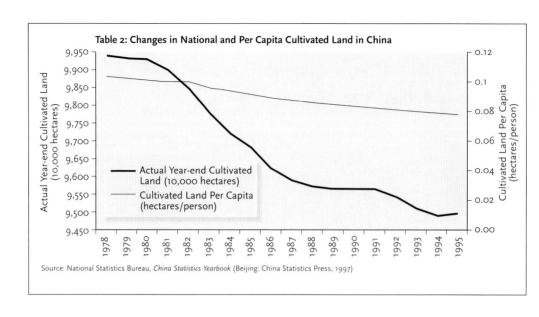

Table 2: Changes in National and Per Capita Cultivated Land in China

Legend:
— Actual Year-end Cultivated Land (10,000 hectares)
— Cultivated Land Per Capita (hectares/person)

Source: National Statistics Bureau, *China Statistics Yearbook* (Beijing: China Statistics Press, 1997)

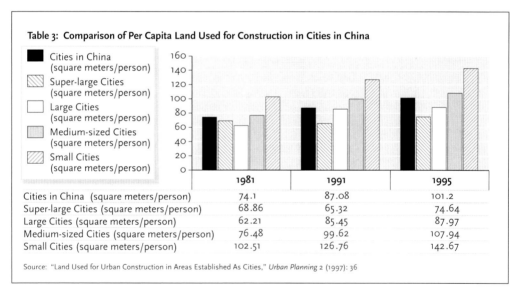

Table 3: Comparison of Per Capita Land Used for Construction in Cities in China

	1981	1991	1995
Cities in China (square meters/person)	74.1	87.08	101.2
Super-large Cities (square meters/person)	68.86	65.32	74.64
Large Cities (square meters/person)	62.21	85.45	87.97
Medium-sized Cities (square meters/person)	76.48	99.62	107.94
Small Cities (square meters/person)	102.51	126.76	142.67

Source: "Land Used for Urban Construction in Areas Established As Cities," *Urban Planning* 2 (1997): 36

struction purposes began to increase. Still, except for small cities that experienced relatively quick improvement, land in large and super-large cities remains in short supply (Tables 3 and 4). Moreover, the constrained supply of urban and residential land has constituted the major reason for the increasing number of storeys in housing in small, medium-sized and large cities in China for over half a century, and this trend can hardly be expected to change in the next few decades.

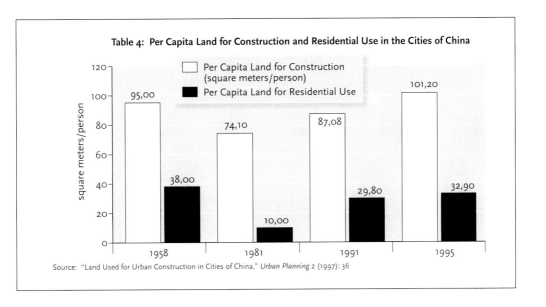

Table 4: Per Capita Land for Construction and Residential Use in the Cities of China

Source: "Land Used for Urban Construction in Cities of China," *Urban Planning* 2 (1997): 36

3. Economy

As a developing country, China's per-capita Gross National Product (GNP) was only US$700 at the end of the twentieth century and is expected to reach the level of moderately developed countries by the mid-twenty-first century. Hence, economic constraints are an objective reality. On the other hand, as shown by the experiences and lessons of the previous fifty years, government policies and political systems also play an important role. In the first thirty years of the planned economy, under the guideline of "production first and life second," government investment in urban housing construction in the unstable political situation was generally insufficient. Indeed, the proportion of GNP invested in housing construction was extremely low, at about 0.78 percent. Despite the growth of urban population, the per-capita floor area kept declining, from 4.5 square meters in 1950 to 3.6 square meters in 1978. The state-set residential standard, in spite of its fluctuations, was also generally at a low level, ranging from thirty-odd square meters per household to fifty-odd square meters. Such a residential standard, together with the constraint of land use, made multi-floor buildings the only choice for housing at that time[5] (Table 5).

During the twenty years of reform and opening-up, state investment in housing increased dramatically. In particular, due to housing funds raised from multiple sources, the total investment in urban housing construction reached 7 to 8 percent of GNP, while

Table 5: Major Changes of State Residential Standards in Urban Areas

In the wave of copying everything from Russia from 1949 to 1957, the Russian residential standards were introduced unquestioningly, referred to as "rational design and irrational application." The 1970s' standards came from "Suggestions on the Revision of Standards for Residential Buildings" by the National Construction Committee in 1973. The 1980s' standards came from "Regulations Regarding Strict Control on Standards of Urban Residential Buildings" approved by the State Council on December 12, 1983. The 1990s' standards were based on "National Standards for Urban Residential Buildings" approved by the National Residential Construction Conference in 1998.

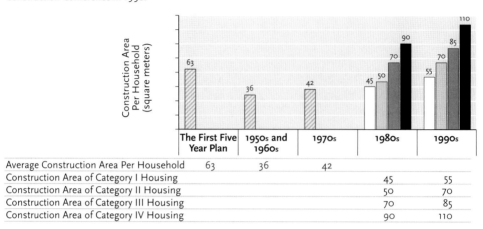

	The First Five Year Plan	1950s and 1960s	1970s	1980s	1990s
Average Construction Area Per Household	63	36	42		
Construction Area of Category I Housing				45	55
Construction Area of Category II Housing				50	70
Construction Area of Category III Housing				70	85
Construction Area of Category IV Housing				90	110

Table 6: Urban Housing Investment as a Proportion of GNP

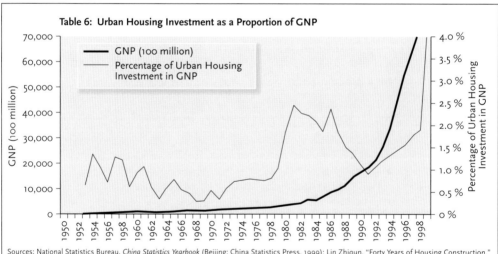

Sources: National Statistics Bureau, *China Statistics Yearbook* (Beijing: China Statistics Press, 1999); Lin Zhiqun, "Forty Years of Housing Construction," *Urban Planning* 9 (1989)

the per-capita floor area in cities increased rapidly to 9.3 square meters in 1998 (Tables 6 and 7). In 1998, the construction area per family in urban areas ranged between fifty-five to sixty square meters and, according to a survey of the State Statistics Bureau in 1999, housing was the first target of residential consumption. Thus, a housing unit with eighty to one hundred square meters of construction area was considered reasonable—not only practically but also economically. Indeed, by 2030, or at least by the mid-twenty-first century, the gross floor area per household may rise to 120 square meters or more.[6] Therefore, taking land use and other factors into consideration, housing will probably continue to take the form of concentrated multi-storey buildings.

4. Society

Society is such a sophisticated concept that it cannot be explained with a simple term, or by statistical averages, especially in a country like China with uneven development. Since the adoption of reform and opening-up policies, social stratification in China has accelerated, producing diversified demands. In a notably short time, suburban villas, urban gardens, luxurious apartment buildings and buildings with mixed commercial and residential functions have sprung up. Yet, while diversified housing is a matter for rejoicing, worries have emerged in the society about housing standing idle, on the one hand, and for families destitute of housing on the other. Moreover, the society in general remains puzzled by this contradiction.

A proper solution to the housing problem mandates a sober understanding of Chinese society. It returns to the cliché: China is a developing country, and no matter how the incomes of urban residents are differentiated, it is still a pyramidally-shaped society in terms of income. For instance, in Beijing—a metropolis serving as the country's capital—an investigation of the social strata showed that rich and powerful people only constitute a minority of the population on top of the pyramid. Typical middle-class families in urban areas, by contrast, only have moderately well-off lifestyles and are average wage earners limited in their capacity to afford housing. The lower-middle and lower-income groups comprise the largest portion of the population, but they have to rely on the social security system for their housing (Table 8). Of course, both the urban spatial structure and the social structure of the population differ remarkably between the country's eastern and western regions, between super-large, large, medium-sized and small cities, and between historical and newly emerging cities. The only thing that can be done is

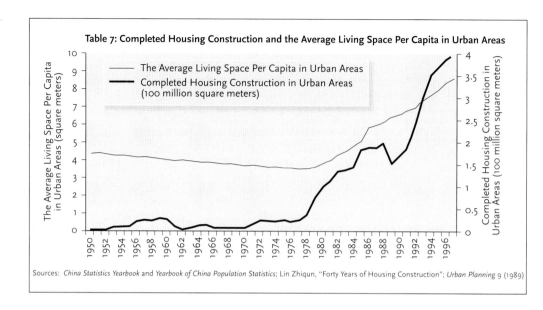

Table 7: Completed Housing Construction and the Average Living Space Per Capita in Urban Areas

Sources: *China Statistics Yearbook* and *Yearbook of China Population Statistics*; Lin Zhiqun, "Forty Years of Housing Construction"; *Urban Planning* 9 (1989)

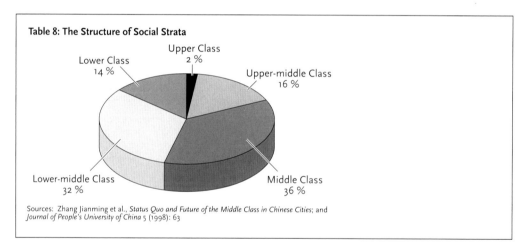

Table 8: The Structure of Social Strata

Sources: Zhang Jianming et al., *Status Quo and Future of the Middle Class in Chinese Cities*; and *Journal of People's University of China* 5 (1998): 63

to conduct specific, in-depth investigations and analyses, and give top priority to the housing issues of the majority of the population and especially the disadvantaged groups, while satisfying demands at other different levels. Therefore, the present market orientation of housing cannot solve the housing problem of all the people in China, and market-oriented housing development cannot represent the entire content of housing construction. Efficiency and fairness will be the issues housing policy should tackle for a considerable time to come. Indeed, it is conceivable that with the improvement of state policy and a housing guarantee system, the maturity of housing reform and the housing market, as well as increasing diversification in investment and operation, Chinese urban dwellers will become more rational in their consumption psychology and behavior, and more conscious in their participation in community building. Eventually, the development of urban housing in China will progressively and steadily proceed along its own track. Everything develops according to a certain objective law, and housing is no exception. Wishful thinking of architects and speculation by realty developers may make a stir for a while, but they will never dominate for long. The original intention of this book is to explore this future road through the examination of its historical background.

Notes

1. Opinions vary in the academic world regarding the division of Chinese history after the Opium War. According to a representative view, the period from 1840 to 1919 was called *jindai*, or "pre-modern times," the period from 1919 to 1949 was referred to as "modern times," and the period from 1949 onward was called the "contemporary age." This division is based on revolutionary movements. According to another representative view, the period from 1840 to 1949 was called *jindai* and the period from 1949 to the present was referred to as modern times. This division gives more consideration to changes in the social nature of the society from semifeudal and semicolonial China to today's socialist republic.

2. The understanding of modernization also varies. The American scholar C.E. Black reckons that human history has gone through three great revolutionary changes. The third is the transition from agricultural civilization, or nomadic civilization, to industrial civilization in different regions and different countries and among different ethnic groups in the world. Social scholars and historians generally understand this third major transformation as modernization. This view is adopted in this book. See C.E. Black, *Motive of Modernization: A Study of Comparative History* (Zhejiang: Zhejiang People's Publishing House, 1989), 1–4.

3. Jiang Tao, *History and Demography—A Study of Traditional Demography Structure in China* (Beijing: People's Publishing House, 1998), 171.

4. Related data concerning the level of urbanization are based on the *Statistical Yearbook on Chinese Population*, 1998.

5. During the period from 1947 to 1957, by imitating the former Soviet Union, the Soviet residential standards were blindly introduced, a practice that was later characterized as rational design but irrational use. Standards in the 1970s were based on "Suggestions of the Construction Commission on Revising the Construction Standards of Housing and Dormitories," issued in 1973. Standards in the 1980s were based on "Regulations of the State Council on the Strict Control of Urban Residential Standards," adopted in December 1983, and, in the 1990s, they were based on the national standards for urban housing construction passed at the National Conference on Housing Construction in 1998.

6. The survey of 5,000 urban households in 10 provinces and municipalities was conducted by the Urban Survey Team of the State Statistics Bureau in 1999.

Part One: Early Development of Urban Housing in the Semifeudal and Semicolonial Period from 1840 to 1949

by
Zhang Shouyi and Tan Ying

Introduction

China is a country with a long history and large population. Big cities appeared early and, in feudal China, were mainly capitals or commercial and handicraft centers where land shortage and crowded living conditions were the two major factors affecting housing form. Because of the highly centralized rule of feudal dynasties, capitals were normally very large. During the Tang Dynasty (A.D. 618–907) many big cities appeared, boasting populations of several hundred thousand and propelled forward by booming commerce and a flourishing handicraft industry. Chang'an (today's Xi'an), the capital of the Tang Dynasty, and Dongjing (today's Kaifeng), capital of the Northern Song Dynasty, were both very large, with populations of over one million. Typical urban problems such as overcrowded living and a prevalence of fire and crime had already appeared and, as a consequence, corresponding measures were taken to tackle them. At this time, traditional Chinese courtyard housing was a popular form that maintained privacy for families while also blending into the crowded urban environment.

However, by the mid-nineteenth century, fundamental social transformation forced the development of urban housing in China into a very different direction. In fact, the period from 1840 to 1949 was an important era in Chinese history. This was a time when China moved gradually from a feudal society into what Mao Zedong defined as a semifeudal and semicolonial organization. Many urban developments were undertaken amid drastic political, economic and social transformation, and urban housing first appeared in the modern sense. Moreover, it was different from traditional Chinese housing in almost all aspects, including investment and construction methods, layout, architectural forms, structure and technology. After some one hundred years, these developments became a coagulated history, starting from initial formation and then going through prosperous times followed by decline, an arc corresponding to China's social and economic development.

During this period the modernization of China's urban housing proceeded in two directions, with the first based on traditional Chinese houses. There, as improvements were made to meet new requirements, they gradually became incorporated into what became modernized urban housing. The second direction involved importing Western forms of housing and adapting them to Chinese lifestyles and particular conditions. Nevertheless, in such a vast country with a large population, China's social and economic development levels were also different, and there were different forms of housing in different regions.

The initial period of China's real estate business and modern urban housing development occurred from the mid-nineteenth century to the early twentieth century. The Opium War from 1840 to 1842 was a turning point, when China began to change into a semicolonial and semifeudal society. As feudal economic structures disintegrated along with the invasion of foreign capitalism and the emergence of a Chinese capitalist economy, the speed of growth was rapid in certain cities, particularly the trading ports. The concentration of population in these cities created an urgent demand for urban housing that was different from previous times. As a result, real estate businesses flourished and urban housing became commercialized and market-oriented, in direct contrast to the traditional mode of development, where each household built its own house according to its individual circumstances. Over time, large areas of urban housing were developed by real estate developers, either for rent or for sale, and entirely new urban housing types emerged.

In particular, the *shikumen linong* housing in Shanghai and the courtyard linong housing in the north were representative of this period. They were outgrowths of traditional houses with new features added to cater to people's new demands. In addition, collateral improvements, represented by progress in urban infrastructure and management, reflected changes of lifestyle and progress in architectural technology. By the same token, this housing also conformed to feudal etiquette, traditional philosophy, the prevailing city environment and available construction technology, and it was reasonable as well as practical.

From early in the twentieth century until 1937, before the outbreak of the War of Resistance against Japan, Western powers stepped up their military and economic aggression against China. During this time, China's national industry and commerce also developed, as trading port cities and industrial and commercial cities in inland areas entered a period of stable prosperity. This was also the peak period in the early development of China's city construction and urban housing development, with distinctive features including diversified means of investment in housing development, enriched housing forms, and rapid progress in building technology. In short, there were different kinds of housing developers, as real estate developers invested in residential construction of varied quality. Specific factories and enterprises also built houses for their employees, and city government became involved in housing development to solve particular housing problems. In terms of housing form, old-style linong housing was still being built and there were various other kinds of housing with different local features. In the meantime, Western housing types were introduced to China in the form of detached houses, apartment buildings and houses with gardens. Generally, these first appeared in the concessions of trading port cities before gradually spreading to other cities. At the same time, Russian- and Japanese-style detached houses, apartment buildings and open-corridor houses were built, along with the development of railways in northeast China. Progress in building technology was embodied in improvements to internal facilities, employment of new materials and construction techniques, increases in the number of storeys in buildings and, in particular, the appearance of high-rise buildings.

After 1937, China entered the period of the War of Resistance against Japan and the War of Liberation. Although population in many cities increased, all city construction and housing development stopped, except in one or two places such as Chongqing. Almost uniformly, urban housing conditions worsened.

In summary, then, during the one hundred years of China's embarkation along the road of modernization, urban housing gradually grew out of traditional forms and evolved into new, diversified housing with distinctive Chinese elements. Influenced by many factors, the general trend can be summarized as follows. First, closed-courtyard houses suitable for large traditional families were replaced by smaller but open housing suitable for the modern, small-sized families. Second, considerable progress was made in architectural technology and building materials. Third, internal facilities and outside environments were modernized. Finally, architectural styles were diversified.

Chapter One: The Emergence of Modern Urban Housing (1840–1910)

1. Social Background

The Chinese economy developed slowly at the later stage of the long feudal period. In the mid-nineteenth century, most Chinese cities remained traditional, as the conceited Qing government adopted a closed-door policy and banned all kinds of foreign trade. Compared with the Industrial Revolution in Western countries, the Qing Dynasty was extremely feeble and, following the Opium War in 1840–1842, Western imperialist powers quite literally forced open its door with their ships and advanced cannons. Subsequently, under the joint action of both internal and external causes, substantial changes took place in China's urban society and economy. However, different from Western cities, this germination of modernization reflected characteristics of China as a semifeudal and semicolonial society. Predominantly, change first took place in two kinds of places. They were the "concessions" in coastal open cities—a tract of land supposedly on lease to, but actually seized by, an imperialist power and put under its colonial rule—and in areas in northeast China also invaded by foreign powers.

1.1. Internal and External Causes of Urban Development

In the late nineteenth century after the Opium War, open cities, and several emerging cities in the north, experienced faster development than those in most other regions. The introduction of foreign capital was one reason for this turn of events, although their prior economic foundation and the rise, in China, of industry and commerce also played an undeniable role. From 1842 to 1860, the Qing government was successively forced to open 16 coastal cities as trading ports, including Guangzhou, Fuzhou, Xiamen, Ningbo, Shanghai, Tianjin and Hankou (Fig. 1-1). In Shanghai, Guangzhou, Tianjin and Hankou, concessions were subdivided for foreign inhabitation. With their own administrative and economic systems, these concessions were effectively states within the state, and quickly became the strongholds from which foreigners could conduct trade and investment activities. Not surprisingly, China became a large market for Western exports and a proverbial paradise for

▲ The New and Emerging Cities in the North
● Coastal Cities with Harbors
■ Later Developed Cities in the Southwest

Fig. 1-1: Chinese cities with rapid development in modern urban housing from 1840 to 1949

adventurers seeking to acquire wealth and secure profits. Subsequently, the input of Western capital, advanced technologies and modern management methods promoted economic development and urban construction. Furthermore, the ideological and cultural influence of these cities began to affect the entire country.

Located at strategic points along water and land transportation routes, the open cities also had a fairly sound economic foundation before their opening to the West. Shanghai Port, for instance, engaged in commercial capitalism using large trading junks before the opening, with from 10,000 to 20,000 workers employed on the docks (Tang Zhenchang, 1989, 102). In the old city proper of Hankou in Wuhan, Embankment Street was lined with innumerable handicraft workshops and stores, presenting a prosperous scene. Guangzhou, the only trading port in China before the establishment of concessions, was thriving and wealthy, with a population of over one million. Throughout, development of modern harbor and railway facilities after the opening further promoted economic development while providing new employment opportunities. Especially within the concessions, the economy developed rapidly, creating a lopsided condition with regard to other areas, and as a consequence, the population swelled quickly. At the end of the nineteenth century, the Western powers intensified their invasion of China. After the 1895 Treaty of Shimonoseki, foreigners obtained official rights for investment, and the operation of factories in China and both modern industry and commerce began to flourish.

From 1896 to 1905, Tsarist Russia and Japan successively acquired privileges to build railways and to construct affiliated enterprises in northeast China. Consequently, cities like Harbin, Shenyang, Changchun and Dalian rose along the railways. Specifically, after the signing of a secret treaty between China and Russia in 1896, Russia established the Mid-East Railway Company, which not only built, operated and maintained railways, but also acquired privileges over land associated with this infrastructure. After the Russo-Japanese War in 1905, the two countries signed a treaty, agreeing that railways and affiliated land south of 50 degrees northern latitude in northeast China were Japan's sphere of influence, subsequently referred to as the Southern Manchurian Railways and Affiliated Land. There, the Southern Manchuria Railway Co., Ltd. was responsible, with its headquarters based in Dalian and its area of operations extending to Shenyang and Changchun. Throughout northern China, such railway-affiliated areas were also constructed on a massive scale as colonies and bases for the invasion of China. Shandong's Qingdao, for example, was occupied by Germany in 1897 and became a new city that developed as a colony.

During the opening to the outside world following the Opium War, many Chinese came to realize the crisis caused by being bullied for lagging behind in modernization. Consequently, they began to take the initiative and to learn and disseminate advanced Western culture, science and technology and to run modern industrial and mining enterprises, in an attempt to rejuvenate the country. During the period from 1860 to 1895, comprador bureaucrats initiated the Westernization Movement, and a number of government-sponsored military enterprises, together with auxiliary government-supervised and merchant-managed concerns, as well as solely merchant-managed enterprises, were established. These earliest Chinese factories and enterprises were primarily located in large open cities, including Shanghai, Tianjin, Hankou, Guangzhou, Nanjing and Fuzhou. In essence, the Westernization Movement and the rise of modern industry were an active absorption of Western civilization, and provided a further impetus to the development of open cities.

In 1900, the Eight-Power Allied Forces, with troops sent by Britain, the United States, Germany, France, Russia, Japan, Italy and Austria, invaded China. Shortly after, facing both internal disturbance and foreign aggression, the Qing government declared a political reform in 1901. Major measures of the reform included the encouragement of industrial enterprises funded by private capital, the establishment of Western-style schools, overseas study and reform of the military system. During this period of reformation, China's national industry made progress and Western culture and scientific knowledge was disseminated, along with advanced technologies, management systems and ideological concepts. By 1910, under all these influences, Shanghai, Tianjin and Hankou became the most important trading ports in central and northern China. In particular, the sparsely populated concessions gradually developed into areas with large populations and bustling business activities. Yantai, Jinan and Tianjin began to construct new urban districts, and the newly emergent cities in the north also underwent preliminary planning and construction.

1.2. Emergence of Modern Urban Facilities, Planning and Administration

Among the most significant developments within the open cities during this period were the start of modern urban infrastructural improvements and the emergence of municipal administrations. In fact, road building was the first step in the construction of the concessions and other new urban areas. To ensure orderly urban development, especially when meeting the demands of industrial development, other urban infrastructure was also rapidly developed, such as the supply of water, power and gas. In 1865, for instance, the Great Britain Gas Company—the first of its kind in China—started to supply gas in Shanghai's concessions. Initially, the gas was only for lighting, although later it was used for cooking and some industrial purposes. In 1881, the Shanghai Tap Water Company was established with British investment and, in 1882, the British-invested Shanghai Electric Light Company was established to supply electric power. In short, by the end of the nineteenth century, public facilities took on their initial form, basically through private foreign investment and operation within the concessions. Meanwhile, many large enterprises also provided services to other areas.

Outside the concessions, construction of urban public facilities also drew the attention of city governments trying to serve the needs of economic development. For instance, the Inland Tap Water Company, set up in 1905, was the earliest water supply plant in Shanghai's Chinese-inhabited area. The Belgian Merchants Power Plant for Streetcar and Electric Light, the largest of its kind in the city, was jointly set up in 1904 by Belgian merchants and the local government of Tianjin; it supplied electric power to the Italian, Austrian and Russian concessions, as well as to the old and new city proper. In 1908, more than ten wealthy Chinese businessmen jointly set up the Hazhen Jiji Water & Power Company in Hankou, and from multiple sources, including private investment, government sponsorship, foreign funding and joint ventures, many urban public improvements covering gas supply, water supply, fire control, power supply, and telephone and telegraph service, began appearing in big cities like Shanghai, Tianjin and Wuhan. However, because only luxury houses in the concessions could have direct access to these modern services, they did not produce a significant influence upon the general urban housing conditions prior to the end of the nineteenth century. By contrast, the majority of residents had to buy water coupons and fetch water from assigned wells, or they had to hire laborers to deliver their water. Furthermore, other improvements like sewage systems did not improve much for the majority. Nevertheless, the creation of urban public facilities did lay a foundation for further city development and the development of modern urban housing.

With regard to urban planning and administration, the concessions and Chinese-inhabited areas of the open cities were independent from each other. Sometimes a concession was divided into several sections subject to administration by different countries. Consequently, these same cities did not enjoy a process of unified planning and the overall structure and sense of organization was often chaotic. Although different districts were formed during different phases of construction, housing was often mixed in with industry and lacked public open space. At the beginning of the real estate boom, most residential quarters were small in scale, ranging from ten to a few dozen houses. Except for a few luxury residential quarters in the concessions, the urban living environment was overcrowded.

From 1870 to the early twentieth century, the open cities experienced steady development. The concession authorities adopted Western urban administrative practices, with stipulations regarding the location, design and construction of residential buildings, enabling the Chinese to follow a clear set of rules when they designed and constructed houses. For instance, the "Rules on Land Leasing in the British, French and American Concessions of Shanghai," created in 1854, stipulated that combustible building materials such as wormwood and timber should not be used in the building of houses. It was also stipulated that the eaves should not stretch to the point of inconveniencing passersby (Luo Suwen, 1991, 11). As time went on, the appendix to the "Rules of the Pidgin Beishou Concession in Shanghai," passed in 1869, stipulated even more detailed provisions concerning house building, and helped promote massive development and an orderly array of residential buildings.

A modern, unified urban plan first appeared in both the newly emerging cities of the north and in occupied Qingdao, and the planning of these cities reflected the reality of China as a semifeudal, semicolonial society. For instance, large tracts of land with favorable environments were allotted to foreigners for habitation, while the smaller tracts with less favorable conditions were allotted to the Chinese. There was a world of difference in the living conditions between the two districts, and their planning largely determined the different directions they would take in the future. In any event, prior to 1910, as construction began to get underway, there was little housing development.

1.3. Urban Housing and the Rise of Real Estate

In the late-nineteenth century, swelling population and expanded concessions in the open cities produced an unprecedented demand for housing, and private real estate development emerged as an important mode of housing construction. The population in urban Shanghai, for instance, totaled around 540,000 in 1852, rising to 1 million by 1900 and 1.29 million by 1910 (Zhang Song, 1993, 91). The concessions there reached 32.82 square kilometers in area after the last expansion in 1914, or an area 16 times greater than the former Shanghai county seat (Fig. 2-5). In 1846, the city proper of Tianjin measured 9.4 square kilometers in area expanding to 13.4 square kilometers in 1900 and 16.2 square kilometers in 1911, with an urban population of 400,000 people (Qiao Hong, 1994, 82). This represented an increase of more than 30 percent compared with the time prior to the opening (Fig. 2-6). Similarly, in 1911, the population in the three towns of Wuhan reached 800,000, more than two times that prior to the opening.

As a result of the Small Sword Society (Taiping) uprising in 1853, wealthy people and refugees in rural and urban areas of Jiangsu and Zhejiang provinces flooded into Shanghai's concessions. The population grew rapidly and, in 1855 alone, the number of Chinese in the concessions increased from 500 to over 20,000. During the period from 1860 to 1862, with the surging movement of the Taiping Heavenly Kingdom, the Taiping army marched into Shanghai. Landlords, wealthy gentry and bureaucrats from the suburbs and from Jiangsu and Zhejiang provinces swarmed into the concessions, where the population rose to a consistent level of 300,000 inhabitants and once hit 500,000 people (Zhu Jiancheng, 1990, 11). As one might imagine, the new immigrants were in dire need of housing and foreign firms such as *laoshaxun yanghang* and *yiheyanghand*, formerly in the opium trade, built rows of simple crude log cabins on cheaply leased or purchased land in the concessions. These log cabins, whose overall form resembled European row houses, borrowed *li* from the Chinese tradition in their names (hence linong architecture), and by 1860, there were around 8,740 residential buildings named with *li* in the British and American concession of Shanghai (Wang Shaozhou & Chen Zhimin, 1987, 6). Furthermore, building for profit replaced building for self-reliance and the real estate business began to emerge in China for the first time.

After the 1860s, Shanghai's concession authorities acquiesced to mixed habitation by foreigners and Chinese. The influx of Chinese strongly boosted real estate development and, during 1865 and 1866, the population in the public and French concessions made up 12.5 percent of the total population of Shanghai, even though they only covered 0.57 percent of the city's area (Tang Zhenchang, 1989, 219). With this pressure, land prices in the public concession soared dozens of times in 1865 alone, making real estate a profitable business. Because log cabins were flammable, the concession authorities banned them in 1870, and the introduction of new facility and building standards made residential construction an increasingly sophisticated undertaking. New methods of design, construction and management were adopted, and real estate development became a specialized business. Moreover, the rise of this business not only promoted the construction of urban housing but also became a main source of local finance. In Shanghai, for example, a large part of the financial revenue of the concession authorities came from taxes on house leases and land use. Meanwhile, the real estate business soon spread to areas outside the concessions, like the southern district, and to other cities such as Wuhan and Tianjin.

The rise of real estate business in the northern open cities also started in the late nineteenth and early twentieth centuries. The earliest example was the construction of Tianjin's New Hebei area. In fact, between 1870 and 1895, Tianjin was the center of the Westernization Movement in northern China, later becoming the city for the implementation of Yuan Shikai's (Sun Yat-sen's) new policies concerning the operation of new types of industry and mining. Because of the expansion of Tianjin's concession, the old city proper had little space for development. Yuan thus decided to develop the New Hebei area along the Xinkai River. Here the government built a regular road network and established factories, schools, government offices and commercial enterprises. In 1903, the new railway station was completed and named the Master Tianjin Railway Station. Between 1903 and 1910, this area developed rapidly and, with the sharply swelling population, Chinese real estate developers constructed residential buildings on tracts of land and then leased or sold them to Chinese residents. By contrast, the newly emerging cities in the north, which were invaded by foreign forces, developed mainly along the railway corridors, and both building and population density was quite low. Moreover, with housing under the unified planning of the railway authorities, real estate business in the modern sense did not occur.

1.4. Housing Conditions of Urban Residents at Different Social Levels

In a traditional Chinese city, there lived landlords, government officials and merchants, as well as the townspeople serving them. Usually the residents resided in different parts of the city according to their wealth, social status and occupation. The houses differed depending on the area, but basically they were built in a traditional manner suitable for a large feudal family. After China entered the semifeudal and semicolonial period, significant changes took place in the urban social and economic structure, mainly as a result of the development of new industries and the influx of people looking for work. Further differentiation occurred in people's social and economic conditions as, besides the traditional scholars, farmers, artisans and merchants, there appeared new social classes including foreign residents, capitalists, compradors, functionaries, industrial workers and vagrants. Naturally enough, families of different classes and incomes had different standards of living and varying demands for housing, further complicating its provision. Generally, a shortage of housing and the polarization of living conditions were common phenomena, roughly dividing into three levels of provision: upper, middle and lower.

1.4.1. The Upper Level

Merchants were the most prosperous among all the occupations in Shanghai. Besides the local merchants, many other merchants from Jiangsu, Zhejiang and Guangdong lived in the concessions, together with bureaucrats, landlords and country gentry, initially seeking refuge from the chaos of war. They all found in Shanghai a new world where they could enjoy life as they pleased, and some of them became wealthy by investing in real estate and running factories. Meanwhile, more and more foreign traders and investors brought along with them their native living habits and built foreign-style garden residences. Also over time, a new group of people—the compradors—emerged. They were Chinese who were directly employed by foreign firms in buying and selling, while also having their own businesses and, generally speaking, they enjoyed a much higher income than regular Chinese employees of foreign firms. In short, the upper level of society in Shanghai was mainly foreign capitalists, wealthy Chinese merchants, bureaucrats and compradors, and they led lavish lives in the paradise of adventurers. Normally, they built their own luxurious residences, but sometimes they also bought or rented houses built by real estate developers.

1.4.2. *The Middle Level*

Along with various urban enterprises and the establishment of different kinds of institutions in cities, the number of office workers engaged in commerce, finance, transportation, education and administration rose appreciably. By and large, though, the middle class represented a small proportion and was constituted by office workers with above average incomes, and owners of small- and medium-scale industrial and commercial businesses. Indeed, the incomes of office workers could vary substantially. Senior employees in large companies and foreign firms earned over a hundred yuan per month, and usually they could afford a very comfortable house with one or two servants. By contrast, office workers with lower incomes could only rent one or two rooms, and some let one or two rooms in their own houses in order to subsidize domestic expenses. For instance, it was recorded that when the renowned writer, Bao Tianxiao, was invited to work for Shibao (Times) in 1906, his monthly pay was eighty yuan (Luo Suwen, 1991, 47–48). In 1911, regular office workers and technicians were paid twelve to twenty yuan a month, while factory workers were paid less than ten yuan. At that time, a monthly income of twenty yuan could cover the food and clothing of a five-member family, and a worker needed at least fifteen yuan a month to support a five-member family. Compared with the upper-level residents, the middle-level residents could only afford smaller dwellings. Nevertheless, many of them began to pursue a new urban mode of life, influencing the direction of residential real estate development, calling for new forms of housing.

1.4.3. *The Lower Level*

A rapidly increasing number of workers was a salient characteristic in the occupational composition of modern cities in China. By the mid-nineteenth century, modern industrial workers emerged in the open cities. Mainly from rural areas, they worked on the docks and in Chinese and foreign enterprises concerned with industry, transportation and other public undertakings. Incomplete statistics show that in 1894, there were 36,000 industrial workers in Shanghai alone, compared to approximately 100,000 industrial and mining workers throughout the country (Ding Richu, 1994, 675).

Among those people moving from rural areas to the big cities were also carpenters, tailors, launderers, shop assistants, women servants and clerks. Together with the industrial workers, they constituted a bulky working class at the lower level of society. They made a living from their labor and their family income was so meager that they could barely cover basic living expenses. Consequently, their living conditions were also extremely crude and simple. Some of them lived in the workshops of factories or stores, and some rented cheap housing. Some investors even built clusters of low-standard houses for rent in areas with factory concentrations, such as Shanghai's Yangshupu district and Tianjin's Hedong and Hexi districts. In such quarters, there were also crude and simple single-storey houses built by local residents, which were partly occupied by the owner and partly leased to others in order to defray costs. Single workers also often jointly rented a house or lived collectively in dormitories, while those with worse economic conditions had to join the vagrants in the slums.

In sharp contrast to the high buildings and bustling downtown areas were the shantytowns on the outskirts of many cities. In the late nineteenth century, the first group of slum dwellers appeared near the Shanghai docks. At the beginning of the twentieth century, along with the development of industrial zones in the open cities, all kinds of shantytowns emerged in wastelands, ruins, graveyards, garbage dumps, and along streams near factories, docks and railway stations. These shantytowns became the principal shelter for poor people who had fled to the cities because of famine or war.

2. Clustered Urban Housing from Traditional Chinese Houses

Clustered urban housing, born out of the Chinese tradition and built by real estate developers, first emerged in Shanghai's concessions. The sale and lease of these properties was primarily targeted for Chinese residents who were able to settle with above average incomes. Over time, these clustered buildings ushered in a new era of urban housing in China.

Owing to the sharp discrepancy between limited land availability and explosive population growth, property, as mentioned before, was expensive in the concessions. It was impossible for the Chinese landlords and wealthy merchants to copy their country mansions, with their spacious rooms and courtyards. Therefore, no matter what the form of the single-unit plan, the construction was characterized by clustered development. The compounds were arrayed in rows, with every two compounds sharing a common wall between them, and as many of these compounds as possible were built according to the lay of land. Consequently, the building density was much higher than in traditional residential quarters.

2.1. The Origin of Old-style Shikumen Linong Housing

The single units of clustered residential buildings, including their floor plans, architectural structure and exterior, were based on traditional local houses. This category of residential buildings can be called the clustered urban residential buildings in a traditional Chinese style, with the most typical of them located in the Shikumen neighborhood of Shanghai (Fig. 1-2). Essentially, it was architecture born out of the houses in the southern parts of the Yangtze River (Fig. 1-3). Most of the houses were two-storey, post-and-panel structures, with a horizontal courtyard in both front and back. Because the entrance of the house was a typical shikumen gate, similar to the traditional gateway of vernacular houses in the south featuring a stone doorframe and wooden plank door, the buildings were duly named the shikumen houses (Fig. 1-4). Clustered shikumen houses were often named *li*, while the regular corridors between the rows of housing blocks were called *nong*[1] meaning "alley." Residential buildings constructed in this fashion thus became called shikumen linong houses,[2] a manner of building which continued until 1930, despite changes. Moreover, because the shikumen linong houses built in the early days used traditional building materials, and fol-

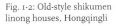
Fig. 1-2: Old-style shikumen linong houses, Hongqingli

Fig. 1-3: A comparison of the traditional courtyard housing south of the Yangtze River and the old-fashioned shikumen housing in early times

First Floor Plan   Second Floor Plan   First Floor Plan   Second Floor Plan

Fig. 1-3a: Floor plan of a two-storey Ming Dynasty house in Jingde town, *Chinese Ancient Architectures*, 474. The striking feature of the Chinese traditional courtyard house is the symmetry and the layers of space in the courtyard. It is arranged by units based on "rooms." Rooms make a unit and units, together with gates, corridors and walls, make a courtyard. A big house, which consists of a few courtyards, contains a group of buildings.

Fig. 1-3b: Xingren Li, a five-room traditional shikumen house, built in 1872, is obviously evolved from the traditional house south of the Yangtze River.
Linong House: 7

Fig. 1-4: Shikumen-style entrance to the traditional courtyard house (left) and the entrance to a shikumen linong house (right)

lowed the traditional structure with the interior divided in the traditional manner, they were called the old-style shikumen linong houses. Compared with the crude log cabins prior to 1870, their rent was higher but their maintenance costs were low. It was easy to lease them and the cost could be recovered in less than ten years. Consequently, tens of thousands of these houses were built in Shanghai each year (Zhu Jiancheng, 1990, 13).

2.2. The Architecture of the Old-style Shikumen Linong Houses

The floor plan of the old-style shikumen linong houses was based on the traditional room, with a standard width of about ten chi, or the length of a wooden purlin. Typically consisting of from three to five rooms, the design of the house maintained a symmetrical layout to the left and right of a middle axis. Normally, a housing unit was divided into two parts—main rooms and accessory rooms. Except for the kitchen, there was no clear-cut division based on function. According to location, the rooms were divided into the guest hall, the guest chamber, secondary rooms, trifling rooms, side chamber, surplus rooms, etc. (Fig. 1-5). At the front, the main hall, guest hall and side chamber formed a small yard with three sides. In the rear, the accessory rooms formed a backyard. If conditions permitted, there would be a well in the backyard that provided water for the family's daily needs. All the building materials came from the local area and the architectural structure followed traditional practice. The main body of the building consisted of the following parts: a mortar tabia foundation, a crossbeam bearing structure, a rowlock wall for enclosure and separation built in hollow bricks, joists sup-

Fig. 1-5: A typical traditional shikumen linong house. Plan and section

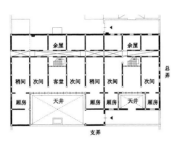

A five-room and a three-room shikumen linong house in Zhaofuli, Shanghai. *Linong House: 7*

Brick and wood structure of Zhaofuli in Shanghai, with a traditional horse head gate

The traditional shikumen linong house in Gongshunlin, Shanghai, adds a back room and another attached room on the second floor. The house depth is over 16 meters with poor light and ventilation. There is an unlighted room in the middle.

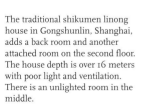

First Floor Plan   Second Floor Plan

porting wooden tiles, a wooden-framed sloping roof and a platform over the accessory rooms.

Clustered construction of old-style shikumen linong houses was small in scale. A main alley and several side-alleys connected all the houses, providing for a compact layout (Fig. 1-6). The main alley was usually bridged over at the entrance from the street, with the name of the *li* and alley indicated on its wall. Sometimes there was also an arch between the gables of the two buildings at the entrance of a side alley, which not only consolidated the wall but also gave it a sense of grandeur (Fig. 1-7). As developers tried their best to build as many houses as possible on the limited land available, alleys between rows of houses were limited in number and usually narrow in size, in order to cut down on construction costs. Such configurations, however, were bad for traffic and fire control. Moreover, the ventilation and lighting relied mainly on the courtyards inside, and here often the extensive depth of the buildings and the smallness of the courtyards were of little help.

Around 1900, rear chambers were added to the old-style shikumen houses because of the explosive growth in popula-

Fig. 1-6: Mianyangli, Shanghai—an early old-style shikumen linong complex. *Linong House:* 9

Site Plan. *Linong House:* 9

Views of Mianyangli neighborhood

Fig. 1-7: The entrances and lanes
of an old-style shikumen linong
housing area

tion and soaring land prices. As a result, the area of the backyard shrank considerably. Furthermore, some rear chambers had two storeys and sometimes a small room was also added over a kitchen in order to increase the construction area on every possible square meter of land. Consequently, the shikumen houses built during this period covered less land per house. One-room and two-room houses appeared and the construction coverage of residential quarters reached 80 percent in some places. Nevertheless, the architectural design did improve to some degree. For instance, overall arrangement of houses was more orderly and attention was paid more to orientation. Moreover, the enclosing wall was lower than before, and, similarly, the two-storey accessory rooms and back chambers were much lower than before, as well as lower than the main rooms, thus ensuring better ventilation and lighting for the main rooms.

The exterior of old-style shikumen houses maintained many characteristics of local houses. A salient feature was the external enclosure by high walls and thick doors to give residents a sense of security. The early houses were, architecturally, rather stark, with conspicuous black doors protruding from the enclosing white plaster walls. The earliest shikumen gates were also crude, with the gable often built into the traditional horse-head wall. Generally, Shanghai's old-style shikumen houses after 1870 were first found in the former British concession, then the former French concession, as well as in the Zhabei and Xinjiao areas, and the residents were mostly the Chinese. As a popular form of housing, the shikumen houses were suitable for traditional large Chinese families, as well as for separate leasing by room.

In Shanghai the shikumen residential quarters gradually became centers of urban activity. Due to their convenient locations and spacious and flexible internal arrangements, productive activities were often commingled in the same buildings with family life. Many commercial firms, entertainment services, newspapers and guildhalls had *li* in their address. At the same time, some family hotels and private clinics also emerged in these areas, and businesses gave a commercial flavor to the neighborhoods (Luo Suwen, 1991, 45.) Finally, the old-style shikumen linong houses later spread to other open cities such as Tianjin and Hankou. In fact, people in Tianjin called similar buildings in the city's Nanshi District tapered-end-style houses (Fig. 1-8). At the end of the nineteenth century and the beginning of the twentieth century, similar shikumen houses emerged in the old city proper of Hankou and on the outskirts of its concessions.

In addition to the old-style shikumen linong houses, there were other clustered residential buildings born out of traditional houses. For instance, the bamboo-tube houses, built in clusters in

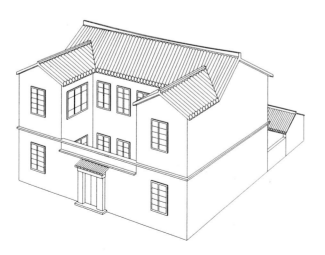

Fig. 1-8: A "tapered-end-style" house in Tianjin

Guangzhou, originated from the local house, characterized by narrow and deep sites. Also, at the beginning of the twentieth century, northern courtyard houses began to emerge in clusters in Jinan's trading area and Tianjin's New Hebei district. These houses were similar to the one-storey courtyard houses in northern China, but simplified in structure, and finally became a mature form of urban housing after the 1920s.

Notes

1. The terms *nong* and *nongtang* (known as *longtang* as well), are mainly used in Shanghai, instead of *xiang* in southern China and *hutong* in the north. They are different expressions for "lane" or "alley."
2. The building of the shikumen linong (or *lilong*) houses is called the shikumen house. Detached individual units of shikumen houses were also built as well.

Chapter Two: An Important Period for the Early Development of Housing in Modern Cities (1911–1937)

1. The Social Background of the Rapid Development of Urban Housing

Between 1911 and 1937, before the outbreak of the War of Resistance against Japan, trading port cities in China developed rapidly, and the cities occupied by foreign countries, such as Harbin, Dalian and Qingdao, also expanded in their own way. It was a thriving period for the early development of housing in China's modern cities. Generally, several major social characteristics were influential. They were: 1) a steadily rising urban population, which maintained the demand for housing; 2) a widening income gap among different social strata, resulting in varied types of housing and housing standards; and 3) a general trend towards small-sized families and varied ways of life, resulting in different demands for housing.

With respect to housing production, self-built houses still existed, but urban housing built by real estate developers made up an ever larger proportion. Meanwhile, city governments participated in different facets of housing construction, including developing appropriate laws and regulations, as well as making direct investments in housing projects. Also, other enterprises like factories and mines often provided housing for their staff and workers. In northern China, for instance, in the newly developed cities that grew up along with the construction of the railways, except for the housing built by the railway authorities for their workers, housing for ordinary citizens was constructed by individuals on land leased from the military and civil authorities. Some of these houses were occupied by local people, and others were constructed for rental purposes. In general, a large number of urban houses were built and in a wide variety of towns.

1.1. The Main Changes in Society and the Demand for Housing

The Revolution of 1911 overthrew the feudal dynasty, paving the way for the rapid development of capitalism in China. During World War I, many owners of foreign-funded enterprises returned to their countries of origin, thus offering an opportunity for China's industry to develop. After the end of World War I, the trading port cities entered a period of greater prosperity and, by 1927, the National Government of Nanjing was founded, putting an end to the rule of the northern warlords. During the period before World War II, society was relatively stable, the economy developed and the urban population in many places increased rapidly. For instance, in 1914, before the outbreak of World War I, the population of Shanghai had increased to 2 million, a figure which rose to 2.64 million in 1927, and to 3.8 million by 1936, or at an average annual increase of from 80,000 to 90,000 inhabitants (Zhang Song, 1993, 91). In 1936, Tianjin's population stood at 1.25 million (Luo Shuwei, 1993, 457), and in 1930 the urban residents of Wuhan reached 1 million, rising to 1.29 million in 1935, the highest population since the founding of this trading port city until 1949 (Pi Mingxiu, 1993, 660).

1.1.1. Trading Port Cities

Population in the treaty port concessions also increased significantly in the prevailing stable social environment. Indeed, many retired warlords and officials and landlords, as well as surviving adherents and nobles of the Qing Dynasty (1644–1911) bought properties in the concessions of Shanghai, Tianjin, Hankou and other cities. They either deposited their capital in foreign banks or invested it in real estate. For instance, Li Hongzhang, a prime minister during the Qing Dynasty, his son Li Jingmai, and grandson Li Guochao, were among the main owners of Shanghai real estate (Zhu Jiancheng, 1990, 15). These people also spent money without much restraint, thus stimulating the development of public service facilities and related ventures in the concessions.

Other areas also made considerable strides during this period. Shanghai's Nanshi district, Zhabei district and the areas by the Suzhou River, for instance, all became densely populated industrial locations. After 1911, Hebei new district in Tianjin became the principal site of the municipal government, and following the construction of the railway, the number of staff and workers employed in government posts gradually increased. Similarly, warlords and officials also bought land there and built houses, allowing it to rank first in terms of population growth in the Chinese-inhabited areas of the country. The Nanshi district between Tianjin's old city area and the concessions also prospered, and, because of the development of industry and commerce, the population of the old city area of Hankou and the trading port area of Jinan also grew rapidly.

One major source of the rising population was the migration of young laborers from rural areas, as well as immigration by impoverished peasants and refugees. In fact, the proportion of industrial workers and other poor people in the total population rose steadily. By 1922, Wuhan had 400,000 industrial workers, making up about half of the city's total population, and by 1927, Tianjin had a total population of nearly 1 million, including over 100,000 industrial workers (Pi Mingxiu, 1993, 695). According to the conservative statistics of the Tianjin Social Bureau, the number of unemployed people in the area under the jurisdiction of the Chinese government in Tianjin was nearly 300,000 in 1928 (Luo Shuwei, 1993, 472). In 1920, the industrial workers of Shanghai totaled 514,000, making up about a quarter of Shanghai's total population (Tang Zhenchang, 1989, 556), although, according to the analysis and calculations made by Zhu Maocheng in his article titled, "The Records of the Survey of Shanghai Workers' Housing and Social Conditions," Shanghai's labor force was about 1.125 million, constituting fully 70 percent of the city's total population.

Unfortunately, as urban population increased, the income gap among residents became wider. A small number of upper-strata residents possessed a large amount of wealth and lived in luxury, while a great number of lower-strata residents were unable to make ends meet and struggled in poverty. Meanwhile, the group in the middle—people with professional skills—was expanding. According to a rough estimate in the mid-1930s, the number of staff working in commerce, finance, transport and communication, culture, education and administration in Shanghai exceeded 200,000 people. Given the consumption level of a family of five in Shanghai, a middle-level family earned a monthly income of sixty-six yuan and a family below the middle level made thirty yuan a month. Therefore, a staff member working in any of the new professions would have no difficulty earning a middle-level income. By contrast, according to a 1926 survey, a worker's family, with his wife and children also working, had an income of twenty to twenty-five yuan a month. If the worker lost his job, or a member of his family was sick, theoretically the worker's family would not have enough money for food and clothing, and available expenditure for housing was correspondingly very low. In effect, a large number of urban residents in the lower-strata could not afford to buy or rent houses or apartments offered on the market. They could only rent a part of a house or part of an apartment. Seizing this opportunity, some people became sublandlords and made a living by letting parts of their houses. The old-style shikumen houses, built up in the central part of Shanghai in the early days, had big rooms but primitive facilities. Shunned by wealthy families, they were often jointly rented by several poorer families. Their basic facilities, like water supply and toilets, were also shared. Some of the families received no sunshine throughout the year, and some lived in rooms without windows. The figures from a report, submitted by the Municipal Council of the Shanghai Public Concessions in 1937, showed that, within the concessions, one house was shared by four families in a total of 22,700 units; one house was shared by six families in 14,000 units, and one house was shared by nine families in 1,300 units. There was even a house where 15 families lived together (Tu Shipin, 1948, part 3, 2). Also, many poor farmers moved into modern industrial and commercial cities because of disasters, poverty and other afflictions. They built various kinds of simple tile-roofed houses and sheds in the suburbs of Shanghai, and some of them had no place to live. In 1936, there were more than 20,000 households living in slums outside the concessions in Shanghai (Tu Shipin, 1948, part 3, 6), and more than 37,000 such families in Nanjing, with a total population of 150,000.[1] In fact, slums could be found on the fringes of downtown areas in almost all large cities. Most of the inhabitants performed low-paid jobs in factories or on the docks. The rest were unemployed refugees.

1.1.2. Emerging Cities in Northern China

From the early days of the twentieth century until the 1920s, along with the construction of railways, Harbin, Changchun, Shenyang, Dalian and other cities in northern China gradually developed from small towns into well-planned cities. Each had a large number of new buildings, and their population was swelled from some ten thousand to several hundred thousand people. Great progress was also made in housing development. The new citizens of the cities included both foreign immigrants and Chinese laborers, as well as other Chinese immigrants. It was a population of different cultural backgrounds and incomes, and so was its living environment. Apartments, built by the railway companies for their employees, were low in density and had adequate amenities. By contrast, Chinese residents were only allowed to build houses on small amounts of land, thus forming crowded neighborhoods. For instance, in Harbin, which was once occupied by Russia, the apartment buildings constructed by the China Eastern Railway Administration for its staff and workers were distributed in the Nangang district within a bucolic environment with complete facilities and with a more than adequate low density of construction. However, in the areas inhabited by Chinese, there were multi-storey courtyard-style residential buildings of low quality and high density. Many Chinese laborers had to live in slums with primitive living conditions.

After 1905, along with the rapid development of the land affiliated with the railways in Manchuria, various types of Japanese-style clustered housing and one-household dwellings were first constructed near the large square in the center of Dalian, and then expanded eastward to the present-day Gorky and Lianhe Roads. As a result, the residential areas inhabited by the Chinese people were pushed to Beigangzi, adjacent to the factory area in the north of the city. The shantytown at Xianglujiao and the residential areas in Siergou, for the lower-strata Chinese laborers, all had shabby houses and a dirty and disordered environment. In addition, between 1897 and 1922, Qingdao, which was once occupied by Germany and later by Japan, expanded gradually on the basis of the plan made during the German occupation, forming a unique pattern. Specifically, high-standard German and Japanese-style modern apartments and garden residences occupied the best areas along the coast. By contrast, Chinese residents and lower-strata Japanese immigrants lived in densely populated neighborhoods around Jiaozhou Road in Dabaodao district. A vast expanse of slums appeared in Taixi Town, where many factories were located. Although recovered by the Chinese government in 1922, Qingdao remained under the control of Japan economically. From 1929 to 1937, as Qingdao was far away from the battlefields, its political situation also remained stable. With an increase of foreign investment and domestic investment by retired warlords and officials, Qingdao also began to develop again.

Finally, after the Incident of September 18, 1931, Japan occupied Northeast China and turned it into a puppet state called Manchukuo. Changchun became the political center, Shenyang and Harbin were the industrial centers, and Dalian became the port, with Mudanjiang and Lüshun as military bases. As priority was given to preparations for war at the time, only residential houses for high-ranking Japanese and Chinese officials were constructed, and the construction of houses for ordinary people stopped almost completely.

1.1.3. Changes in Family Size, Their Way of Life and Their Influence
Another factor affecting the demand for housing was the change in the size of urban families and their way of life. Generally, small families were common in cities during this period. In feudal society, along with the rise and decline of the economy and the influence of natural and man-made calamities, each Chinese family had on average from two to nine members. By the end of the Qing Dynasty in 1911, each household had from five to six members on average, and the disintegration of economic self-sufficiency was the most impor-

tant reason for the decline in family size. On one hand, those farm-ers who immigrated to cities to work had a meager income, which restricted the number of family members they were able to support. On the other, such immigration broke down traditional large fami-lies, with several generations living under one roof. In fact, family size continued to shrink until the Second World War, a trend made all the more obvious in cities by large floating populations. For instance, from the beginning of the twentieth century until the 1930s, household size in Tianjin declined from 5.6 to 4.8 people, and surveys conducted in Nanjing, Shanghai and Beijing on urban families indicated that each family had 4.39 members on average (Wu Wenhui, 1935, 23). In the emerging cities of Shandong Province and northeast China, the proportions of immigrants and floating populations were very high. Among them, single-person households and nuclear families made up the overwhelming major-ity; farmers seeking jobs in cities, as well as refugees, also had small families. For example, a survey conducted in 1933 of 180 slum-dwelling families in Nanjing indicated that 75 percent had from two to five members, with an average of 4.12 members per family (Wu Wenhui, 1935, 22).

For the middle class, change in the traditional concept of the family was another reason behind the shrinking family size. At the beginning of the twentieth century, scholars who accepted the pro-gressive outlook from the West began vehemently to criticize the traditional Chinese marriage and family system in the name of free-dom and democracy. During the May Fourth New Cultural Move-ment of 1919, some progressive intellectuals put forward various ideas for changing the old family system and promoting equality, freedom and liberation of women. As members of floating popula-tions, many people broke the shackles of the large feudal families and established small, independent nuclear families. Meanwhile, between the 1920s and the 1930s, some famous large urban fami-lies disintegrated and moved out of the residences where they had lived under one roof for generations (Luo Shuwei, 1993, 596). Not surprisingly, the trend toward smaller families directly affected the evolution of housing types. Simultaneously, along with changes in urban residents' ways of life occasioned by their higher demands for better living environments, the functional arrangements of housing were quickly improved. Over time, the plan layout and exterior of residences gradually shifted from traditional, reserved, isolated and separated houses into a more Western and more open style of living.

1.2. Multiple Channels in the Supply of Urban Housing

Due to greater demands for housing, real estate developed vigorously not only in the trading port cities, but also in many inland cities such as Chengdu and Beijing. Large amounts of urban housing constructed in this manner gradually became an important component of the urban housing stock, vividly reflecting changes in the economy, technology and culture of the time.

1.2.1. The Prosperity of Housing Real Estate

In the trading port cities, economic development and population growth caused a continuous rise in land and dwellings prices. In the concessions in particular, increases in housing costs outstripped population growth. In Shanghai, for example, the population in the public concessions in 1930 was nearly three times that of 1901, but the number of houses was only 1.8 times greater. What's more, the population density in the concessions was 15 times that of the areas inhabited earlier by the Chinese, and the rent in the public concessions in 1930 was eight times higher than in 1901.[2] Indeed, written documents indicated that in the thirty years from 1903 to 1933, the price of land in the public concessions of Shanghai increased ten times (Wang Shaozhou, 1987, 568).

Before the end of World War I, mainly foreign firms invested in and operated housing real estate ventures. But after 1910, a large number of Chinese real estate developers—mostly former landlords, warlords, bureaucrats, politicians, compradors and business people—also participated in the business. In addition to collecting rent from houses and land, they participated in other real estate business activities with foreign real estate agencies. For instance, the Zhang, Liu, Xing and Pang families were originally powerful landlords in Nanxun, who later became the most well-known real estate owners of old Shanghai (Zhu Jiancheng, 1990, 15). In the 1920s, Bei Runsheng, a former comprador who made a fortune by selling pigments, invested almost all his assets in real estate and became one of the largest Chinese real estate owners. In fact, it was very common for financial institutions to engage concurrently in real estate activities in order to secure needed investment. Usually, financial institutions were glad to make such investments without undue risk through mortgage loans, and, with the passage of time, often the same financial institutions took part in real estate directly. In addition, individuals also engaged in real estate business through investments or loans, and some entrusted banks with the design, construction and leasing of their properties.

As time went on, real estate dealers, who became owners of large-scale projects, began making specialized demands in design, construction and budgeting. Gradually the construction of houses drew the attention of Chinese and foreign architects, as well as modern construction firms. For instance, there were many clustered urban houses designed by Chinese architects in Shanghai, Tianjin and Wuhan, and builders turned themselves from traditional clay-and-wood workshops and artisans into formal construction companies using modern building materials construction technologies. Also, rising population brought prosperity to cities in northern China, activating a booming real estate economy. During the Japanese occupation from 1914 to 1922, for instance, real estate owners in Qingdao constructed new residential developments and then rented them to Chinese residents and lower-strata Japanese on land leased from the city government. Such practices continued for years, but the scale of real estate development couldn't match that of the trading port cities.

1.2.2. Housing Construction by the City Government

In 1927, after the founding of the Nationalist Government in Nanjing, each city established a new city government. Usually, a Municipal Council was placed in charge of urban construction. Its tasks included devising laws and regulations for construction, building infrastructure, standardizing the leasing of houses, planning and constructing new residential areas, improving slum areas and constructing houses for ordinary citizens. City governments, however, played slightly different roles in housing development in trading port cities, such as Shanghai, Tianjin, Wuhan, Guangzhou and Xiamen, as well as in Qingdao and Nanjing, the political center.

In an attempt to raise the quality of planning and design of residential areas so that they could rival those in the concessions, some city governments planned and constructed new residential areas, know as model quarters or model villages. These quarters and villages were supposed to serve as examples for urban housing development elsewhere. The usual development procedure included: planning in a unified manner, subdividing the land, putting forward the requirements for housing design and selling these designs for construction to individuals or real estate developers. Usually such housing was large in scale and designed by Chinese architects, with the plans often obviously reflecting the absorption of Western planning ideas. Although not many of these residential areas were completed, some planning ideas were of major significance. Between the end of the 1920s and the early 1930s, for instance, the

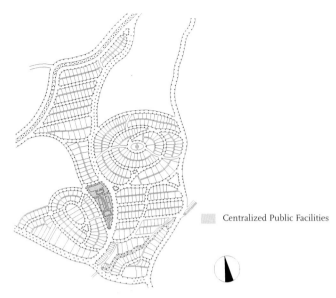

Fig. 2-1: Site plan of the Model Residential Area in Guangzhou (*Contemporary Cities and Architecture*, 44, originally from *Implementation Report by Guangzhou Municipal Government in the Past Two Years*)

Centralized Public Facilities

Guangzhou Municipal Government decided to start housing construction in new areas. When completed, the new Dongshan District in Guangzhou was composed of high-class residential districts with detached garden residences as the mainstay, featuring a bucolic and quiet environment. These residential areas had markets, gardens, primary schools, kindergartens, public halls, libraries, police stations, post offices and other service facilities, and earned the sobriquet of the Model Residential Areas of Guangzhou (Fig. 2-1). Similarly, in 1919, the Xiamen Municipal Government started the construction of municipal works such as embankments, roads, docks, parks and the demolition of city walls. To help small real estate owners whose houses were demolished during this construction, Xiamen also started to construct model villages. For instance, the One Hundred Family Village had rows of 100 houses each, with public facilities, and were constructed for residents who had to be removed from the site where the Zhongshan Park was being constructed. The 1930s witnessed the construction of three model villages of this kind in Xiamen (Guo Husheng, 1993). In Hankou, the new model village, whose construction started at the end of the 1920s with investments by the Hankou government, was located at the lower section of the present-day Liberation Road. This village was designed by Yu Bojie, with new-style shikumen houses as the predominant form. The overall layout of the new model village was proactive, with well-defined roads, green land and a sports ground (Fig. 2-2). In addition, universities in Nanjing and other cities built houses for their faculties in a similar manner.

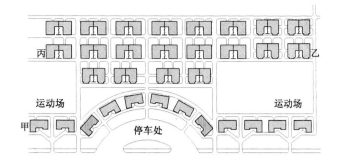

Fig. 2-2: Site plan of a model village in Hankou (*Contemporary Cities and Architecture*, 185, originally from *Business Report* by Hankou Official Business Administration, 1930)

运动场   运动场

甲   停车处

丙   乙

Demolishing slums and building houses for common people were important achievements of China's city governments in the 1920s and the 1930s. In 1928, the Shanghai Municipal Government began to consider the construction of houses to be rented to common people at a low price, together with the establishment of shack quarters, a plan which was implemented in 1930 and later became an important task of the Shanghai Administrative Committee of Common People's Welfare (Huang Jiantong & Li Pei, 1989, 159). Before the War of Resistance against Japan, Shanghai constructed seven residential areas for common people, involving close to 2,000 houses. In the 1930s, when Shen Honglie served as mayor of Qingdao, one of his achievements was to change the slums of Taixi Town into the "courtyard for common people" (Yang Bingde, 1993, 292). In the same period, the Nanjing Municipal Government also performed similar work.

In addition to their direct involvement in housing construction, city governments also promulgated requirements for construction materials, the space between houses, and the width of the lanes leading to dwellings in order to facilitate both traffic and fire fighting. Moreover, this activity played a key role in controlling, guiding and improving the living environments of cities. For instance, the "Interim Regulations of Qingdao City on Construction," set forth in 1932, specified the ratio defining the construction density, the width of roads and the height of buildings, as well as the stipulation that no single-storey houses were allowed to be built in commercial centers. There were some regulations on maintaining a certain amount of open space and restricting the height of buildings in high-class residential quarters. For instance, the "Construction Regulations of Shanghai," which were revised in 1937, required that the ground coverage of two-storey buildings and those lower than two storeys not exceed 70 percent of the foundation area; for three-storey buildings and higher, the ground-floor area was not to exceed 60 percent of the foundation area. Further, the height of buildings constructed along a highway was not to exceed 1.5 times the width of the road, and those exceeding the figure were to be set back storey-by-storey, according to a certain proportion. There were also specific regulations on the width of major and secondary roads, and others governing the windows of various dwellings. However, in spite of governments' involvement in housing development, compared with the total amount of urban construction, their activities were few, and some of their more ambitious plans were not put into practice.

1.2.3. Housing Development by Railway Companies
in Northeast China

Many foreign railway staff and workers came to live in the emerging cities of northeast China. Their houses were constructed by the railway companies in a unified way, with characteristics that reflected different users and standards of living, although each type of house had a standard design. Among them, the China Eastern Railway houses developed by the Russians in Harbin, and the Manchurian Railway residential areas developed by the Japanese South Manchuria Railway Co., Ltd., in Dalian and Shenyang, were most representative of this new type of modern urban housing. In concept, these projects were China's earliest large-scale residential areas designed according to modern planning concepts. The various types of urban housing were usually of good quality, such as the large-scale Manchurian Railway housing in Shenyang of the 1930s, where the notion of a "neighborhood unit," influenced by Western architectural ideas, was adopted. The neighborhood unit had four large roads on each side as its boundary, with narrow roads laid out in-between. At its core was a primary school, with commercial and service facilities scattered along the large roads on the four sides. Each neighborhood unit had a public bathhouse and a club. The community center, jointly used by many neighborhood units, had a post office, shops, a police station, a central park and other public buildings (Fig. 2-3). The China Eastern Railway residential areas in Harbin were also of a high standard, with a commodious environment and furnished apartments for rent. In fact, all employees working on the railways, ranging from high-ranking officials to ordinary workers, lived in the apartments, distinguished only by different space standards.

Throughout, construction activities on land associated with the railways were under strict control. In Dalian, for example, when Japan took over in 1905, much of the urban construction had already taken shape. To keep the city beautiful and clean, while not letting the Japanese lose face, the provisional ruling authorities

Fig. 2-3: Master plan of the residential area of the Manchurian Railway in Shenyang (*Collection of Essays from the Fifth Conference on Contemporary Architectural History*, 121–122)

Fig. 2-3a: Master Plan

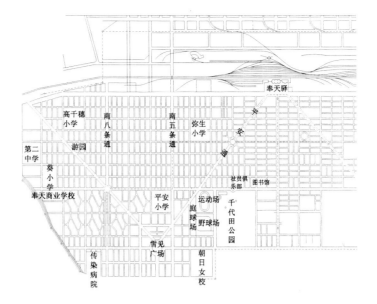

Fig. 2-3b: Site plan of the residential area of the Manchurian Railway in Shenyang (Volume 16, No. 5)

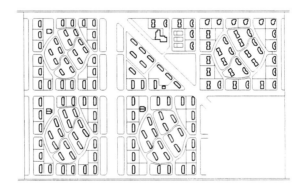

worked out regulations for the control of housing developments, which gradually became perfected after several revisions. The construction regulations started with fire protection, specifying that permanent architecture must adopt a fireproof structure, partition walls must be designed as fire walls, and so on. Second, the regulations for urban streets specified the minimum height of the eaves of permanent buildings, the maximum and minimum amounts of building coverage and continuity of buildings along streets. Thanks to those efforts, Dalian had a tidy road network, with buildings along the main street continuing at three storeys, mostly made of brick, stone and concrete, rather than of traditional wood construction.

1.2.4. Housing Development by Industrial and Mining Enterprises
In the modern industrial and commercial cities of China, housing
for a large number of workers was a different story. In general, there
were several ways to solve the prevailing housing shortage. Workers
could either rent houses from a landlord outside the factory, or, like
many single workers, they could live in the factory's dormitories or
workshops. Some even built shacks by themselves. More often than
not, however, large factories and mines provided housing for workers, although often with bad living conditions. For instance, as the
leading industrial city of modern China, Shanghai had a large number of cotton mills, mostly concentrated in Yangshupu, and housing
for workers was built near the factories. According to a survey conducted at that time, factory housing was generally divided into three
classes (Zhu Maocheng, 1926, 6). The first-class housing had two
storeys, and in 1926, the monthly rent for this kind of dwelling
ranged from six to nine yuan (Fig. 2-4). The second-class housing
was comparatively low, made up of one-storey houses with attics,
and the monthly rent ranged from two yuan to four yuan. The third-
class housing, which was also the worst, consisted of one-storey
buildings built with lighter materials, to which workers usually
added attics. However, when compared with rent in the open market, rent of the factory houses was fairly low. Furthermore, workers
who rented houses on the strength of their employee's cards also
had the right to let a part of the house to others. To reduce expenditures, three or four families with from ten to twenty members often
jointly rented a two-storey house with an area of seventy square
meters, lowering the monthly rent per family to one or two yuan
(Fig. 2-12). Such houses were severely overcrowded and the indoor

Fig. 2-4a: Workers' houses built
by factories and enterprises in
Shanghai

Fig. 2-4b: Workers' houses built
by factories and enterprises in
Shanghai

and outdoor environmental quality was poor, providing the inhabitants with no joys in life.

Another example was the workers' residential village built by the owner of the Kailuan Coal Mine in the 1920s. Original construction of the Kailuan Mine started in the early 1880s, located near a small town called Tangshan to the north of Tianjin, an out-of-the-way mining area. Most miners were from the poverty-stricken areas in Shandong and south Hebei province, several hundred kilometers away. Those who came to the mine to look for temporary employment usually rented houses in Tangshan City. To stabilize the workforce and guarantee a supply of laborers to the mine, the owner of the Kailuan Coal Mine built a workers' residential village nearby to encourage workers to settle down with their families. By 1932, over 10,000 staff and workers of the Kailuan Coal Mine lived in various kinds of houses, making up 25 percent of the total employees (Guo Shihao, 1985). Nevertheless, in general, the houses built by factories could not satisfy workers' demands for housing.

2. Diversified Forms of Urban Housing

After the 1920s, large tracts of urban housing of different kinds gradually assumed a leading position in the housing construction of Shanghai (Fig. 2-5), Tianjin (Fig. 2-6), Wuhan and other large cities, as well as in the emerging cities of northern China. As mentioned, housing was mainly developed in two directions, roughly simultaneously. The first was housing developed on the basis of China's traditional houses, and the second was housing forms imported direct-

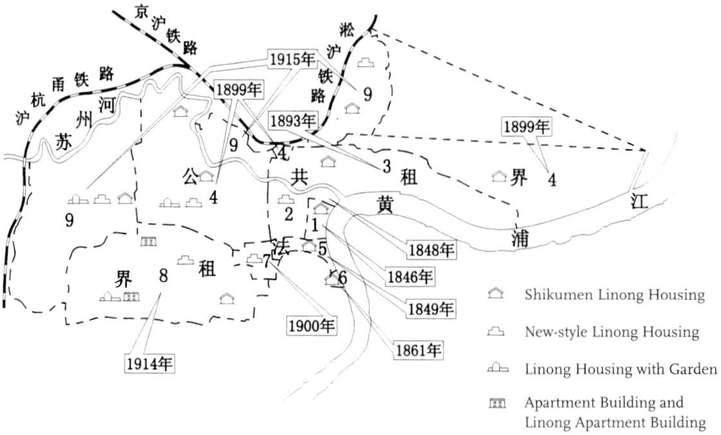

Fig. 2-5: The distribution of different types of housing in Shanghai from 1840 to 1949

△ Shikumen Linong Housing

△ New-style Linong Housing

△ Linong Housing with Garden

▥ Apartment Building and Linong Apartment Building

Fig. 2-6: The distribution of different types of housing in Tianjin from 1840 to 1949

△ Linong with the Traditional One-storey House

▤ Rough One-storey House

▥ "Tapered-end-style" Building

△ New-style Linong

△ Linong Gardens House

▥ Linong Apartment Building

(Drawing from *Linong House*: 26)

ly from abroad. During this period, diversified housing demands, investments and operations, plus regional differences, resulted in a wide variety of housing. Generally, housing had the following characteristics: a varied appearance of small houses, together with apartments; sophisticated indoor facilities; improvement of the external environment; the use of new materials and new technologies; and the employment of various kinds of unit design. In addition to the changes and development of traditional Chinese courtyard-type houses, terrace houses, apartments, open-corridor housing and high-rise apartments based on models from foreign countries were introduced. The trend toward smaller family size and increased land prices and rents made the design of small dwellings more and more popular. A large number of houses in the shikumen linongs of south China, for instance, were turned from an original five-room or three-room configuration into one-room or one-and-a-half-room dwellings. In addition, apartment buildings and other more compact housing types appeared, with small floor-space allowances for each household.

Along with the appearance of new types of housing, the indoor design of high- and medium-class houses completely broke away from tradition, with more clearly specified functions and facilities. As wealthy and powerful residents in the concessions raised new demands for their living environments and housing, residential areas of a far better quality began to appear. Along with the development of urban public facilities, some newly built houses had garages, running water, storm-water drainage and gas, with all pipes laid underground.

In the late 1920s, large amounts of imported construction materials, such as cement and timber, came onto the Chinese market, and patterned floor tiles began to appear in houses. Reinforced concrete and other new building technologies were also used in housing development, and new buildings had more and more storeys. China's urban development at that time absorbed various architectural styles from other countries, often reflecting extraordinary splendor. As a house was often the status symbol of its owner, people attached more and more importance to architectural style. Hence, buildings in the traditional European style, the Western classical style, the Russian style, the Japanese style, the International style or whatever style was in vogue in the world at the time, were built one after another in Chinese territory. Later, they also became rich and valuable resources for the indigenous development of Chinese urban housing.

2.1. Clustered Urban Housing Developed on the Basis of Traditional Chinese Houses

Clustered housing, developed on the basis of traditional Chinese dwellings, had the following characteristics. They were at once houses developed out of traditional residential architecture and out of the large-scale construction being practiced in cities, with many families living together in the same compound. Often they were built with indigenous features in order to adapt to both the local climate and lifestyle. Generally, houses were constructed in an area and then sold, or rented, to particular families as commercial ventures, rather than as isolated efforts on the part of individual families to provide for their own shelter. As time went by, the size of houses became smaller, as demonstrated, for example, by the evolution of shikumen linong houses in Shanghai. Initially, each house was built for one family and, later, individual rooms in the house were rented out separately. Large residential compounds with shared courtyards were also built with the intention of renting rooms to different families, effectively reducing the living space available for each. These types of large residential compounds were common in Harbin and Qingdao.

2.1.1. New-style Shikumen Linong Houses and Guangdong-style Houses

Around 1919, a new type of housing, known as "new shikumen linong houses," made its appearance in the Western concessions of Shanghai. It was the direct result of population growth, reduced family size and discrepancies in income. These houses were normally large in size and neatly arranged. The main lanes and branch lanes, with their own distinctive functions, produced a well-organized and rhythmic appearance. Examples of this type could be found in the Jianyeli, Junyili, Siwenli and Yingchunfang neighborhoods of Shanghai; among them, the Siwenli residential area, whose construction began in 1916, was particularly notable, covering an area of 3.21 hectares and incorporating 664 dwelling units (Fig. 2-7). Compared with the old-style shikumen linong houses, the new-style shikumen linong house had several distinguishing characteristics. First, the houses were smaller, but the functional layout of their plans and the quality of their internal facilities were improved over prior models. Second, they were usually constructed on a large scale and, consequently, the overall layout was more reasonable and tidier. Finally, Western building materials and technologies were used.

Accommodations in most of the new-style shikumen houses were a single room bay in width, with a few containing two bays, and both the covered area and building area of each building was about one-fourth that of the old-style shikumen house. In order to increase the living capacity of the houses, great efforts were taken in planning and design. Each house was composed of main rooms and subsidiary rooms, and in-between was a small longitudinal courtyard. The subsidiary rooms at the back were generally constructed in two storeys, although some of the new-style shikumen houses were three storeys high. The platform on the top of the subsidiary rooms could be used for drying clothes, and with the floors of the main rooms reaching higher than those of the adjacent subsidiary rooms, the main rooms could still receive adequate sunshine and ventilation, even with a narrow distance between them. Such configurations also made the houses aesthetically appealing (Fig. 2-8).

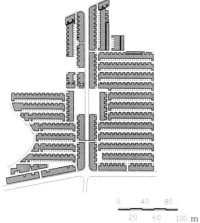

Fig. 2-7a: Master plan of
Shanghai Siwenli, the largest
new-style shikumen housing
development

0   40   80
20   60   100 m

Fig. 2-7b: Individual house plan

天井 天井

上 上

后厢房

客堂 客堂 前厢房

天井 天井

First Floor Plan

天井 天井

上晒台 下
上晒台 上晒台 下

后厢房

前楼 前楼 前厢房

阳台 阳台

天井 天井

Second Floor Plan

In plan layout, each room was considered a basic unit and a traditional symmetrical arrangement was maintained. Distinctions
were made between living rooms and bedrooms. In single-room
and double-room houses, subsidiary spaces were added, in line with
needed functional requirements. Each house would have a kitchen
with a chimney and running water, and a few first-class houses were
built with bathrooms and garages. The depth of the new-style house
was reduced to twelve meters or less, a measure which effectively
eliminated the dark rooms commonly found in deeper old-style
shikumen linong houses. The new-style houses all had a small yard
in front of the main rooms, and normally, a yard at the back as well.
The main gate was still rendered in the shikumen style and was
often eye-catching.

The new-style shikumen linong houses appeared more spacious
than the old-style houses, mainly because the walls of the yard were

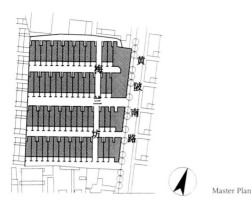

Master Plan

Fig. 2-8a: Shanghai Meilanfang, a typical new-style shikumen linong housing development

Meilanfang, located on 596 South Huangpi Road, occupies a land area of 0.53 hectares. It has 70 units in three-storey buildings. Most of the units have only one main room on each floor. Eight units facing the street use the first floor as shops.

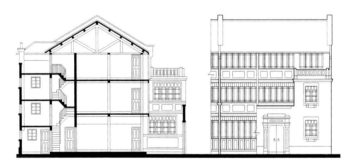

Fig. 2-8b: Plan, section and facade of the house. The house is a brick and wood structure with a "Ren" style truss.

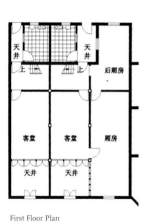

First Floor Plan

Second Floor Plan

Third Floor Plan

Fig. 2-8c: General views of
Shanghai Meilanfang

lower and the lanes were wider. In order to accommodate the passage of cars, the width of major lanes reached four meters, which
also met the demands for fire fighting. The branch lanes were generally no less than 2.5 meters wide, enough for a rickshaw to pass,
and the back lanes were about 1.5 meters wide (Shen Hua, 1993,
26). Improvements were also made in orientation, view and ventilation, and many new-style houses were built with balconies, making
them look more ornate.

In addition to an added number of storeys, considerable changes
were made in the structure of the new-style linong houses. These
included: 1) the use of reinforced concrete posts and concrete slabs;
2) the use of solid brick bearing walls; and 3) the use of cement
paving in lanes, small yards, kitchens and toilets. Wooden floors
were used in the living rooms, and those who could afford them covered their floors with imported patterned floor tiles. Almost without
exception, pitched and gabled roofs were used over the main rooms,
and were covered with tiles. Changes in building materials added
color to the monotonous gray tones, and the machine-made red
apartment tiles replaced the earlier black clay tiles. Red and gray
bricks were frequently used to construct walls, which were also
sometimes decorated with granitoid, or stones set in cement.
Influenced by foreign architectural styles, Western methods of
detailing were largely adopted in both the old- and new-style shikumen linong houses, with the first incorporations coming by way of
decoration on gates. In the hierarchical Chinese society, the size,
material and decoration of the gates of a house reflected the status
and wealth of its owner. In southern China, the door frames of rich
and influential families were often made of stone, with "lucky" brick
carvings above the door. This architectural element was used in
many old-style shikumen linong houses, and Western carvings also

Fig. 2-9: Overdoor ornamentation of Shanghai shikumen linong houses

Fig. 2-10: Gable ornaments and overhead buildings spangalane

Fig. 2-11: Other ornamental
arrangements with Western
influences

began to appear above the door frames. As new-style shikumen linong houses were developed further, Western-style decorations became prevalent everywhere—on doors, on gables and on the overhead buildings spanning across lanes (Figs. 2-9 and 2-10). They also appeared on windows, brackets, arches and rails. Some decorations were often quite complicated and delicate (Fig. 2-11).

The new-style shikumen linong houses were distributed adjacent to the old-style shikumen linong houses centered in the Huangpu district of the concessions in Shanghai, as well as in the Nanshi and Zhabei districts (Fig. 2-5). This type of house also appeared in the expanded British concession in Tianjin (Fig. 2-6) and in Hankou.

The Guangdong-style houses, a kind of low-standard, simple house of small size, evolved from a type of "shop house," prevalent in southern China, where the first floor of this two-storey structure was normally used for commerce (Fig. 2-12). A single room in width and without a courtyard in front, these houses had a small yard at

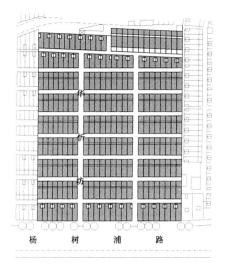

井

坊

坊

杨 树 浦 路

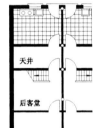

First Floor Plan

天井

后客堂

客堂

亭子间

天井

后楼

前楼

Second Floor Plan

Fig. 2-12: Huaxinfang, a Guang-dong-style linong housing area in Shanghai

It is located at 1991-2009 on Yangshupu Road in Shanghai with an area of 1.3 hectares. It was developed by Sheng Xisun as employee housing for Huasheng Textiles. It consists of 213 units of Guangdong-style housing and 13 units of shikumen housing.

Fig. 2-12a: Master Plan

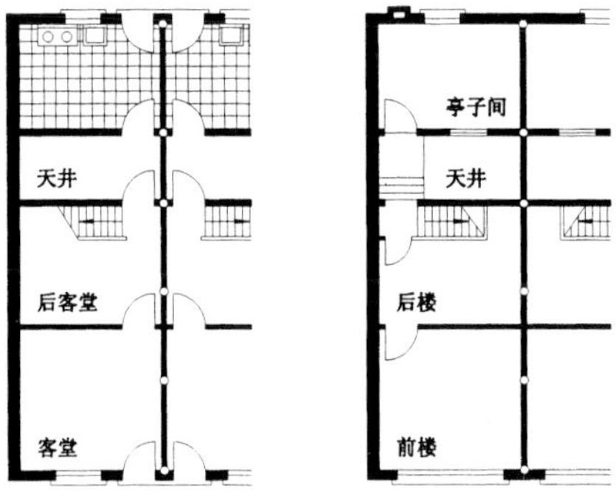

Fig. 2-12b: Plan

Fig. 2-12c: View of Huaxinfang

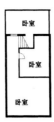
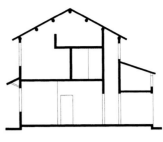

Fig. 2-13: Basic layout of a late Guangdong-style house for workers

Fig. 2-13a: South Xinhuali, a late Guangdong-style house with less depth and no back courtyard

Fig. 2-13b: Street view of south Xinhuali

Fig. 2-13c: Compressed layout of a late Guangdong-style workers' house

First Floor Plan   Second Floor Plan

the back and some subsidiary rooms. Small and simple, they were at first inhabited by people of Guangdong origin and by Japanese immigrants, hence the name Guangdong-style house. Later they were rented to workers and others in the lower social strata, and many factory-made houses for workers were simplified versions of the Guangdong-style house, so small that one floor was only a little more than twenty square meters in area (Fig. 2-13). Except for the kitchen, no special function was designated to each room, and rooms were simply divided into front room, back room and living room. Many of these kinds of houses were built after 1910, often together with shikumen housing. The Guangdong-style houses built after 1919 were even smaller and lower, though their building materials were improved.

2.1.2. Courtyard Urban Houses in North China

Primarily because the population density in northern China was lower than in the south, the traditional courtyard houses in northern China were usually constructed with one storey around a large yard. In the early twentieth century in cities having trade relations with foreign countries, housing developers linked the courtyard houses together, and built them on a large scale. Each housing area was also named as *li*, although there were different kinds, such as single-storey houses in a row, or houses with two-, three- and four-sided courtyards. In order to build more houses while guaranteeing sunshine for the main rooms, the yards were compressed into a rectangular shape, with the north-south side longer than the east-west. Originally, only one family lived in one courtyard. Later, the rooms of each courtyard house were rented separately, as had happened to shikumen housing in Shanghai. After the 1920s, few changes were made to the layout of individual courtyard houses, but principal rooms in some of these houses were built as two-storey structures, and improvements were made in the overall layout, building materials, structure and detail design.

The first large-scale development of courtyard-style houses in Tianjin was initiated by Chinese real estate developers in the Hebei Xinqu and Nanshi districts—located between the old city and the French and Japanese concessions. Of particular note was the large-scale courtyard linong complex built in Dongxingli in the form of sixteen square lots. Each lot had from four to seven single-storey three-sided courtyard houses constructed upon it, and each house

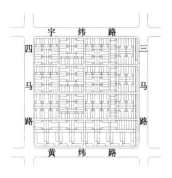

Fig. 2-14a: Master plan

0   50
⌐——————⌐
            m

Fig. 2-14b: Each house is a brick and wood structure and has a simple facade, decoration and facilities.

Fig. 2-14: Dongxingli, a northern courtyard housing area in Tianjin (*Contemporary Cities and Architecture of China*: 112)

Dongxingli, built around the 1930s, is located in the New District north of Hai River. It is a relatively large neighborhood with northern courtyard houses. The total area looks like a grid with 3 streets horizontally and vertically. It divides the area into 16 squares, each of which contains 4 to 7 courtyard houses facing different directions. The construction density is up to 70% of the site area.

Fig. 2-15: A view of northern courtyard housing blocks near Damalu in Yantai

had three principal rooms and wing rooms on both sides and, between them, side rooms used as kitchens and bathrooms. Built of bricks and wood, these houses were decorated and furnished in a simple manner. Today, unfortunately, new multi-storey apartment buildings in Dongxingli have replaced these old-style courtyard houses.

By contrast, the courtyard houses are well preserved in the Damalu area of Yantai (Figs. 2-15 and 2-16). In particular, houses in the Qinganli of the Damalu district were commercially built relatively early and were of good quality. This development consisted of four lanes, each with a length of seventy meters. There were nineteen houses altogether, and among them eighteen dwellings were constructed in the style of the traditional four-sided courtyard, and one was made with two yards. The arrangement of the rooms in the courtyard also followed the Chinese tradition, but Western building techniques were used for some. For example, the houses on the north side were two-storey houses made of bricks and concrete with open corridors. The pillars, beams, staircases and the flat roofs were all made of reinforced concrete, and Western decoration was used for the eave, column cap and handrail details.

In Jinan during the 1920s and 1930s, a number of courtyard houses were built in the Shangfu district and on its periphery. Most were three-sided and four-sided single-storey courtyard houses built of red bricks and stone. They were also of good quality and Western details were adopted. Some houses along streets were of two storeys. Similarly, housing for miners in Kailuan was built on a courtyard configuration (Fig. 2-17). In order to meet the traditional living habits of the miners, who came from the countryside of northern

Fig. 2-16: The appearance of
northern courtyard housing

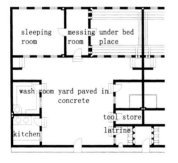

sleeping room	messing room	under bed place
wash room	yard paved in concrete	
		tool store
kitchen		latrine

Plan

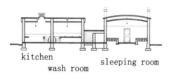

kitchen
wash room   sleeping room

Section

Fig. 2-17: Housing for employees
in the Kailuan Mining Administration

China, single-storey structures were built of limestone and were outfitted with *kang*—a large stove-heated bed which also served many daily functions in vernacular houses in the north—a kitchen, a cooking stove and a toilet. The houses were joined together and each had a yard. Other modern improvements were also provided, such as running water, electricity and sanitary facilities.

In Qingdao, Dalian, Harbin and some other cities in northern China, courtyard houses were originally built by immigrant Chinese families. In the early twentieth century, population in these centers increased quickly. Land was in demand and the size of urban families became smaller. As a result, several families would often share one courtyard house. After the 1920s, as the population rose, workers and poor people from elsewhere constituted the majority of the urban population. To meet their needs a simpler type of courtyard house, often in primitive condition, was built in the Chinese-inhabited areas (Qing Zhiqiang, 1992, 224). Specifically, this type of house was built in the Dabaodao district of Qingdao, the Xiganglu district of Dalian and the Daowaiqu district of Harbin. Typically, a dozen or even several dozen families could live together (Fig. 2-18). A big courtyard was designed according to the size and shape of the piece of land and from two to four two-storey or three-storey buildings with open corridors were built around the courtyard. These buildings were rented on the basis of individual rooms. Sewers and public toilets were built and public staircases were provided at the corners of the houses. Generally, these buildings were constructed at high densities and had poor sanitary conditions. In addition, open corridors were not the best choice for the cold weather of northeastern China. The main purpose was to provide quick and cheap housing for poorer workers. Originally, this kind of housing was built with bricks and wood, and houses along the street were provided with different kinds of Western and Chinese decorations—although

Fig. 2-18a: Compound houses in Qingdao

the insides of the houses, as a rule, were decorated in a Chinese style. Sometimes this kind of complex would consist of two or three yards. After 1920, reinforced concrete was used in some parts of the buildings, and after the 1930s some of the buildings were built as four-storey structures in a Western style. Usually, these buildings were concentrated in neighborhoods and commercial areas inhabited by Chinese, and the courtyards were closely connected and formed compact environments where people could seek peace. The largest such complex occupied an area of 3,000 square meters and was well appointed (Fig. 2-18b).

Fig. 2-18b: Compound houses in Qingdao

2.2. The Introduction of Western-style Urban Housing to Chinese Cities

As mentioned earlier, from 1910 to the 1930s, different kinds of urban housing were introduced from foreign countries to the cities with which they had trading relations, as well as in the emerging cities of northern China. Common characteristics included: a division of the inside space of the house according to functional requirements, the use of Western building methods, and improvement of the external environment and public facilities. In short, the construction quality and amenities of this kind of housing were satisfactory, and most are still used today.

Not surprisingly, Western-style urban housing started in the concessions and eventually spread to other areas. They were mainly built by real estate developers and gradually evolved into high-standard, high-quality apartment buildings. As the heights of the buildings increased, their density was also lowered, adding further to their amenity, and usually the exterior environment was much better than that of the shikumen linong houses. In addition, facilities were also improved; many dwellings had rooms and toilets for servants, and some even had staircases for emergency use. Over time, however, this form of housing reflected the ever-increasing gap between the rich and poor.

In the emerging cities of northern China, new houses were developed emulating, at least in part, the construction of railway company housing. As mentioned earlier, at that time, houses built by the Manchuria Railway Company and China Eastern Railway Company for their employees used standard designs no matter what kind of houses were involved. Even in the workers houses, all the bedrooms, kitchens, bathrooms and storerooms were also built to meet basic needs. Higher-grade houses were more spacious and better equipped, and various kinds of houses were built to meet the demands of different people, including: detached and semi-detached houses, terrace houses, duplex arrangements and apartments.

As northern China was comparatively sparsely populated, most buildings were low in density and did not have many storeys. As time went on, however, increased population changed this situation and more and more people lived closer together. In Dalian, for example, houses built before 1910 were detached houses with a floor area of from 150 to 200 square meters. After 1910, denser urban housing began to be built. From 1921 to 1928, as the rising population imposed a strain on available land, there was a construction boom and many terrace houses were constructed. After the 1930s, clustered houses with relatively small amounts of available floor space were built in urban areas, served by public staircases and with only thirty square meters for each family (Sha Yongjie, Lu Wei & Ji Yan, 1998, 107).

2.2.1. Western-style Terrace Houses

When the old concessions in Shanghai developed into bustling commercial centers, some of the old shikumen linong houses were turned into shops, while others were rented to middle- and lower-income residents. The rich people who used to live there moved on to the newly developed concessions in search of a more comfortable life, as well as a quiet and pleasant environment. In short, shikumen linong houses could no longer suit the needs of the elite. Consequently, a new type of Western house appeared in concessions around 1910, with Spanish, British and French inspiration. After the 1920s this kind of house was also built in Tianjin, Hankou, Yan-

Fig. 2-19: Terraced houses of different styles

tai and some other cities having trade relations with foreign countries. At the same time, among the houses built for railway workers in Shenyang and Dalian, a Japanese form of clustered housing was adopted (Fig. 2-19).

The floor space of each of the new-style linong houses was about 150 to 300 square meters per family. Usually three, but sometimes more than a dozen houses were joined together, and some two-storey houses were built with one family living upstairs and another downstairs, each with their own entrance. In terms of outdoor open space, the family downstairs had a courtyard

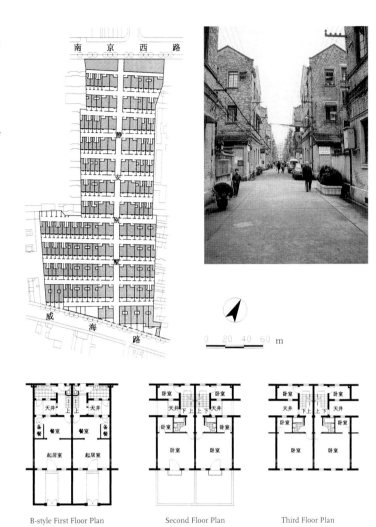

Fig. 2-20a: Jingan Villa, Shanghai, a typical new-style terrace housing area

Jingan Villa, developed by Zhang Tanru and located on 1025 Nanjing Road with a site area of 2.35 hectares, is the largest new-style terrace housing area in Shanghai. There is a main lane in the middle and on each side there are 24 secondary dead-end lanes. It has 183 units of new-style three-storey terrace housing.

Master Plan

Unit Plans

B-style First Floor Plan   Second Floor Plan   Third Floor Plan

and the family upstairs had a balcony. Although the living area of this kind of house was small, the environment was comparatively pleasant. Primarily because of new living habits and market conditions, the new-style linong house was built according to living requirements reflected in the layout of Western-style houses. Generally, the houses were three-storey buildings with both principal rooms and subsidiary rooms (Fig. 2-20). The living room, bedroom, bathroom, reading room and dining room were located in the main part of the building, which typically faced south, and where the ceilings were higher. The kitchens and rooms for servants were placed on the north with lower ceilings, and sometimes there was an extra toilet for servants, as well as a storeroom and a yard at the back. In addition, an entrance hall, a food-preparation room, a closet and a

garage were also built, and some houses even had fireplaces, serving
both for heating and for decoration. In the clustered houses of cities
in northern China, solariums were also sometimes built, and the
new-style linong houses of the Machangdao and Anlecun districts
in Tianjin had basements containing a boiler room, servant rooms,
a kitchen and a storeroom. Otherwise the main entrance led to the
second floor, leaving the lower ground floor for the same purpose as
a basement (Fig. 2-22).

In both the new-style linong houses and higher-standard houses, sanitary and sewage facilities were well equipped, and some
houses even had two bathrooms. The billing, management and
maintenance of water, electricity, gas supply and the telephone system were usually well handled. Typically, departments and special
companies were made responsible for the maintenance of telephone lines and pipes, and also provided for garbage disposal and

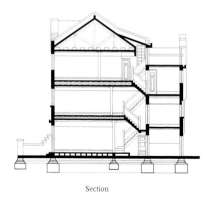
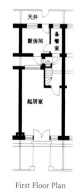

Fig. 2-21: Jincheng Li, Shanghai,
a new-style terrace house

天井

厨房间

备餐室

起居室

Section

First Floor Plan

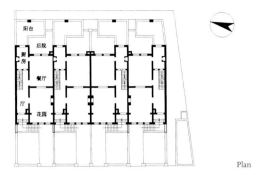

阳台
后院
厨房
餐厅
厅
花园

Plan

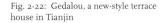

Fig. 2-22: Gedalou, a new-style terrace house in Tianjin

The building is located at 285-293 Hebei Road and was designed in 1937 by P. Bonetti, an Italian architect. The house is in the typical Italian architectural style. It is a structure of wood and brick. It has gardens in front and at the back of the building and also a garage at the first level. The entrance stairs lead directly to the second floor, where the living room and dining room are located. The bedrooms are on the third and fourth floor. Because the facade is decorated with glazed bricks, which look like knots, it was called the Gedalou—Knots House.

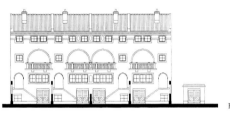

Facade

Section

fire-fighting. The bearing walls of the Western-style urban houses were made of bricks. Floors of the main rooms were made of wood and the floors of moisture-prone places, like the bathroom and *shaitai* (a flat roof for drying clothes), were constructed from reinforced concrete (Figs. 2-21 and 2-22). Nevertheless, sloped wooden-frame roofs still occupied a dominant position, as imitations of Western-style sloped roofs were often incorporated. Elsewhere, there were some flat roofs made of reinforced concrete with waterproof layers.

Compared with the traditional Chinese houses, the rooms of Western-style terrace houses were wider but shorter in depth, and provided for more sunshine and better ventilation. Invariably, there was a yard surrounded by low walls in the front of the house, where grass and flowers were also planted, and it became a pleasant place to relax. The entrance of the house was often placed off to one side of the courtyard, making it more usable, and the houses were usually compactly laid out. Roads were wider and there was more space provided between houses, making them highly sought-after by middle- and upper-income families.

Following the expansion of the concessions in Shanghai, development of the new-style linong houses shifted from the east to the west of the city. They were mostly found in areas to the west of Jing'ansi Street, and somewhere between Chongqing Nanlu Road and Xiangyang Nanlu Road. The most representative houses built during the 1920s and 1930s were in the Simingcun, Jing'an Villa, Huaihaifang, Mofancun and Changlecun residential areas. During the same period, a lot of the new-style linong houses were also built in Tianjin, with those built in the expanded British concession becoming known for their quality. In particular, new-style linong houses in the Shengshengli, Anlecun, Gedalou and Tongleli districts, as well as in Machang Villa, were very well made and with an appealing outer appearance (Fig. 2-22).

2.2.2. Large-scale Development of Semi-detached and Detached Houses

In Harbin, with a relatively sparse population and low density, heating was the most important concern in housing design. Housing for the China Eastern Railway worker was mostly in the form of terrace houses, and the city saw the earliest examples of semi-detached urban housing in China, mostly built as single-storey structures to accommodate ordinary staff members and from two to four families. In some cases, two-storey houses were built, one family living upstairs and one downstairs; the floor space owned by each family ranged from twenty to seventy square meters, with from one bedroom to as many as five bedrooms. Some of the houses had one room, others two, while the biggest had more than five rooms. The floor space of each dwelling in one building was not the same and, in that way, it could satisfy the functional demands of different families (Fig. 2-23). Throughout, practical requirements determined the design of each dwelling and it usually included a small entrance hall, a living room, bedroom(s), a children's room, a kitchen and a bathroom. Typically, a five-bedroom dwelling also had a workroom and a room for servants. Two families usually shared one entrance hall and a kitchen in the houses where four families lived, and usually they were assigned to single workers. Also, as previously mentioned, the China Eastern Railway worker housing was built in a unified way, and so it had its own characteristics. To the east of the

Fig. 2-23: Different combinations of one-storey houses for the employees of the China Eastern Railway

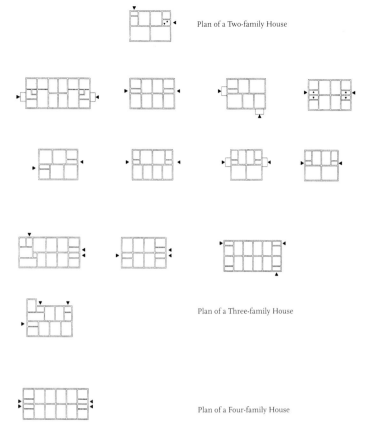

Plan of a Two-family House

Plan of a Three-family House

Plan of a Four-family House

former China Eastern Railway Administrative Bureau on Xidazhi Street, for example, the designs followed the pattern of the so-called small neighborhood common in Europe at the time (Fig. 2-24). Altogether there were forty neighborhoods connected by roads, and there were about ten buildings in each neighborhood, mostly consisting of single-storey houses. Invariably, buildings were placed at the edge of the roads and formed a large open space in the center of the neighborhood, providing a good place for social interaction and outdoor activities. Wells, sewage pools, public toilets and cold storage were also built for public use, and greenbelts were connected with the parks at the road intersections. As a consequence of these improvements, this residential area in Harbin possessed many features of a residential area of a modern city, and, therefore, became a valuable model. Although the form of each building was simple and looked enclosed, primarily because of the cold weather, the whole neighborhood was pleasant.

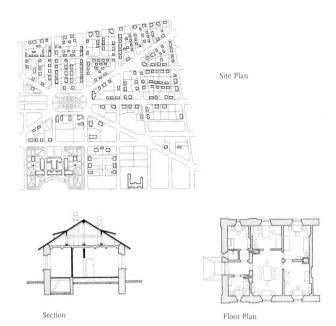

Site Plan

Fig. 2-24: Site and floor plans of houses for employees of the China Eastern Railway (Theses of the Third Conference on the Modern Architectural History of China, 82–84)

Section

Floor Plan

Of the Manchurian Railway employee houses built in Shenyang and Dalian, many were semi-detached and detached units. Often serving as residences for high-ranking officials—many of them foreigners—most of these houses were designed with noticeable foreign features. Usually, furnishing and decoration of rooms was in a Japanese style, including the use of *tatami* with small bedrooms, big closets, sliding doors and a Japanese square bathtub (Fig. 2-25).

After the 1920s, Western-style houses with gardens were built in the trading cities to meet the luxurious lifestyle preferences of wealthy Europeans and high officials. These linong-style garden houses were built mainly in the Xuhui and Luwan districts in Shanghai, whereas in Tianjin they were built mainly in the German,

Fig. 2-25: Hefeng, Japanese-style houses for employees of the Manchurian Railway

First Floor Plan of a Two-storey Detached House

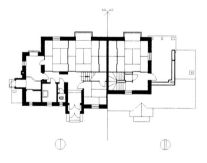

Floor Plan of a Two-storey and Two-family House

British and Italian concessions. Because of their quality, the price of the houses was very high. Each house had a big courtyard, and the road between two buildings in the development was wide enough for cars to pass. In general, the overall environment of the houses was quiet and well maintained (Figs. 2-26 and 2-27). Whether semi-detached or detached, these three- and four-storey houses had windows on at least three sides and most accommodated from one-and-one-half to two bedrooms. The houses were also well equipped with a kitchen, a bathroom, built-in closets, modern heating and other amenities. Steel-framed windows, often extending to the floor, were used to provide better lighting and a view of surrounding areas and, usually, part of the flat roof was used as a deck. Most noticeably, the

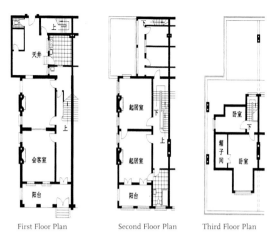

First Floor Plan   Second Floor Plan   Third Floor Plan

Fig. 2-26: Typical semi-detached garden linong houses on 1156 Liyang Road, Shanghai

The houses are located on the south of Liyang Road and were built in 1914 on a land area of 4 hectares. It consisted of 70 units of semi-detached garden houses lined in four rows. The lanes are about 10 meters wide with enough room for parking. It is convenient and accessible to automobiles, since both the ends of the lanes are connected to the main roads, Changchun and Liyang.

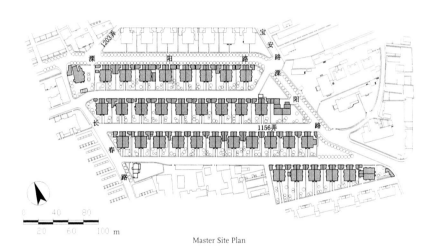

Master Site Plan

Fig. 2-27: Shangfang Garden, Shanghai, a typical detached garden-style housing estate

It is located on 1285 Huaihai Road, with a site area of 2.66 hectares, was developed by Xingye Bank of Zhejiang Province and built in several phases starting from 1938. A total of 68 three-storey detached and semi-detached garden houses were lined in five rows, and a few new-style terrace houses and apartments buildings were located in the north of the estate. The main lane was about 10–15 meters wide with temporary parking, and the secondary lane was about 6 meters wide and accessible to automobiles.

Each house in the northern section occupied an area of 400 square meters and was built with a garage. The houses conformed to one of five designs. The two rows in the south had an area of 200–250 square meters and conformed to one of four designs. Generally speaking, houses were light and spacious with tasteful decoration, gas and bathroom facilities. It was an ideal neighborhood in which to live.

Master Site Plan

Floor Plan of Design B

Third Floor Plan

Second Floor Plan   First Floor Plan

width of the rooms in these houses was large while depth was small. The height of each floor was reduced incrementally, with the height of the first floor generally running to 3.6 meters, the second floor to 3.3 meters and the third floor to 3.0 meters. The kitchen was comparatively small, although served by gas. Many of these features reflected the influence of new architectural trends in foreign countries, with various outward appearances including English, Spanish and modern styles. Nevertheless, regardless of style, all the houses were designed to make the most of their interior and exterior accommodations. On the whole, there was not much difference between linong garden houses and new-style linong houses. The only difference was that the flat roofs of houses were covered by red clinker bricks and sometimes flowers were planted. Another new feature was the introduction of corner windows, providing occupants with a broader view.

2.2.3. Multi-storey Apartment Houses

In Harbin, two-storey high-grade apartment buildings appeared early on, again because they were economical and easy to keep warm (Liu Songfu, 1991, 82). The buildings were designed with standard units, each accommodating from two to four households sharing one staircase (Fig. 2-28). Within each apartment there was an entrance hall, a livingroom, bedrooms, a children's room, a kitchen and a bathroom. Large apartments had a study and a sunroom, as well as a stairway to the kitchen. Overall, apartments ranged in size from two to five bedrooms and, in layout, attention was paid to the reasonable division of rooms. On average, each family possessed a floor area of 50 to 100 hundred square meters, and

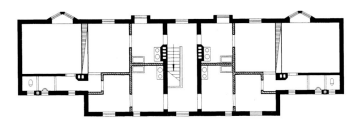

Fig. 2-28: Apartment Housing for the Manchurian Railway

Shannan Village, a housing estate with four-storey apartment buildings, was developed by Puitang (a church) and built in 1940. It occupies an irregularly shaped piece of land of 1.62 hectares and has 16 independent apartment buildings, each of which consists of eight three-room apartments. It has a total of 128 apartments and 86 garages. Apartments are of a brick and concrete structure and well decorated and equipped. The ratio of space between buildings and building height is 0.5-0.8. Because of well-used space between buildings, the apartments are well lighted and ventilated. The free layout and well-developed landscape create a pleasant living environment.

Standard Unit Floor Plan (Theses of the Fifth Conference on Contemporary Architectural History of China, 124)

these dwellings were occupied primarily by foreign staff who had come to China earlier.

In the trading cities, the development of apartment buildings was a combined result of increased urban population, land shortage and the concentration of urban housing. In the concessions of Shanghai and Tianjin in the 1930s, for instance, a pressing problem was rising population and insufficient land and, therefore, multi-storey apartment buildings were built to accommodate these exigencies. Most were middle-grade or high-standard apartments for people to rent. Some stood alone in crowded neighborhoods, while others were developed together as a larger complex. Although they were well designed, usually the floor space of each apartment was comparatively small and the building area of each household ranged from 40 to 150 square meters. Whether large or small, every apartment had its own kitchen and bathroom and most had separate livingrooms and bedrooms, with more expensive apartments having a separate diningroom, a servant's room and a garage. The main bedroom had its own bathroom and some units even had back doors and special staircases for servants. Although none of these houses was very large, the layout of rooms on the same floor made them look spacious and convenient to use.

In areas where many apartment buildings were constructed, the outdoor environment was usually well appointed. Because of the low density of buildings, communal space was large and the increased green open space presented inhabitants with a pleasant place for social interaction. Generally, the design of houses differed according to location and building standards. Among the different types were one-staircase units for two households, one-staircase

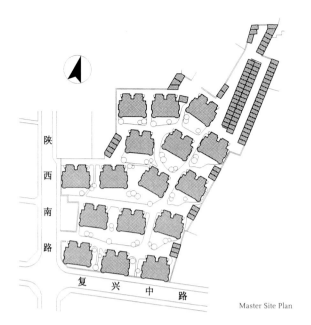

Fig. 2-29: Shanghai Shannan Village, a housing estate consisting of multi-storey apartment buildings

陕西南路

复兴中路

Master Site Plan

Plan of a Standard Building

units for four households, and multiple units, with both a small depth and a larger depth unit, allowing windows on three sides (Figs. 2-29 and 2-30). Where small apartment buildings were located along streets, the first floor was used for shops, although lone apartment buildings on small lots could also be found in the concessions in Shanghai and Tianjin. Many were apartments with their own access and some were served by inner corridors. Generally, each family had from one to three rooms. These houses were suitable for middle-class families, and some were constructed by for-

Fig. 2-30: Shanghai Garden
Apartments

These garden apartments are
located on 1173 West Nanjing Road
on land of .90 hectare. They were
built in 1931 and have four rows of
apartment buildings and two rows
of garages. There are a total of 60
apartments designed with 2 to 5
rooms to suit different family
sizes.

The three and four-storey buildings have a brick and concrete
structure with flat roofs and thick
walls. They are also furnished
with hardwood floors and top-
quality decoration, kitchen and
bathroom facilities. The generous
space between buildings provides
areas for landscaping. The buildings have convenient access both
to public transportation and shopping.

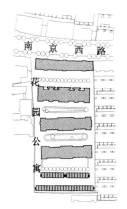

Master Site Plan

Standard Floor Plan

Fig. 2-31: Individual multi-storey apartment buildings in different cities

eign companies for their employees. Functional and financial factors were major considerations in these designs, with the result that they were usually simple and practical (Fig. 2-31).

The building structure of the apartments was sound, even though internal renovation was carried out to differing standards. The buildings with four storeys or more were constructed of reinforced concrete, and the first-floor walls were built of machine-made red bricks. All external and internal walls, from the second floor and above, were made of light, hollow bricks, in order to make them easier to build, and reinforced-concrete rib floors were surfaced with hardwood mosaic. In the kitchen and bathroom, places were set aside for pipes, with cement mortar used to paste mosaic and red tiles on the floors made of concrete and coal cinder. Coatings of thermal protection and waterproof layers were added to the house roofs and, overall, both the structure and building methods were similar to those used today.

In addition, there was another kind of small apartment with long open corridors. It was low-standard housing built extensively in Dalian after the 1930s, and copied one of the standard designs of the Manchurian Railway employee housing, with a public staircase linking every floor and a long open corridor linking every household. Usually, each household occupied one bay of the building, with a floor space of twenty square meters, into which was crammed a bedroom, a small square hall, a kitchen, a bathroom and a closet.

2.2.4. High-rise Apartment Buildings

Apartment buildings of seven storeys or more with elevators sprang up in Shanghai after the 1930s (Fig. 2-33). The rationale behind this phenomenon was as follows. First, significant progress had been made in building technologies, often using a lot of cheap imported materials. Second, there was a steep rise in land prices within the downtown area, making tall apartment buildings the only choice. Commonly, a layout of inner corridors was adopted and, depending on the location of the apartment building and its prospective inhabitants, floors were constructed with a mix of apartment units with differing numbers of rooms (Fig. 2-32). Typically, they ranged from one-and-a-half-bedroom apartments to five-bedroom apartments, but most contained two or three bedrooms. With respect to the plan, attention was paid to the connection of bedrooms and bathrooms, as well to the arrangement of the kitchen with the dining room and the living room with the balcony. Attempts were also made to give each apartment a good view. The rooms were fully furnished with *qian-qing* (early Qing) closets, and corridor closets were installed to make full use of the available space and to make the rooms look neat. Gen-

Fig. 2-32: Picardi Apartments, a high-rise apartment building in Shanghai

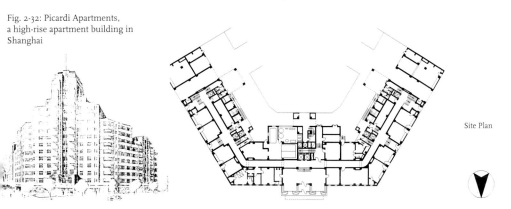

Site Plan

Fig. 2-33: Some well-known high-rise apartment buildings in Shanghai (clockwise)

Spacious staircase and mailboxes, Changchun Apartment Building

Broadway Mansion

Changchun Apartment Building

Embankment Building

Cathay Mansion—the north building is today the Jinjang Hotel

Fig. 2-34: Sheds in slum areas of
Shanghai

erally, the floor height of apartment buildings was around 3.5 meters
and the ceiling height was about 3.2 meters. These tall apartment
buildings were also well equipped. Besides electricity and running
water, gas, heating, hot-water facilities and a garbage chute were
provided. In the corridors there were boxes for milk and papers and,
in some high-class apartments, kitchens were equipped with refrigerators. Typically, there were two elevators—one for people and the
other for goods. In addition, there was a subsidiary staircase for
service people to use. In some large apartments, one elevator was
used exclusively by two or three families on the same floor, in order
to guarantee privacy. A long inner corridor was generally divided
into several sections with a door between each section. This not only
guaranteed the privacy and quietness of each section, but could also

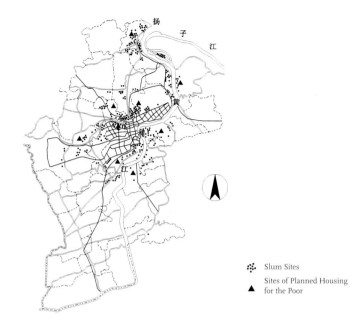

Slum Sites

▲ Sites of Planned Housing for the Poor

be used for dispersing individual living spaces within an apartment, or for internal communication.

Influenced by modernism, most apartment buildings in Shanghai featured a simple and modern style of exterior, such as those of the Embankment Building (Hebin Da Lou) and the Broadway (Bailaohui) Mansion, and some of the buildings were decorated in an artistic manner. The entrance hall was usually lavishly designed, and in order to attract tenants the design and use of materials for the floor, walls and roof of the lobby were often elaborate. In these regards, representative tall apartment buildings in Shanghai were the Picardi (Bikadi) Building, the Embankment Building and the Junling Building. Apartments were mainly for rent; the Hammierdeng Mansion and the Broadway Mansion combined public functions, hotel rooms and apartments by placing them on separate floors.

2.3. Housing for Average Residents Built by City Governments

Slum-dwellers usually came to cities from the poor villages to avoid poverty and war, although, as large as Shanghai was, there was no place for them to reside (Figs. 2-34 to 2-35). Usually, they built houses of reed mats and grass with an area of only five or six square meters. Effectively, these shacks were only shoulder height, like pigstys. Shantytowns were also common in trading cities and the cities in northern China; those who lived in crude tile-roofed houses

- ●   Slum Sites

- ▨   Sites Available for Slum
Development and Housing
for the Poor

- ■   Sites Planned for Slum
Development and Housing
for the Poor

Fig. 2-36: Locations of housing
for the poor in Nanjing

were called "the populace" and those who lived in thatched cottages
were called *Penghu*. The living environment of shantytowns was of a
very poor quality—damp, dark and dirty. Inhabitants received water
from a fire hydrant by the roadside, with typically one fire hydrant
being used by several thousand people, and sewage was simply dis-
posed of around the dwellings.

In order to solve this housing problem and the poor environment of the shantytowns, in the 1930s the Nanjing city government
adopted some measures to improve living conditions and to generally set an example for other cities to follow. According to the "Survey on *Penghu* Families in Nanjing," presented by the Sociology
Department of Central University in 1933, the slums were harmful
to the city in four respects. They harmed its appearance, its public
health and fire-fighting capacities, its public security and its decency
(Wu Wenhui, 1935, 102). One outcome of this survey was the establishment of the Shack Improvement Committee, which aimed to
demolish the slums and move the inhabitants into newly constructed housing. Initially, the government planned to take over 200
hectares of urban land to build houses for slum-dwellers. After the
land was cleared, roads, ditches and toilets were built and clean
water was supplied. Then the slum-dwellers moved in and were
required to build their own dwellings in orderly rows. Each family
occupied an area 5.5 by 4 meters; the finished dwelling was normally divided into two rooms and was required to be 2.6 meters high,
with walls made of clay or bamboo with clay floors. The frames of
the houses were usually made of wood covered with reed mats and

with cogongrass placed on top.[3] Later, gray tiles replaced the reed mats and cogongrass for fire-prevention purposes. It cost about thirty yuan to build a dwelling like this, and every slum-dwelling family received ten yuan from the government for this purpose—the rest came from their own pocket. In addition, the government spent about forty yuan on each family for public facilities, such as schools and toilets, and an administrator was placed in charge of the management and doubled as a teacher. From 1935 to 1937, such houses were built in the Sisuocun, Shimenkan and Qilijie areas of Nanjing, and of the 7,759 slum-dwelling families who needed relocation, 4,111 families settled down in one of these three places (Fig. 2-36).

By 1935, populace housing was being built by the city government and, in order to keep them as low-rent houses, the "most important principle," in the guidelines of the time, was to "control construction cost and maintenance costs."[4] The houses were 2.4 meters high, and were built with brick walls and gray-tiled floors. The frames of the houses were made of China fir and covered with reed mats. Every family owned a house, measuring 3.5 by 4.5 meters, with a small kitchen on the side. Including the land price and the expenditure for infrastructure and public facilities, the average cost came to 120 yuan.[5] In both the shack district and the populace housing, the principles of layout were the same. There were eight households located in one row, fifteen rows formed a block, and nine blocks formed a district. Among the nine blocks, one was set aside for public facilities and a green public open space (Figs. 2-37 and 2-38). A similar layout was adopted by the city governments in Shanghai and Qingdao when they also built housing for the poor.

Both the shacks and populace housing came to be called "workers' residential areas" in Nanjing and, originally, the government planned to build nine such districts. Starting from 1935, about 5,000 slum-dwelling families and other working poor would be relocated to these districts every year.[6] After the outbreak of the anti-Japanese War in 1937, the building of the houses had to be stopped, and those already completed were badly damaged. A plan to build

Fig. 2-38: Plan of housing for the poor in Qili Street in Nanjing

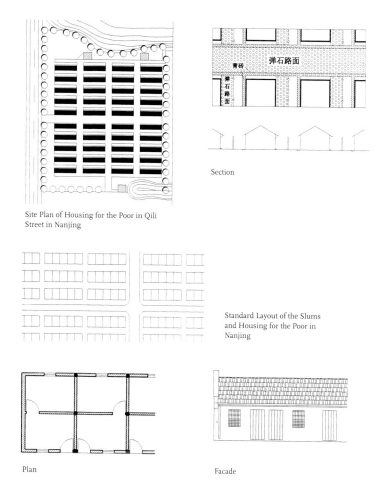

Section

Site Plan of Housing for the Poor in Qili Street in Nanjing

Standard Layout of the Slums and Housing for the Poor in Nanjing

Plan

Facade

such houses was discussed again in 1948 but was not put into practice. At the same time, a Relief Camp and a School for Women to Learn the Trade were both constructed in Nanjing, to house more than 1,000 homeless refugees.

Notes

1. The numbers are from the report "The Past and Future of the Workers' Housing in Nanjing," submitted by the Nanjing municipal government in October 1935. The report mentioned that this number was based on a recent survey, but there were still many families not registered.
2. Luo Zhiru, *Shanghai in the Statistics Table* (Shanghai: City of Shanghai, 1932), 16, 21 and 24.
3. "The Past and Future of Workers' Housing in Nanjing" (Nanjing: Nanjing Municipal Government, 1935), 3.
4. Working Affairs Bureau of Nanjing, *Work Report* (1937), 128.
5. "The Past and Future Workers' Housing in Nanjing," 13.
6. Ibid., 9.

Chapter Three: A Languishing Period in Early Modern Urban Housing (1937–1949)

1. Damages Caused by the War and a Deterioration of Living Conditions

In 1937 war broke out between Japan and China. Soon large pieces of territory in China's north, east and south fell to the invading Japanese troops; cities were destroyed and construction activities stopped. For ordinary urban citizens, the problem of housing shortage was made all the more serious because of a large influx of refugees. Most of them saw their income fall and, therefore, their ability to pay rent diminished. It was not uncommon that many families shared one house, resulting in serious overcrowding. Slums that had emerged earlier in the suburbs increased each year as the war went on. In Shanghai, for instance, statistics indicated that there were more than 50,000 households living in slum conditions by 1947[1] (Fig. 3-1). In Shanghai and Nanjing, some of the housing for ordinary city residents was also destroyed by war.

When the Japanese were defeated, a civil war ensued and the real estate business was not able to recover from depression. Beside some housing construction invested in by government institutions for their employees, most construction activities were devoted to

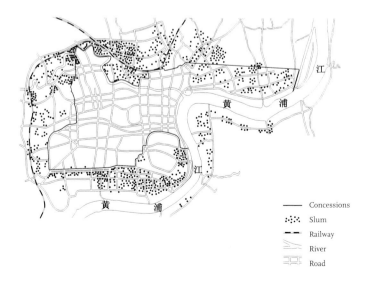

Fig. 3-1: Distribution of the slums in Shanghai before 1949

江

黄　浦

黄　浦

—— Concessions
∴∷∴ Slum
– – Railway
River
Road

repairing houses damaged during the previous war. In Changchun and Harbin, which had been occupied by the Japanese and served as their strategic bases, there had been some construction, but little housing was built for ordinary people.

2. The Lopsided Boom in the Concessions

The concessions in Shanghai and Tianjin became so-called isolated islands among the Japanese-occupied areas and provided the rich with a haven largely free from war damage. Between 1937 and 1945, the population of Shanghai increased by some 2 million people, reaching 6 million by the year 1945. Under these circumstances, some housing was still constructed to cater to the needs of the rich. It included the new style of linong houses, garden-like houses and apartments. Among representative buildings from this period were the Shangfang *huayuan* (employee garden housing of 1938), the Shanghai *xincun* (Shanghai village of 1939), the *fulü xincun* (Fortune Village) and the *yiyuan* (comfortable garden) in Shanghai and the *quilini* (luxury lane) and the *yunchengli* (lucky city lane) in Tianjin. Because these projects were built for powerful officials and wealthy businessmen, they were spacious and occupied large areas of land. For example, the high-grade detached and semi-detached garden-like houses all had large green spaces. The ratio between the height of the house and the distance between houses was more than 1:1, and interior decoration was completed to very high standards. The facade of the houses usually varied, some having rather complicated features. There was, however, no new development of housing types per se.

3. Population Surges in Cities in Southwest China and Housing Development

In 1938, the Nationalist government shifted its capital from Nanjing to Chongqing and devised a construction plan, emphasizing industrial construction in the southwest, using heavy industry related to military purposes. Since southwest China was weak in terms of industrial development, factories in the east were moved to the southwest. Through financial re-allocations, investment and loans, the government encouraged local and outside industries to participate in this industrial construction. By the end of 1940, close to 450 factories had moved from the coastal areas to the hinterland, recruiting 12,000 skilled workers and more than 20,000 technicians and engineers from the coastal areas (Qi Dayun, Ren Antai, 1991, 190).

The shift of factories and population to the southwest gave impetus to the economic development of Chongqing and Chengdu, where building activities blossomed. The government had built some public buildings as well as housing, but there were few well-planned and large-scale housing projects besides the construction of *Chengdu xincun*. As Chengdu's population swelled from 460,000 in 1937 to 830,000 in the early 1940s, the supply of housing fell well short of demand. With the leadership of the mayor, a plan was devised to build what was to be called the *Chengdu xincun*, between the then Huaxi University and Sichuan University. Land for roads, housing and public buildings was planned, and after neighborhood communities were designated, price tags were placed on the land for public sale. This plan boosted the development of the urban district of Chengdu. However, a lack of financial and personnel resources during wartime made construction difficult, and not much came of the project. At the same time, in the old districts of Chengdu, Chinese developers built some one-storey clustered urban housing and Western-style clustered housing like that found in Shanghai's new linong, although here again nothing new was to be found.

With its ups and downs, the early period of China's modern city housing development left a special page in the history of China's urban housing development, reflecting a transformation from traditional to modern urban housing. It created a unique city landscape with an invaluable architectural heritage. Traces of that particular time can still be found in most affected cities, and in the decades that followed, the utilization, transformation and renovation of the old houses, while protecting their representative architecture, became a topic of concern for professionals in particular, and for the public in general.

Notes

1. Urban Economy Research Group in the Department of Economy of Shanghai Social Science Academy, *The Evolution of Slums in Shanghai* (Shanghai: Shanghai Social Science Academy, 1962)

Part Two: Housing Development in the Socialist Planned Economy from 1949 to 1978

by
Zhang Jie and Wang Tao

Introduction

After the founding of the People's Republic of China, socialist public ownership within a planned economy was established. By acquir-
ing privately owned houses and by developing public properties, the
majority of urban housing gradually became publicly owned.
Between 1949 and 1978, China's urban housing development was
always constrained and influenced by the state's policies of industrial development, which gave priority to heavy industry. Throughout,
the state adopted a strategy of high accumulation and low consumption in order to guarantee large sustainable investments for heavy
industry. Consequently, a dual social and economic structure was
shaped in both the cities and countryside, with rules and regulations
concerning urban residents' salaries, welfare and household registration. This system, in turn, effectively constituted the basis of
urban housing development. Guided by the principle of "serving
production as well as people's livelihood," industrial production pre-
conditioned housing development, with the objective of meeting
basic residential needs while giving priority to industrial development.

Under the socialist planned economy, China developed a complicated urban housing welfare system, whereby the State kept control of housing development and readjusted policies in the light of
situations reflected in the national economy. This system divided
urban residents into different categories and imposed control over
them. As a result, people whose work units were of a different ownership—implying a different social status—ended up living in different housing conditions. With this system, two types of housing
also appeared in cities: houses managed by enterprises or institutions, and publicly owned houses managed by urban housing management departments of local governments. Furthermore, both had
a profound influence on the formation of the cityscape.

The state policy of "production first and livelihood second" kept
urban housing standards at a low level. As far as planning and
design were concerned, the objective was to keep housing construction costs and standards of provision under control and, in order to
develop rapidly, the state propagated standard designs for housing.
However, although industrialization of housing was an objective of
this approach, it did not make much progress, being restricted by

prevailing levels of economic and industrial development, as well as by less than favorable levels of investment. In fact, during a thirty-year period, industrialized housing did not advance much beyond brick and concrete structures with a low level of technological involvement. Moreover, because of active state involvement, urban housing development—including planning and design—was only able to make progress when the national economy was prosperous. When the national economy met with difficulties, housing development slumped accordingly.

Generally, housing development in this period can be divided into three stages. The first was from 1949 to 1957, corresponding to the First Five-Year Plan, when the national economy recovered. This was a time of stable and normal urban development in China, when the level of investment in housing was about 10 percent of the total investment in capital construction, and the housing systems, designs and technical standards provided the foundation for housing development for the next thirty years. In the early days of the Peoples' Republic of China, massive housing construction began to ease housing shortages and, as the First Five-Year Plan was put into practice, the emphasis shifted towards production, supported by building standards, methods of design and industrial procedures introduced from the Soviet Union. In the later period of the First-Five Year Plan, the adverse effects of unbalanced industrial development emerged and, under the state policy of "production first, livelihood second," housing construction standards dropped for the first time. Subsequently, in an attempt to seek a mode of housing construction that suited China's situation, the Central Party Committee (CPC) put forward the policy of "let a hundred flowers blossom and a hundred schools of thought contend." Encouraged by this, architects made fruitful studies about housing standards, construction costs and residents' living habits. Aesthetic issues also became less important and the controversy over socialist realism and functionalism was brushed aside in favor of a more pragmatic attitude. Unfortunately, however, all of this resulted in poor housing design for a long time to come.

The second stage lasted from 1958 to 1965, beginning with the Great Leap Forward and followed by readjustment and rectification of the national economy. These ups and downs in political and economic development also caused jolts in housing development. The Great Leap Forward and the People's Commune Movement resulted in a serious imbalance in the structure of the national economy and housing development was sacrificed. Investment in housing development dropped sharply and housing construction standards declined to the lowest level since the founding of the People's Republic. To practice strict economy became the prevailing principle, as the key problem was how to cut costs. Meanwhile, strongly influenced by ideology, the People's Commune Movement appeared in cities, albeit for a brief period of time and, starting from 1961, economic readjustment and rectification occurred, enhancing urban housing development. Influenced by an atmosphere conducive to research, insightful ideas about housing design were expressed; discussions about housing layout promoted research and development of small apartment buildings, as well as the diversified design of residential areas. But as a leftist ideology gained ground again, the idea that "thrifty was revolutionary" became predominant once more in housing circles.

The third stage lasted from 1966 to 1978, covering the Cultural Revolution and its immediate aftermath. The political turmoil sweeping the whole country did devastating damage to China's social, political and economic development, with the result that housing development stopped and did not recover again until the 1970s. Population growth and backward agricultural practices forced the state to impose strict control over the use of land in order to guarantee grain production, and land shortages in cities hindered housing development. To keep city size from expanding and to save land, high-rise buildings were encouraged by the state, while the general building density of residential areas was increased.

Although housing development turned out for the better during the later period of the Cultural Revolution, the leftist idea of taking class struggle as a key component was not brought to an end. Instead, its influence lasted until 1978. Then a crumbling economic situation, a virtual standstill in housing development and a swelling population created extremely serious housing shortages, and reform became inevitable.

Chapter Four: Economic Recovery Following the Soviet Model and Reflections During the First Five-Year Plan (1949–1957)

In the early period of the People's Republic of China, the housing shortage was the major problem. In the planning and design of housing, the simplest methods were adopted in order to build as many houses as possible and in the shortest possible time. Starting from 1953, with economic and technical assistance from the Soviet Union, China embarked on the road to socialist industrialization and the establishment of a planned economic system. Moreover, this period provided two cornerstones for subsequent urban housing development: namely that housing construction should serve China's industrialization and, second, that it should follow the Soviet Union's model of housing development. By the end of the First Five-Year Plan, some unexpected circumstances had arisen. In 1956, for instance, Stalin was criticized at the Twentieth Congress of the Soviet Communist Party. At the same time in China, the consequences of imbalanced development of industrial and agricultural development also began to emerge, forcing China into a discussion about the path it had taken towards socialism. Meanwhile, those in urban housing who mechanically followed the Soviet model were criticized, thus beginning basic questioning of whether the Soviet model was appropriate for China's particular circumstances.

1. The Social and Economic Background of Urban Housing Development

The period from 1949 to 1952 brought economic recovery to the newly founded People's Republic. The major tasks facing the government included: holding down rising prices, suppressing inflation and ensuring the supply of basic daily necessities. This work was largely completed by 1952 and, with help from the Soviet Union, China began its First Five-Year Plan in 1953 with the establishment and operation of a planned economic system of socialist industrialization.

1.1. Establishment of a Planned Economic System
When the People's Republic of China was founded in 1949, the national economy was in a shambles. To control inflation and

reduce the financial deficit, the new government decided on a policy of managing the economy in a unified manner. Personnel, material and financial resources were centralized to promote a quick recovery and to guarantee the balance of revenues and expenditures.[1] Soon after, this policy proved to be effective, boosting the government's confidence about centralized management. As China began its First Five-Year Plan with the help of the Soviet Union, imitation of the Soviet model further strengthened the planned economic system in a centralized direction.[2] Enterprise and local government personnel, financial and material resources, as well as production, supply and distribution functions were all placed under the unified management of relevant departments of the central government. This arrangement also ensured the policy of giving priority to the development of heavy industry. Under such circumstances, the construction, distribution and management of urban housing were also centralized, paving the way for the establishment of a welfare housing system.

1.2. Policies Giving Priority to the Development of Heavy Industry

Based on Marxist economic principles and considering the experience of the Soviet Union in giving priority to the development of heavy industry, China devised its own policies of industrial development. During the process of expanded production—according to Marxist economic principles—the production of the means of production being used to make the means of production increases fastest, followed by the production of the means of production used to make the means of subsistence (i.e., production of the means of production increases faster than all other forms of production). Consequently, priority was given to the development of heavy industry by the Chinese government in its First Five-Year Plan.[3] The strategy of putting emphasis on the development of heavy industry had profound effects on China's economic and social development, and it also determined the direction of policies concerning urban development, whereby housing was essentially considered to be non-productive.

Owing to these preferential policies, heavy industry grew rapidly, resulting in a rapid development of the national economy. According to the goals set forth in the First Five-Year Plan, the total output value of industry and agriculture would increase at an annual rate of 8.6 percent, and the gross value of industrial output would increase by 14.7 percent annually. In fact, the actual increases of the gross value of industrial output was 18.4 percent during this period, surpassing the figure in the plan. Compared with 1952, the production of the means of production increased 210.7 percent, an average annual increase of 25.4 percent. Also showing the obvious effects of the new economic policies, the proportion of production of the means of production in the gross value of industrial output increased from 35.5 percent in 1952 to 45 percent in 1957.[4]

The distribution of capital construction investment also pointed to a policy that favored heavy industry. Of the 58.84 billion yuan in capital construction investment during the same five years, 52.4 percent was used in the industrial sector, 88.8 percent of which was for heavy industry, with more than 10,000 factories and mines under construction. Of these, 921 exceeded their quotas, some 227 more than stipulated in the original plan.[5] The proportion of socialist industry—including publicly and collectively-owned enterprises as a whole—rose from 44.8 percent in 1952 to 72.8 percent in 1957, as the transformation of capitalist industry was carried out through state enterprises in all industrial sectors. In fact, by 1957, the proportion of capitalist industry in the gross value of industrial output was below 0.1 percent.[6] As a consequence, investors in urban housing development and owners of urban housing became predominantly public or state-owned entities.

1.3. Establishment of a Binary Economic Structure and a Low-wage System in Cities

As it was recovering from the damages of war, the greatest difficulty facing the Chinese economy was how to find sufficient capital for the establishment of its heavy industry and expanded production. Public accumulation at the time could hardly meet the needs. Through a highly centralized planned economy and management system, the government used administrative forces to organize and allocate social and economic resources, in what amounted to compulsory accumulation for industrialization. Also, taxes and unequal exchanges of industrial and agricultural products, as well as rural resources, were employed by industries to support their expansion and development. To maintain a high growth rate for industry, and to avoid urbanization's and industrialization's rivalry for resources, the government devised a series of supplementary systems and measures for the sole purpose of sponsoring industrialization. This resulted in a pattern where cities developed industries, while agriculture was the single and only concern in the countryside (Wang Jieye, 1996, 2-3). In addition, to keep the cost of industrial production under control, the state put most of the national income into expanded industrial development and adopted a system of low wages in cities—a system that lasted from 1949 until 1978. Under such a policy of high accumulation and low consumption, people's livelihoods were placed below production and, in order to meet the basic needs of city dwellers, they were provided with subsidies and other welfare supplements including housing. This is the primary reason why urban housing developed at such a low level and for such a long time.

1.4. Urbanization and City Development

During this period, and particularly during the First Five-Year Plan as construction of more than 900 large-scale industrial projects began, the new government, with the strategy in mind of developing heavy industry first, adopted a guideline for urban development that can be summarized as "focusing on key projects and advancing steadily." Six new cities were built, twenty cities were greatly expanded, and seventy-four cities were expanded on a smaller scale. The population of cities and towns kept rising steadily, with an average annual increase of 4.45 million people, or an increase of 7.06 percent, as compared to 2.24 percent for the national population as a whole. Urbanization also rose from 9.05 percent to 13.08 percent in these eight years, at an annual average of 0.5 percent, or slightly higher than the comparable average world figure (Zhou Yixing, 1997, 108). These rates indicate that economic growth and urbanization were well coordinated during the First Five-Year Plan, even though the explosion of urban population put greater pressure on urban housing than before.

Less than one-third of the 694 key industrial projects of the time were located in coastal areas, with the remainder located in China's hinterland (Dong Jianhong, 1955, 1–12). This was done for the purpose of national defense and also in an attempt to narrow the gap among regions in terms of production. Almost all newly built cities were located in regions where raw materials and other resources were plentiful, and were sited around industrial construction projects.

Throughout, the economic focus was on heavy industry, and one task facing these cities was to transform their consumption-based economy to one that was production-based. According to Marxist theories, cities in socialist countries are the bases for production of means of production rather than of consumption, and the working class should comprise the majority of the urban population. Therefore, the Municipal Planning Commission, established in 1949, argued that even the historic capital of Beijing should also be a large industrial city, as well as a political center. Later, this statement was reiterated twice, in Beijing's city plans of 1954 and 1957.[7] With a strong concern for economy and planning, most new industrial areas were constructed on the periphery of existing cities, surrounded by large living quarters that comprised the major part of urban housing growth in this period.[8]

1.5. The Soviet Union's Influence

For historical and ideological reasons, the newly founded People's Republic of China had close cooperation with the Soviet Union on political, economic, military and cultural matters. Soon after World War II ended, the Soviet Union devoted considerable effort to the reconstruction of cities and houses and, consequently, had gained much experience. Furthermore, the Soviet model profoundly affected China's economic and urban development at that time and, during its economic recovery, China began fifty construction projects, all with the help of the Soviet Union. Indeed, as stated earlier, the ideas of compiling the First Five-Year Plan, establishing a highly centralized planned economic system and giving priority to the development of heavy industry, all came from the Soviet Union. Also, a core component of heavy industrial development in the First Five-Year Plan was 156 key industrial projects that received direct Soviet assistance in technology, equipment and personnel. Against this backdrop of the New China imitating the Soviet Union, it was only natural to find similar influences in the planning and design of urban housing.

2. Urban Housing Development and Related Policies

In general, urban housing development in China took place under a policy framework that stressed production over matters of social welfare and resulted in several new types of housing and changes in patterns of property ownership. The urban housing system that emerged also required different approaches to management and construction, under the dictates of a planned economy.

2.1. Urban Housing Development Policies

In the economic development of the New China, as described earlier, urban housing construction was considered as the production of the means of subsistence—a non-productive component in the accumulation of capital. Furthermore, when priority was given to heavy industry, consumption was required to give way to production, so as to concentrate all powers and resources in the rapid development of heavy industry which, it was believed, would boost

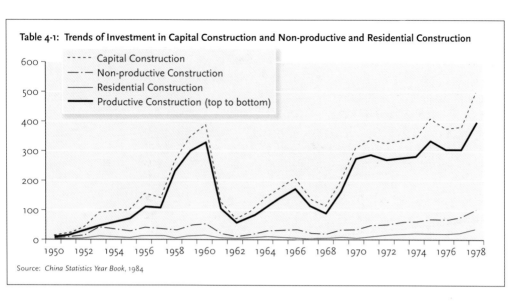

Table 4-1: Trends of Investment in Capital Construction and Non-productive and Residential Construction

- ----- Capital Construction
- —·— Non-productive Construction
- ——— Residential Construction
- ——— Productive Construction (top to bottom)

Source: *China Statistics Year Book, 1984*

the national economy as a whole. Consequently, urban housing construction was always placed in a secondary position (Table 4-1).

In the years before the First Five-Year Plan, city construction in old cities focused mainly on improving sanitation and infrastructure.[9] In the First Five-Year Plan it was clearly stated that the principle of building socialist cities was one of shifting from "cities of consumption" to "cities of production." The construction of municipal works was concentrated in newly built industrial cities and industrial areas located in the suburbs of older cities. Living quarters for workers—known as "workers' new villages"—were built near the factories in order to shorten commuting time and make full use of the municipal infrastructure. Workers' new villages constituted a major part of urban housing growth in this period, with relatively little reconstruction in the old districts of cities. In Shanghai, for instance, the total floor space of housing was 4.8 million square meters more in 1957 than in 1950, and 57.7 percent of this was housing for workers (Table 4-2).

Before the founding of the People's Republic, private ownership of urban housing was predominant. In Wuhan, for instance, private housing accounted for 84.32 percent of all units (Cai Derong, 1987, 35). After the founding of the People's Republic, the new government adopted a system of public ownership by taking over the properties of the former Nationalist government, confiscating properties from imperialist countries and from bureaucrat capitalists.[10] However, the new government did not deprive private urban house owners of their property in the same way they deprived land owners in

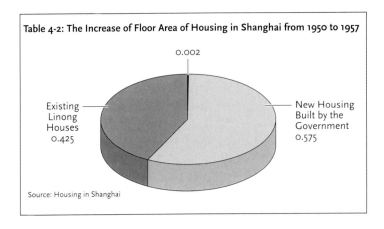

Table 4-2: The Increase of Floor Area of Housing in Shanghai from 1950 to 1957

0.002

Existing Linong Houses 0.425

New Housing Built by the Government 0.575

Source: Housing in Shanghai

rural areas of theirs during the agrarian revolution because, gener-ally, private ownership of urban housing was considered as capital-ist rather than feudalist in nature. And, in the new democratic revo-lutionary period, house ownership of a capitalist nature was to receive the same protection as other ownership of private capital, with the sole exception of bureaucrat capital.[11] Thus, between 1949 and 1956, government policies were protective with regard to medi-um- and small-property owners in cities and, in 1956, the majority of urban housing was still in private hands. Since the economic strength of the state was limited at the time, buying and selling of private houses and the existence of a rental market eased the pres-sure of housing shortages to some extent. In Beijing, for example, there were 1.2 million houses at the beginning of the new republic, with only 280,000 publicly owned houses. The rest were privately owned and half of these were rented houses. More specifically, at that time there were 410,000 households in Beijing and 330,000 households lived in rented houses, although without a uniform rental rate. By contrast, publicly owned houses were managed by a government department, with rents set at reasonable levels after the department had earned a little profit and after it deducted expendi-tures for routine management and repairs.[12]

As the so-called socialist transition period came to an end, China entered a period of complete socialism and quickened its steps toward a socialist system of public ownership. As the socialist trans-formation of the ownership of the means of production was com-pleted, in 1956 the government put forward "Current Information of Privately-owned Houses in Cities and Suggestions on their Socialist Transformation" (Bi Baode, 1994, 22-23) and started to shift private houses more vigorously into public ownership. Conse-quently, in the two decades that followed, the proportion of privately owned houses throughout China kept declining and, by 1978, only 9.9 percent of all houses were owned privately (Wang Xiaoming, 1988, 59).

2.2. Establishment of an Urban Housing System and Housing Construction

In the early period of the People's Republic, the economy was weak and commodities were scarce. The government continued with a free or semi-free system of supply that had been used by the Communists before they came to power. Under this system, consumer goods were divided into various categories and provided to all government officials and city residents. The purpose of this policy was to guarantee the supply of the most basic consumer goods, and housing was among the items provided.

2.2.1. *The Formation of the Welfare Housing System*

After China embarked on the path of industrialization, a policy of low wages and low consumption was implemented. Government officials and city residents were supposed to pay rents for their housing, although housing was not regarded as a consumer good. By the 1950s, China's economy had recovered considerably and, in 1955, the State Council issued the order that a wage system would be instituted for all civil servants, replacing the earlier system of free supply. At the same time the State Council issued its "Interim Measures Regarding the Collection of Rents for the Publicly-owned Apartments of the Government Agencies under the Central Party Committee." From this, housing rents were readjusted with reference to the standard for civil servants, and most rents were set at lower rates than before.

But why were they lower rents? Earlier in this chapter, the policies employed by the government to make agricultural resources serve industry so as to give priority to the development of heavy industry were discussed. In cities, the government kept strict control on consumption and pay raises, thus effectively controlling urban populations with regard to the supply of basic consumer goods, which were both rationed and subsidized. As levels of industrialization rose, people's wages were still kept at a low level, so that resources could also be used for industrial accumulation. Essentially, this was the reason for the low rents and the welfare allocation of housing. The advantages of such policies were that all housing became controlled by the government, which could then decide on the scale of its production, space standards, consumption and distribution, and also with the advantage that the government could make timely adjustments depending on economic situations. In effect, under policies that discouraged consumption, employees received low wages but only a very small amount of their wages were used to pay rents, forming a system whereby the government assigned housing to low-paying city residents who only paid a nominal rent.

2.2.2. The Management System of Urban Housing Construction Under a Planned Economy

The highly centralized system of the planned economy also found its way into city construction, mainly in the construction, management and distribution of publicly owned housing. Within this system, sources of investment for urban housing became narrower, with more than 90 percent of the investment coming from the state. On May 8, 1956, the State Council issued its "Decision on the Enhancement of Construction Work of New Industrial Areas and Newly-built Cities." This document stressed that "in order to make the construction of dwellings, shops, schools and other cultural facilities in the newly built industrial cities and workers' towns economical and reasonable, they should gradually meet the requirement of unified planning, design, investment, construction, distribution and management." Moreover, the responsibilities and powers of the competent departments and local governments in the construction of new industrial areas were also clearly spelled out. The competent departments were to be responsible for the construction of infrastructure, roads and houses within the newly built factory complexes, including living quarters for employees. Local governments were also made responsible for the construction of infrastructure and roads used by the general public, as well as other public facilities. However, one result of this approach was uncoordinated investment in housing among different branches of government.

Under this system, each enterprise was responsible for constructing housing for its own employees in the following manner. First, housing construction was placed on the yearly agenda of capital construction, and the department, at a higher level, appropriated funds. Land was provided by a local government free of charge, and a division within the enterprise would be set up to take charge of the construction and distribution of housing. Unfortunately, local governments did not have sufficient funds to build cultural, recreational and sanitary facilities for the general public. On the other hand, each enterprise, regardless of how big or small its living quarters were, was required to construct a complete set of facilities to meet the basic needs of its employees. Consequently, in addition to being an economic entity in the city, each enterprise was also self-sufficient. Residents could get daily necessities and enjoy leisure-time activities without going out of the compound of their living quarters. In this manner the city became comprised of "work unit communities," as they were called.

Geographically, the location of work unit communities had its own special characteristics. Usually, the living quarters were constructed in close proximity to the workplace to save travel time. This was particularly the case in the newly built industrial areas of the city suburbs, where living quarters were a consideration when choosing the location of a factory. As infrastructure provided by the city was usually not sufficient in areas where factory building took place, independent facilities in the compound of the living quarters became all the more comprehensive, often ranging from independent heating plants to employee hospitals, and some even had their own middle schools. Invariably, emerging districts in cities were formed of many such "work unit communities" dotted along the road network. In old city districts, the planners also tried, as much as possible, to construct living quarters near workplaces but, more often than not, they were separated because of the comparative difficulty in obtaining a large enough tract of land. In spite of this limitation, however, people in the old districts were able to take advantage of the city's existing cultural, recreational and health care facilities, and consequently the infrastructure that was needed in their living quarters was not so complete as in the newly built districts. Throughout, it was also not uncommon for neighboring enterprises to build and to share a common set of facilities.

In the matter of the management of publicly owned housing stock in cities, as early as December 20, 1948, the Central Committee of the Communist Party issued "The Decision on Matters Regarding Publicly-owned Housing Stocks in Cities," which set up the Management Committee of Publicly-owned Housing in Cities. Under this committee a management department was organized and placed in charge of the management and distribution of all urban publicly owned houses. As more and more former private houses were confiscated, and as the state became the sole investor in real estate, the amount of publicly owned housing increased rapidly and, in 1956, the Party Central Committee established the Ministry of Urban Services, under which there was an urban real estate management bureau in charge of urban housing.

In terms of ownership, urban housing was divided simply into private housing and publicly owned housing. The latter was further divided into two types: 1) houses managed by relevant departments of the city, and 2) houses managed by a work unit. There was very little new private housing because of a lack of investment. Low rents also made it difficult to keep formerly private housing in good condition, and much of it was plunged into a state of disrepair. In addition, since this kind of housing was usually located in the city's old districts, it often lacked adequate infrastructure. *Dazayuan* (a shared large courtyard compound) was a typical example, and overcrowding rendered the surrounding environment unpleasant. One *siheyuan* (courtyard house), or a house formerly used by one family, now became the dormitory of a work unit and the dwelling of several families. This created a lot of disturbances and inconvenience, and many people had to live without tap water and toilet facilities.

Organizations and work units in China fell roughly into two categories: state-owned or otherwise. The first category included all institutions and departments directly belonging to the Party Central Committee, a province, a municipality, a prefecture or a county, as well as certain other enterprises. The second category was comprised of mainly collectively owned organizations or institutions. The state was placed in charge of the planning, investment, construction and distribution of housing for officials and staff members working in state-owned organizations. Those working in non-state-owned enterprises were not entitled to newly built houses or apartments and had to rent old houses or apartments. As one might imagine, a big difference existed in the conditions of housing between these two types of dwellers, although the matter was not decided so much by each individual's income as by the nature of the organization in which they were employed. A survey conducted in 1983 indicated that for a staff member working in a Beijing-based organization belonging to the Party Central Committee, the average investment for housing and average floor space were 1,880 RMB yuan and 8.29 square meters, respectively. For a person who worked in an organization belonging to the municipality, the figures were 490 yuan and 5 square meters respectively (Deng Qing, 1995, 23).

In 1955, after a stratified wage system was put in place, the Party Central Committee worked out a corresponding standard for housing. This became the basis on which organizations constructed and distributed their houses and flats. Effectively, the distribution of newly built housing in cities and towns depended mainly on a person's official position, almost continuing the previous allocation or system of semi-free supply.[13]

2.2.3. The Growth of Urban Housing Development

The period from 1949 to 1957 was a time when China's urban housing construction grew at a relatively rapid rate. The proportion of investment in urban housing construction, as a proportion of total capital construction investment, remained at around 9 percent.[14] With investment from the state, more than 110 million square meters of housing were completed in this eight-year period and, during the First Five-Year Plan, the amount of floor area of completed housing accounted for 35.5 percent of the total floor area of all building construction (Wang Xiaoming, 1988, 57). In Beijing, for example, the floor area of completed housing rose steadily each year, and so did the proportion of the floor area of housing in total building construction (Table 4-3).[15] Moreover, this growth somewhat improved the living conditions in cities. However, because the original housing shortage was serious and the speed of new housing construction did not keep up with the speed of population increases, the supply of urban housing once again fell short of demand.

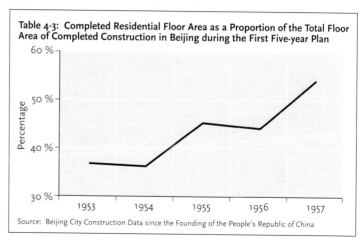

Table 4-3: Completed Residential Floor Area as a Proportion of the Total Floor Area of Completed Construction in Beijing during the First Five-year Plan

Source: Beijing City Construction Data since the Founding of the People's Republic of China

2.2.4. Housing Conditions of Urban Residents

The housing conditions of urban residents in this period were varied. This was because the transition to an exclusively public-owned housing system was not yet complete. Generally, urban housing could be divided into old residences and newly built, publicly owned housing. A considerable number of urban residents lived in old houses or flats and their living conditions often differed. According to a survey conducted in Beijing's old residential areas in 1955, the average floor space per person for a workers' family was 4.51 square meters. Families with an average floor space of 5 square meters per person accounted for 77 percent of those surveyed, and the actual average floor area per person for the general population was only 2.69 square meters. Most lived in rented houses or flats that were privately owned, hence their rents were relatively high. Most of the houses were siheyuan or linong houses built before 1949 and, usually, one original house was shared, as mentioned earlier, by several families. Outdated infrastructure made water and power supply unsatisfactory and sanitary facilities were miserable.

In the newly built, publicly owned urban housing, the average floor space per person was from four to seven square meters, and differences existed between the housing related to organizations of different kinds. As mentioned earlier, people working for departments directly belonging to the Party Central Committee enjoyed better and larger houses than those working in other enterprises. These houses were usually equipped with good infrastructure and other service facilities. But, as the standard was kept low in the first place, it was not uncommon for several families to share one kitchen and one lavatory, although generally these houses were in better condition than those in the city's old residential areas. However, under the guideline of "reasonable design and yet unreasonable use" during the First Five-Year Plan, one apartment was often shared by two or more households, causing much inconvenience.

3. Stages of Development in the Planning and Design of Urban Housing

In an attempt to address its housing problems, China went through various stages of development. At first, Soviet practices were emulated closely, giving rise to standardized forms of unit and building arrangement, before fundamental differences with prevailing Chinese circumstances became widely recognized and were adjusted for. The resulting modifications, as well as reflections on matters of formal expression, allowed China to realize its own housing solutions to pressing problems of shortage.

3.1. Easing of Shortages During Economic Recovery

During the economic recovery of the early 1950s, the government concentrated its efforts on the rehabilitation and stabilization of the social and economic order. The government attached great importance to the housing problem, as they realized that housing shortages were affecting social stability. Through improvement of existing infrastructure in cities, the government also elevated the living conditions of residents of the existing houses and, at the same time, large quantities of simple houses were constructed quickly.

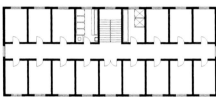

Fig. 4-1: Five-thousand room housing project at Heplingli, Beijing

Plan

3.1.1. Design of Housing: A Cheap Way to Ease Housing Shortages

In an attempt to solve the serious problem of housing shortages in the early days of the People's Republic, the government constructed many semi-temporary, low-rise apartments and dormitory-like apartments in the newly built industrial cities and in industrial areas on the outskirts of existing cities (Fig. 4-1). As the purpose was to construct apartments that would accommodate as many families as possible, and as quickly as possible with a limited budget, the simplest design was adopted that would facilitate the construction process. Most had only one storey, and each family was assigned from one to three rooms, depending on the household size. In most cases, kitchens, toilets and showers were shared. In a few areas, the linong-style housing was copied for the design, with some new developments (Fig. 4-2).

Many cities also redeveloped or upgraded slum areas, along with improvement of the urban infrastructure and the living environment generally. Before 1949, infrastructure in most Chinese cities, and particularly in slums, was grossly inadequate, and poor living conditions and an unpleasant environment were causing health problems for the residents. During the First Five-Year Plan, the State pointed out that "in cities with no concentration of industries, planning shall be performed only for industrial areas and plants. No

Fig. 4-2: Caoyangxincun Village, Shanghai

reconstruction is to be done on the old cities, and existing buildings are to be made use of wherever possible..." (Dong Jianhong, 1955, 12). Consequently, as not much building construction was going on in existing cities, most investment in urban construction was used to build infrastructure in slum areas and to redevelop the houses there—for example, the earth work and tidying up of Longxugou and Taoranting in Beijing. Between 1949 and 1956, Shanghai saw piped running water increase by 24.9 percent, and more than 1,000 water supply outlets were added to the city, most of them located in the slums.

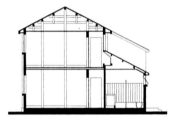

Section

Second Floor Plan

First Floor Plan

3.1.2. Residential Area Planning: The Neighborhood Unit

The *hanglieshi* (lined up in rows) residential area was made up of low-rise north-south apartments lined up in parallel rows as it was the easiest and most viable form of construction. With respect to climate in most regions of China, the north-south layout had many advantages. It enabled full use to be made of sunlight in the winter,

Fig. 4-3: Site plan of Chaoyang-
xincun Village

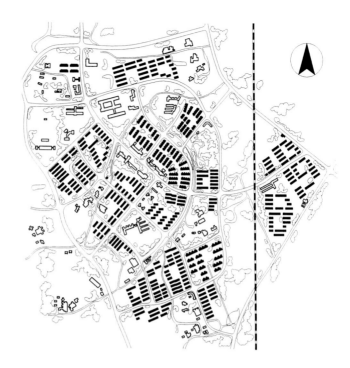

and avoided scorching heat from the sun in summer, as well as providing for good ventilation. For these reasons, the north-south layout was also traditionally a dominant orientation in Chinese urban
housing for several thousand years. Moreover, as most newly built
housing did not have heating systems, the layout became even more
important to the livelihood of residents. Further, with the limited
budget available, the use of natural conditions to raise the living
standards of residents became the easiest and most effective choice.
In addition, the hanglieshi was easy to construct, saved land, and
the cost for laying pipelines and wires was low. Its major defect was
the sheer monotony of the outdoor space provided.

"The Neighborhood Unit," which had been introduced to China
before the founding of the People's Republic, was now used in planning residential areas. With the development of large-scale urban
housing, the organization and management of supplementary facilities for residents became an important issue in planning residential areas. In Shanghai, the Caoyangxincun village, for instance,
whose construction began in 1951, adopted some features of neighborhood units. This residential area had a total area of 94.63
hectares. It was 0.6 kilometers from its center to its edge, requiring
from seven to eight minutes to walk. Public buildings were erected
in the center and, in order to maintain "public buildings on a certain

scale and in line with residents' economic conditions," Caoyangxin-cun village housed more population than a neighborhood unit would normally have stipulated (Wang Dingzeng, 1956, 1). The planning of the Caoyangxincun residential area was also a success because it provided for an effective inner road structure and allowed the whole project to be well integrated with its surroundings (Fig. 4-3). However, after the introduction of the Soviet Union's ideas about residential area planning, and for ideological reasons, Caoyangxin-cun was criticized as the embodiment of capitalist urban planning.[16]

3.2. Learning from the Soviet Union in the First Five-Year Plan: Copying and Formalism

In 1953, after its successful economic recovery, China began a planned and large-scale socialist development. For economic, tech-nological and ideological reasons described earlier, the Soviet Union's mode of socialist industrialization became the object from which China learned. This Soviet model, although having profound influences on China's social and economic development, also left its mark on China's urban planning and design. Standard design methods and forms of residential area planning were widely adopt-ed. In short, learning from the Soviet Union in an all-around way was the predominant feature in housing construction in this period, and the actual differences between the two countries were over-looked.

3.2.1. Introduction of a Standard Method of Design from the Soviet Union

Although there had been some urban housing development during the economic recovery, housing shortages were still a problem fac-ing Chinese cities after 1953 and, as China embarked on the road of socialist industrialization, the idea of industrialized housing was brought to China from the Soviet Union. In the Soviet Union, the policy of industrialized building was initially raised at the First and Second Construction and Architectural Conferences of the Soviet Communist Party. The advantages of industrialized building were that it could quicken construction speed, lower costs and save labor; its major features comprised design standardization, mass produc-tion of components and systematic construction. After China began the First Five-Year Plan, this quick potential answer to the housing shortage was introduced, giving rise to the concept of a standard design for China's urban housing (Min Yulin, 1955, 1). Moreover, implementation of the policy of rapid industrialization created many tasks, and standard design had the advantage of boosting design efficiency in a country that lacked sufficient technicians in architectural design and construction.

The standard design was first used in northeast China in 1952, under the guidance of Soviet experts. By 1953, the total area of housing under construction, employing the standard design, reached 679,000 square meters, accounting for 34 percent of all construction.[17] The National Construction Commission entrusted the Ministry of Construction Engineering and the Ministry of Urban Construction with the task of drafting the standard design for industrial and civilian architecture. Specifically, the Ministry of Urban Construction was in charge of the standard design for the construction of housing and ended up with six versions for the following six areas: the Northeast, the North, the Northwest, the Southwest, Central China, and the Southeast. The basic material structure of housing was to be made with brick and concrete, and standard units were to be assembled to make standard apartment buildings. In addition, the reference design included the building, its structure, its water supply and drainage, as well as its heating and lighting (Zhou Jinxiang, 1985, 348).

3.2.2. Standardized Housing Design in its Early Stages and the Contrast with Particular Chinese Situations

The following were the cardinal principles in the standard design of housing. A unit was to be designed with standard components conforming to a construction module. Various combinations of such standard units were to form different buildings, and when the different buildings were put together, they formed residential areas. The most fundamental "cell," so to speak, in the design of housing was the unit. A residential unit consisted of several households all using the same staircase, and its advantage was that each apartment was independent and therefore quiet. Compact placement on the same level meant that the pipes and wires were congregated, lowering costs and maintaining a relatively high construction density. Also, basic units, with different compositions, when placed in the middle or at the end of a building block, could form residential buildings of different lengths, shapes and heights, thus satisfying the different requirements of different groups. The standardized building components were produced in large quantities in factories, which accelerated construction speed (Min Yulin, 1955, 5).

It is obvious that the standard design of the Soviet Union was the product of a planned economy. For instance, the quota-target system, formulated by the state, provided the basis for the standard design. Through fixed construction prices and a fixed amount of floor space per person or per family, the state could determine precisely the scale and output of housing construction. This was especially important to the centrally controlled economy under which the state was the sole investor. When assembled together, standard plans gave rise to a standard collection of designs, which became the basis of the planning and construction of all residential areas in cities, as well as the production of specific building components.

Along with the standard design for housing came the system of production targets and the inner-corridor housing plan from the Soviet Union. However, the Soviet standard was nine square meters of floor space per person, and there was a big gap when compared with China's then per-person floor space of four square meters. As a consequence, the Chinese put forward a principle to guide their own standard design practice. This guideline—"rational design and irrational use"—assumed that living standards would rise as production grew rapidly, and because housing generally could be used for a rather extended length of time, architects should base their design on long-term targets. The guideline further suggested that, at least for the time being, several families could share a bigger unit in the belief that the inconvenience would soon end as socialism developed. This principle combined short-term goals with long-term goals, but put emphasis on the latter. During the initial stages, it also meant that the amount of floor space provided was much higher than the actual amount enjoyed by Chinese citizens. In fact, most houses built before 1954 had higher standards than ordinary Chinese people could possibly enjoy, and were designed according to the standard of six square meters per person and some even targeted for the long-term standard of nine square meters (Zhou Jinxiang, 1985, 348). However, because these apartments were bigger than what one family was supposed to enjoy—most being three or four-room apartments—they were normally shared by more than one family. Each room was so big that usually more than one person would share one room, creating much inconvenience within a family or between families (Fig. 4-3). This notion of doubling up was to have an influence on urban housing design for a long time to come. In addition, since there was a big difference between the Soviet Union and China in geography and climate, the inner-corridor unit plan did not accord with Chinese people's living habits, and did not provide residences with sufficient sunshine and ventilation. This was particularly bad for shared apartments. It was inconvenient to keep the door open for ventilation, and families with only northern rooms did not get any sunshine. These problems were largely overlooked initially, but as the standard design was popularized, such designs were widely adopted, and these apartments became a dominant form in the development of urban housing in China.

3.2.3. Housing Forms Under the Ideology of "Socialist Content, and National Form"

After World War II, modernism greatly influenced reconstruction in Europe and to some extent America. Under the influence of architectural theories from the Soviet Union, modernism was criticized in China as a capitalist aesthetic. To counter modernism, the Soviet Union proposed the theory of social realism, which gave birth to a predominant design form characterized by "socialist content and national form." The new republic needed new forms for its architecture, and Chinese architects sifted through their architectural heritage for the national form that would convey this socialist content. After studying Chinese architectural history, some finally found a solution in the composition of a traditional "big roof" with Soviet-style elevations, and decorative carvings from Western architecture combined with classical Chinese components and patterns. In fact, this practice was the goal toward which many of the first generation of Western-trained Chinese architects strove. Indeed, before 1949, Chinese architects had made many experiments in this respect and, after the founding of the People's Republic, this architectural form enjoyed high esteem and was regarded as a form that best embodied the great New China and its national characteristics—before coming under criticism for economic reasons in 1955 (Fig. 4-4). Finding inspiration from vernacular Chinese architecture was also another way to build houses with "socialist content and national form." The stepped gable wall, the highly decorated *chuihuamen* gateway and window lintels, for instance, were used in the construction of some

Fig. 4-4: No. 301 Standard Housing Design in North China

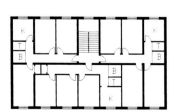

Fig. 4-5: An apartment building at Jingshanhoujie, Beijing

apartment buildings on university campuses in the early 1950s (Fig. 4-5).

In general, the public's hope for good housing at the beginning of the Republic, combined with an optimistic economic situation during the First Five-Year Plan, caused architects to pay much attention to the artistic form of urban housing, although in retrospect some bent too far in the direction of formalism. It was effective in helping shape the urban landscape quickly during post-war reconstruction, but some practical functions of housing were overlooked in favor of formal architectural concerns. For example, in housing projects that featured the big roof, the placement of balconies was made in consideration of compositional dictates, rather than in acknowledgment of the direct needs of dwellers.

3.2.4. Perimeter Block Neighborhoods: a Type of Residential Area That Appeared Under Soviet Influence

Soviet influence could also be found in the overall layout of residential areas and was most strongly represented by the appearance of perimeter block neighborhoods. Normally found in Europe, this type of residential area usually has a distinct axis, with buildings arranged along the streets. Houses stood either north-south or east-west, with public buildings located in the center of the residential area, exhibiting a strong sense of order and formalism (Figs. 4-6 and 4-7). However, for those considerable number of east-west houses in this type of residential area, access to sunlight and ventilation was far from satisfactory, and noise from the street was often disturbing. In addition, the resulting orderly and stern ambience of the neighborhood was not ideal for many residents.

Fig. 4-6: Student dormitories on Beijing University campus, 1952

Fig. 4-7: Plans of the residential area of Changchun No. 1 Automobile Plant

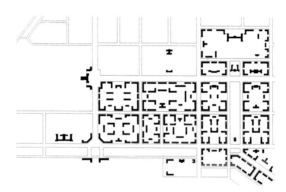

Detailed Plan of the Residential Area

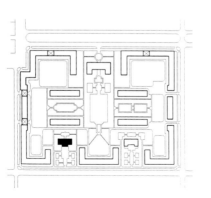

Neighborhood Layout

3.3. Reflections on Learning from the Soviet Union in the Later Stage of the First Five-Year Plan

China entered an era of contradictions and puzzlement in the mid-1950s. The Soviet Union, which had been the model for China to follow, found itself shaken by some unexpected political events, and Sino-Soviet relations soured. The policy of making use of agricultural resources to develop heavy industry actually damaged agriculture, which in turn eroded the development of the national economy as a whole. China entered a period when it began to re-examine its road to development. One view favored quick growth, while the other view opposed it. At this time Mao Zedong put forward the policy of "let a hundred flowers blossom and a hundred schools of thought contend," encouraging free discussion and examination of socialist development, as well as of other issues. The architectural community re-examined the thorough copying of the Soviet Union and, within a few years, the earlier standards of urban housing were being applied less rigidly. The focus of this period was still learning from the Soviet Union, but it was "a process that rejected the backwardness of Soviet practices and was highly selective" (R. Maikefakuer and Fei Zhengqing, 1990, 130).

3.3.1. Housing Design: Combining Soviet Experience with Chinese Characteristics

The impact of the imbalanced development of industries on economic growth became obvious in early 1955. The architectural community began to criticize the waste in non-productive buildings.[18] In July of that year, the First Five-Year Plan for national economic development was officially ratified. In order to continue with the policy of developing heavy industry first, the state began to reduce the scale of investment in non-productive capital construction, and reiterated that money must be saved in non-productive buildings.[19] In his report on the First Five-Year Plan for national economic development, Vice-Premier Li Fuchun said that the cost of non-productive construction should be 15 percent lower than their budget, resulting in a big drop in housing investment (Table 4-4). In addition, the Ministry of Architectural Engineering revised its space standards to meet the requirements for lowering the standard housing design and housing construction standards for non-productive purposes, with the result that floor space per person was reduced from between six and nine square meters to between four and five square meters (Fig. 4-8). This policy change, essentially due to economic reasons, was a seminal decision in combining standard design with the prevailing Chinese situation.

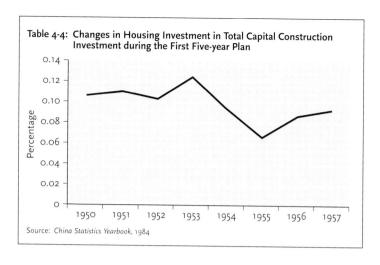

Table 4-4: Changes in Housing Investment in Total Capital Construction Investment during the First Five-year Plan

Source: *China Statistics Yearbook*, 1984

In practice, however, this policy, advocating economy and influenced by leftist thinking, went astray. In housing construction, practicing thrift was stressed to such an extent that the fundamental utilization of the house was overlooked and form in architectural design gave way to solely economic considerations. Architectural theorists harshly criticized formalism and the valuing of traditional approaches, with the expensive big roof becoming the first target, along with its architectural advocates. Soviet influence was clearly visible in this criticism, as the doctrine that valued what was old—i.e., "socialist content and national form"—was also being criticized in the Soviet Union. At the meeting of the Central Committee of the Soviet Communist Party that took place on November 8, 1955, such a practice was criticized as having ignored the purpose of technology and economy in building construction and management. It was considered wasteful, it deviated from reality and it hindered the

Fig. 4-8: The Baiwangzhuang residential area in Beijing

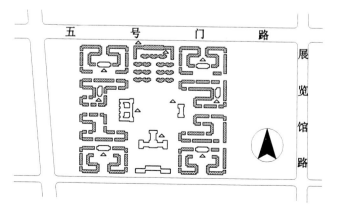

rapid development of socialism (Chen Jun, 1982, 47). Subsequently, the question of whether to practice thrift or not was elevated to become a highly political issue in the Anti-Rightist Movement started in 1957, even though the factor of economy had always been an important element in housing construction since the founding of the People's Republic. Effectively, ideology made thriftiness a principle that prevailed over everything else; it also became a principle employed to popularize low-standard housing at times of economic distress.

In 1955, as emphasis once more shifted towards economy in housing construction, industrial methods which could furnish large quantities of low-cost housing quickly became popular, and the promotion of a standard design became urgent. As mentioned earlier, entrusted by the State Construction Commission in 1955, the Bureau of City Construction went about the appraisal of the standard design of residential buildings throughout China and solicited plans for standard housing designs with the aim of popularizing selected plans. Subsequently, at a meeting of appraisal held at the end of 1955, an exhibition was staged in order to ask the experts and the general public for comments and suggestions. The principal criticisms of the standard design included: 1) dogmatic emulation of plans from the Soviet Union; 2) not enough consideration on matters related to inhabitants' livelihoods; and 3) inconvenience in the utilization and allocation of space (Li Yiguang, 1956, 99). The focus of the criticism lay on the specification of the standard design for housing and blind modeling of the Soviet Union, combined with excessive emphasis on thrift. In sum, this was seen to result in what was termed "rational design, but irrational use" for housing development.

The direct results of these discussions and research were new attempts by Chinese architects to cater their designs to particular situations in China, and these experiments headed in two directions. The first was the adaptation of the standard design to Chinese circumstances. As described, major problems of the standard design were housing orientation and ventilation. Since each apartment consisted of many rooms and each room was rather large, when shared by several families, the family that ended up with rooms that faced north received no sunlight at all throughout the year. It was also difficult for the flow of air when an apartment was shared by a few families. Moreover, considerable unlighted space existed in the corners of the buildings. With this in mind, a single-unit plan composition of the standard design, called the 2-2-2 composition (i.e., three two-bedroom apartments served by one staircase), was considered to be comparatively reasonable. This was the configuration whereby an apartment was shared by three families, each occupying two rooms, and the two families at each end of the apartment would each have one room facing south and one room facing north. The family in the middle had two southward facing rooms and, in a revised design, the rooms in the middle were shared and rooms at both ends of the apartment were made smaller but inhabited exclusively by one family. Each family, therefore, had at least one room facing south. Balconies were no longer mere decoration, and each family also had a balcony facing south.

The second revision resulted in the emergence of new unit types. The existence of several families sharing one apartment was caused by disparities between the high levels of housing design and low levels of actual living standards. Moreover, the composition of an apartment was directly affected by its size. Therefore, new types of apartment designs appeared, notably open-corridor apartments.

Under the policy of "let a hundred flowers blossom and a hundred schools of thought contend," China lowered its housing design standards and reflected on the practice of the sharing of an apartment by several families and, from this reflection, the idea of creating apartments used exclusively by one family was proposed and later put into practice. The lowering of design standards made rooms smaller, and normally each family occupied only limited space. Moreover, under this constraint, the former inner-corridor composition could not guarantee that all families had rooms facing south and good ventilation, with only one staircase serving multiple apartments. Thus the open-corridor apartment came into being, with the corridor usually located at the northern side of the apartment and with each apartment consisting of one or more parallel bays of the same depth along the corridor. Bedrooms were located on the south side, while toilets and kitchens were located on the north side near the corridor. The advantage of such an arrangement was that one stairway could continue to serve the whole apartment building. While leaving room for each family to enjoy its own apartment, it had at least one room facing south and good ventilation. In theory, the long corridors in the housing plans were more suitable for one- to two-storey structures, but were wasteful in space efficiency. In reality, however, the corridors were used by families as storage spaces and were welcomed by residents. The Xingfucun neighborhood apartment buildings in Beijing of 1957, for instance, were representative of the open-corridor apartment (Fig. 4-9). In addition, based on further research, Chinese architects also proposed other housing designs that suited China's particular situations. These

Fig. 4-9: The design of housing made in 1955–56 after standards were lowered

厨房 厨房 居室 居室 居室 居室 厨房 厨房

居室 居室 居室 居室 居室 居室 居室

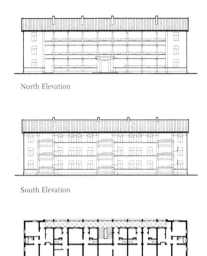

North Elevation

South Elevation

Plan

Fig. 4-10: Xinfucun Village, small-sized, open-corridor apartment buildings in Beijing

Apartment Plans

View of a building block

included configurations with short open corridors and horizontally aligned stairways.

Housing structures of this time were mainly made of brick and wood, or brick and concrete. Most used wooden frames and prefabricated slabs. The advantages were savings in industrial raw materials and ease of construction. Block masonry construction was among the earliest industrial housing systems and was used in the Hongmaogou residential area in Beijing in 1957 (Fig. 4-10). Each floor was 2.8 meters high and the exterior walls were constructed with two layers of bricks with one layer of concrete beam above. The vertical walls were bearing walls. The masonry unit had forty-seven modular scales and was manufactured by brick production machines. Usually two tower cranes installed the masonry blocks at the construction site. Masonry unit systems became even more sophisticated in the following thirty years of development. In Beijing, for example, from 1955 to 1979 some 103,000 square meters of housing employing masonry units were completed (Hu Shide, 1993, 16).

3.3.2. Planning of Residential Areas

While discussions over the standard design were still going on, a controversy started over whether to adopt parallel row-housing layouts or perimeter block neighborhood layouts in the planning of residential areas. Supporters of the perimeter block idea maintained that it saved land, had a complete form and was convenient for the placement of public buildings. If each perimeter block neighborhood was considered as a small cell, when many of them came together, they would give shape to a sophisticated network of streets,

Fig. 4-11: Hongmaogou, masonry housing in Beijing

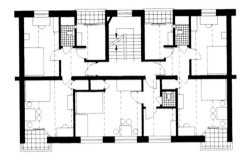

squares and ultimately the city landscape. Also, it was condoned by progressive Soviet ideology, and it was believed that the neat formation of this planning model embodied the spirit and order of a socialist society.

However, as the government began to emphasize thrift in housing construction and the big roof was criticized by the architectural community, the formalist streak of perimeter block neighborhoods was cast in doubt (Ji Ping, 1956, 103). Major problems for this kind of planning were claimed to lie in its unsuitability for China's geography, climate and environment, as well as to people's living habits. Buildings placed along the street produced annoying noises for residents, as noted earlier. Moreover, with a limited housing budget, it was important to build north-south houses and make full use (also noted earlier) of natural ventilation. Unfortunately, the two features were usually sacrificed in the perimeter block neighborhood in favor of a more complete form, and some architects believed that instead of paying attention to the form of the residential area, more consideration should be given to particular situations and requirements (Wang Hua, 1956, 53) (Fig. 4-9).

At the end of the First Five-Year Plan, as mentioned earlier, the Soviet Union's idea of complete planning for a residential area was introduced to China and put into practice. The general plan of Beijing City, which was issued in 1957, stated that residential areas from thirty to sixty hectares would become basic units where citizens could live[20] (Figs. 4-11 and 4-12). Furthermore, the idea of residential area planning was thought to be the embodiment of socialist ideology in the composition of an urban society. In "Planning and Construction of Residential Areas in Cities," it was stated that "in

Fig. 4-12: The Xizhaosi residential area in Beijing

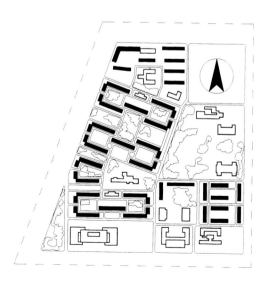

big cities of a socialist country, the social and political life of the people should be organized around areas that were facilitated by a complete network of institutions that provided socialist culture, education, as well as other necessary provisions and that such an approach, in spatial terms, would occur in residential areas" (Li Pin Nie Fu, 1958, 23).

Generally, residential areas were divided into three or four levels. Caoyangxincun in Shanghai, for instance, consisted of eight "villages." In planning terms, each village could then be divided into three levels: the village, the neighborhood and residential clusters. Correspondingly, social administration was also organized at four levels: the neighborhood committee (63,400 people), the village committee (8,000–10,000 people), the work area (2,000 people), and the small group (300–500 people). In fact, except for the attached ideological labels and its administrative structure, residential areas were not much different from neighborhood units in Western countries, except that a residential area was usually larger than a neighborhood unit and, indeed, as noted, Caoyangxincun was criticized for bearing the mark of the idea of the neighborhood unit. Nevertheless, by 1957, as eight villages (residential areas) were completed one after another, Caoyangxincun was accepted as a complete residential area.[21]

Notes

1. Sun Jian. *The Economic History of the People's Republic of China (from 1949 to the early 1990s)*. (Beijing: Chinese People's University Press, 1992), 66. In March 1950, the government issued "The Decision on the Unification of the Country's Financial and Economic Work." With this decision, the country's revenue and expenditure, the dispatch of materials and the management of cash were all brought under the control of the central government.

2. Zhao Dexin, ed. *A History of Economy of the People's Republic of China, 1949–1966* (Henan: Henan People's Publishing House, 1988), 389–392. To guarantee the implementation of the First Five-Year Plan and to make limited financial, material and technological resources serve the needs of reconstruction, the government had no other choice but to adopt centrally controlled measures. These included central government control of key projects of capital construction. During the First Five-Year Plan, state budgetary investment accounted for 90.3 percent of total investment of capital construction. It also included unified management of materials. In 1953 the state planned to distribute 227 types of materials and the figure reached 385 in 1956. In addition, enterprises turned over most of their profits to the central government to ensure the implementation of the state budget, and, finally, use of labor and the wage system were under the control of the central government.

3. In August 1952, the Financial and Economic Commission of the Central Party Committee issued "Construction Tasks During the Five Years and Attached Charts." The major content, with respect to industrial construction of the First Five-Year Plan period, was that priority was to be given to heavy industry, and that light industry was to be subordinated. In heavy industry, emphasis would be placed on such industries as steel, iron, coal, electricity,

petroleum, machine building, military industry, non-ferrous metals and fundamental chemistry. Emphasis in light industry construction would be on textiles, paper-making and pharmaceuticals. Other sectors might develop according to actual needs and consideration of whatever personnel or physical resources they had, provided they didn't hinder the development of heavy industry.

4. Sun Jian, 171–172. During the First Five-Year Plan, total investment in capital construction reached 55 billion RMB yuan, of which 42.5 percent, or 25,026 billion yuan, went to industrial sectors. In this same period, capital construction created 49,218 billion yuan worth of added fixed assets, of which 20,064 billion yuan were added industrial fixed assets.

5. On January 9, 1952, the Financial and Economic Commission of the Party Central Committee issued "Interim Measures on Capital Construction." Based on the principle of planned and centrally controlled management, construction projects were divided into two types: within quotas and outside quotas.

6. State Statistic Bureau, *Statistical Yearbook of China, 1984* (Beijing: China Statistic Publishing House, 1984), 194.

7. Editorial Committee of the Urban Development History of Beijing, *Beijing's Urban Development Since the Founding of the People's Republic of China* (Beijing: Chinese People's University Press, 1985), 23–47.

8. *People's Daily*, editorial, "Strengthen the construction of new industrial areas." August 13, 1954. "Some of these key projects are new construction, reconstruction or extension of existing projects in old industrial cities, but most of them will be constructed near cities where there are no modern industries."

9. *People's Daily*, editorial. "Carry out the policy of putting emphasis on city construction," August 11, 1954. "Between 1950 and 1954, the state spent more than 10 trillion yuan (old currency) on the construction of public utilities and improvement of environmental sanitation. According to statistics from 20 cities at the end of 1953, these added to the existing facilities over 1,900 km. of pipes of running water, over 1,400 km. of sewer and nearly 2,000 public buses, tramcars and trolley buses. In 1952 alone, some 5 million square meters of housing for workers were constructed in Beijing, Tianjin, Shenyang, Anshan and Shanghai. Filthy ditches—Shishahai, Longxugou in Beijing and the Qiangzi and Jinzhong rivers in Tianjin—which had been a source of contagious disease for years, received a thorough cleaning, creating a clean and comfortable living environment for millions of laboring people."

10. Bi Baode, *Studies on China's Real Estate Market* (Beijing: Chinese People's University Press, 1994), 21. As major cities were liberated, people's governments in those cities, based on policies, edicts and documents regarding the abrogation of imperialists' privileges in China, the confiscation of bureaucrat capital and the return of it to the state of the people, were laid down in "The Proclamation of the Chinese People's Liberation Army" (issued on April 25, 1949). "The Common Program of the Chinese People's Political Consultative Conference" laid down the takeover or confiscation of real estate previously possessed by imperialists, bureaucrat capitalists, war criminals, collaborators and counter-revolutionaries in cities. In January 1951, the Government Administration Council of the Central People's Government issued "The Directives on the Confiscation of Properties Possessed by War Criminals, Collaborators, Bureaucrat Capitalists and Counter-Revolutionaries." It issued in June of the same year "Decisions on the Confiscation of Properties of Counter-Revolutionary Criminals." After this, more real estate was confiscated.

11. *People's Daily*, Xinhua letter box, "On the nature and policies of urban house property and rent," April 25, 1949. Land and house property in cities should

not be handled in the same manner as the land problem in the countryside. Generally, private ownership of urban housing is capitalist rather than feudalist in nature. And, in the new democratic revolutionary period, housing ownership of a capitalist nature shall receive the same protection as other ownership of private capital, with the sole exception of bureaucrat capital.

12. Editorial Committee of the Urban Development History of Beijing, 187.
13. "Decision on several issues about enhancing the construction work of new industrial areas and new industrial cities," issued on May 8, 1956.
14. During the economic recovery period, investment in housing accounted for 11 percent of the total investment in capital construction. During the First Five-Year Plan, investment in housing accounted for 9.1 percent of the total investment of capital construction. *Statistical Yearbook of China.*
15. Editorial Department of Editorial Committee of the Urban Development History of Beijing, *Materials about Beijing's Urban Development Since the Founding of the People's Republic of China,* VI (Beijing: Editorial Committee of the Urban Development History of China, 1993), 380.
16. Yang Tingbao, "Report on the Fourth Congress of International Architects' Association," *Journal of Architecture,* 55:2, 69. "In terms of layout of housing, the neighborhood unit is adopted by capitalist countries while the large neighborhood is adopted by the Soviet Union and other peoples' democratic countries. . . The major difference between the two is that the latter considers the city as a whole, and each neighborhood is an organic part of the city, while the former does not have anything to do with the city. This reflects the difference in social systems."
17. "Standard design work for the past three years," materials from the national standard design conference of the Design Bureau of the Ministry of Architecture and Engineering of the Central Party Committee, February 12, 1954.
18. Editorial, "Opposing waste in housing construction," *People's Daily* March 28, 1955.
19. Li Fuchun, "Practice strict economy and strive to complete the construction of socialism," the vice-premier's report at the conference of high-ranking cadres, June 13, 1955, and Bo Yibo, "Opposing extravagance and waste, guaranteeing the quick, better and economic completion of capital construction projects," again delivered at a conference of high-ranking cadres, June 30, 1955. Also, the "Decision of the Central Party Committee on practicing strict economy," July 4, 1955.
20. Editorial Committee of the Urban Development History of Beijing, *Beijing's Urban Development Since the Founding of the People's Republic of China* (Beijing: Chinese People's University Press, 1985), 3.
21. Refer to section 3.1.2. in this chapter.

Chapter Five: The "Great Leap Forward" and Readjustment: Seeking a Road for Self-Development (1958–1965)

Between the end of the 1950s and the mid-1960s, China's social and economic development experienced its first major setback and subsequent readjustment. During this period the general development strategy was almost the same as that pursued in the First Five-Year Plan, with the only difference being that, after China had broken ties with the Soviet Union, it sought a road toward self-determination, with greater attention focused on the speed of development. The "Great Leap Forward" that started in 1958, however, pushed to extremes the principle of giving priority to heavy industry. Consequently, the national economy deteriorated rapidly and the social economy was on the verge of imminent collapse. Although the economic readjustment that started in 1961 remedied and corrected many of the shortcomings, the leftist ideology of the Great Leap Forward still controlled the country.

Housing was still in a secondary position in national economic development, although the urban welfare housing system established in the previous period was extended and strengthened. Nevertheless, during the Great Leap Forward the principle of economic savings in housing design was taken to extremes and a large number of low-quality houses, unsuitable for use, were completed. By contrast, after adoption of the policy of "letting a hundred flowers blossom and a hundred schools of thought contend" and following a thorough review of housing design principles learned from the Soviet Union, together with an attachment of greater importance to research, an objective and realistic spirit was injected into housing design during the period of readjustment and rectification. Subsequently, housing design began to consider residents' demands and actual economic conditions more seriously, and the range of housing types was enriched.

In cities, rapid development of industry and population growth added pressure on available land resources and, where possible, the larger cities extended out into the suburbs. The design of entire residential areas was also popularly adopted by cities. In addition, people's commune buildings appeared, and a planning ideology, based on the idea of the people's commune, began exerting an influence on the form and structure of Chinese cities.

1. The Social and Economic Background of Developments in Urban Housing

Along with the basic fulfillment of the socialist transformation of private ownership of the means of production, China transcended perhaps the most profound social change in its history. After that, revolutionaries were confronted with a brand new problem—how to build a new society. To accomplish this, the Chinese government began to shift its focus to the general line of socialist construction adopted at the Second Session of the Eighth National Congress of the Communist Party of China, held in May, 1958. Essentially this line of thinking meant going all out, aiming high and achieving greater, faster, better results—and more economically as well. Encouraged by the economic achievements during the First Five-Year Plan (1952–1957), the government was full of confidence in the policy of developing heavy industry as its economic mainstay. Nevertheless, due to both international and domestic changes, a leftist viewpoint gained the upper hand, and their optimistic estimations of the situation touched off the Great Leap Forward in industrial production and the social experiments of the people's commune. Some years later, this approach led the Chinese economy into a quagmire, and, although the government started economic readjustments in 1961, a leftist ideology still played a significant role.

Between the end of the 1950s and the mid-1960s, China's urban housing development can be divided into two main stages. They are: the Great Leap Forward and the associated period of the people's commune (1958–1960) and the period of economic readjustment (1961–1965).

1.1. The Great Leap Forward in Economic Development

After the First Five-Year Plan, as the Chinese government stressed further the policy of giving priority to heavy industry, a sense of impatience grew. In 1958, the Central Committee of the Communist Party of China (CPC) put forward the slogan for economic development of "Catching-up with the United States and Exceeding the United Kingdom" and set out a series of unrealistic production targets to develop heavy industry and to harness fully the strength of the nation.[1] After that the Great Leap Forward in economic development started, with the upshot that the emphasis on heavy industry became even more imbalanced.

More specifically, the Great Leap Forward focused on rapid development of the iron and steel industry. The Chinese government believed that iron, steel and machine industries were the basis of all modern industries and that iron and steel output was the symbol of national strength. Unfortunately, their unrealistic targets in these regards put great pressure on other industries.[2] On the one hand, they had to make way for iron and steel production in terms of both capital and other resources, and on the other, they were required to provide corresponding supplementary work for the fulfillment of the high-output goals. The direct result of this was activities aimed at reaping immediate rewards, destroying the balanced development of the national economy. Moreover, due to excessively large-scale capital construction, the portion of the national income used in accumulation increased by a large margin. The accumulation rate in 1957 was 24.9 percent, rising to 33.9 percent in 1958, but also with a corresponding substantial decrease in non-productive accumulation (Table 5-1). This was the very reason why the proportion of overall investment in urban housing, and the construction standards that went with that investment, dropped rapidly.

The negative effects of the Great Leap Forward on urban housing development were also reflected in the rapid changes of urban population. According to the original plan, 1,135 large and medium-sized projects would be constructed in 1958, but actually 1,587 such projects were constructed, or an increase of 595 over 1957 (Sun Jian, 1992, 245). One cause was that a large number of rural laborers were absorbed into the cities during the expansion of heavy indus-

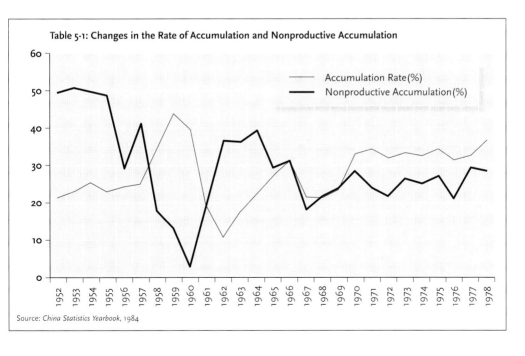

Table 5-1: Changes in the Rate of Accumulation and Nonproductive Accumulation

— Accumulation Rate(%)
— Nonproductive Accumulation(%)

Source: *China Statistics Yearbook*, 1984

try. In 1957, China had 193 million rural laborers, a figure which dropped to 155 million in 1958, or a reduction of over 38 million within one year. The ratio between agricultural and industrial laborers decreased from 12.8:1 to 3.5:1. Another cause was the fluctuation of the urban population, which, in turn, resulted in the rise and fall of qualitative housing standards.

1.2. The "People's Commune Movement"

When China started the Great Leap Forward in 1958, another national campaign—the People's Commune Movement—unfolded in rural areas throughout the country. The principle economic reason for starting this movement was that the Chinese government believed that collectivization could raise grain output to meet the tremendous demands placed on agricultural resources by the Great Leap Forward. In addition, the people's commune was regarded as an advanced form of social organization, conforming to the communist ideal.[3] In essence, some people truly believed that communism could be realized soon after rapid economic development and reform of the social system was fulfilled smoothly.[4] The Great Leap Forward further aroused this optimistic and radical sentiment.

The idea of the people's commune was based on Marx's theory of urbanization. Marx believed that the capitalist form of production was the source of contradictions between urban and rural areas, as well as urban pathology. In a socialist society, the cities and countryside should be combined, and the people's commune was regarded as a form of social organization, with a communist orientation, that could eliminate differences between town and countryside. Under the guidance of a leftist ideology, the people's commune in China's rural areas developed rapidly. The concept was first put forward in July 1958 and, on August 29, the Political Bureau of the CPC Central Committee formally adopted the "Resolution on the Establishment of the People's Commune in Rural Areas." By the end of September, 265,000 people's communes had been created, and 99.1 percent of the rural households had joined them (Sun Jian, 1992, 251). Initially, the people's commune followed the principle of distribution according to need, as the wage system was regarded as an embodiment of a capitalist hierarchy and was replaced by a supply system.[5] In March 1960, the Central Committee of the Communist Party of China required all cities to expend every effort to mobilize the masses and to organize various forms of people's commune on a trial basis. By the end of July, more than 1,000 urban people's communes had been set up in the large and medium-sized cities, and over 77 percent of the total urban population in China had joined (Sun Jian, 1992, 269). Needless to say, both eventualities unavoidably effected the planning and design of residential areas.

1.3. The Period of Economic Readjustment

In 1961, confronted with results contrary to expectations, the CPC Central Committee put forward the "Eighth-Character Principle"— readjustment, rectification, supplementation and improvement— and started to take action in the national economy.[6] The main aspects of this readjustment included: reducing the scale and number of the capital construction projects, readjusting agricultural production, reducing urban population, and reducing the formation of cities and towns (Zhang Bingchen and others, 1991, 27).

Readjustment achieved positive results within a relatively short period of time. In 1962, the total value of agricultural output increased by 6.2 percent over that of 1961, and the total value of industrial output value decreased by 16.6 percent. More important, the ratio between industrial output value and agricultural output value changed from 4:1 in 1960 to 2:1 in 1961 and the ratio between light industry and heavy industry was reduced from 42.4:57.5 to 47.2:52.8. Meanwhile, the scale of capital construction was reduced to a level whereby it could only maintain simple reproduction and, in 1962, the investments in capital construction totaled 7,126 billion yuan, or a reduction of 5,616 billion yuan from 1961, the lowest level since 1953 (Table 5-2).

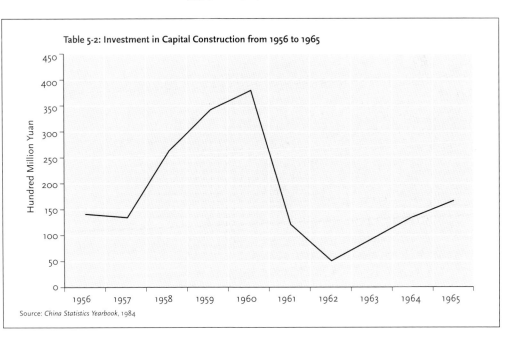

Table 5-2: Investment in Capital Construction from 1956 to 1965

Source: *China Statistics Yearbook*, 1984

During readjustment, the CPC Central Committee maintained that great importance should be attached to investigation and study as principal components of its efforts, and under a relatively objective and thoughtful atmosphere, China conducted a self-examination of the extremes of the Great Leap Forward. Along with the unfolding of these efforts, and the gradual restoration of the national economy, the government's attitude of "seeking truth from facts" brought forth a relatively rational and stable period of housing development.

2. The General State of Urban Housing Construction and Relevant Policies

As mentioned, the radical industrial policy of the Great Leap Forward led to abnormal development in urbanization. In the three years from 1958 to 1960, the average annual growth rate of heavy industry was 49 percent, and the direct effect of this rapid growth on urbanization was that the number of cities increased by 42 percent, the number of staff and workers all over the country increased by 28.68 million, and the urban population increased by 10.41 million annually. The proportion of urban population in the total population increased from 15.4 percent in 1957 to 19.7 percent in 1960 (Table 5-3). The rapid growth of urban population, on the one hand,

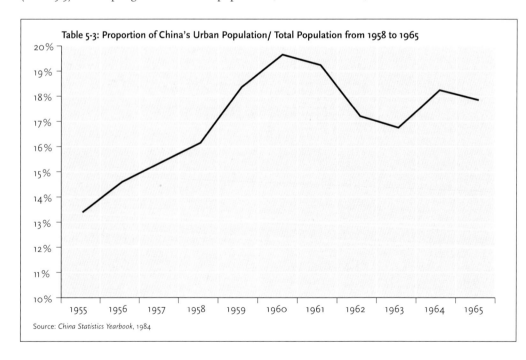

Table 5-3: Proportion of China's Urban Population/ Total Population from 1958 to 1965

Source: *China Statistics Yearbook*, 1984

meant decreased numbers of rural laborers, and intensified the reduction of agricultural output. On the other hand, it brought forth tremendous pressure on cities, and they had difficulties in dispensing wages, supplying grain and constructing housing.

2.1. Abnormal Development of Urbanization

One of the main measures China adopted after the beginning of the economic readjustment in 1961 was a reduction in the urban population, as well as in the number of cities and towns. By June 1963, China had laid off a total of 19.4 million urban staff and workers, and urban population decreased by 26 million. Most of the staff and workers, who had been laid off, were employees who had come from rural areas after 1958. They were sent back to the countryside to engage in agricultural production, thus decreasing the state's expenditure on wages and the supply of commodity grain in cities, while also strengthening agricultural production. Meanwhile, the criteria for establishing cities and towns were raised, resulting in a reduction of their number. From 1962 to 1964, for instance, the number of cities decreased from 208 to 169, and the number of towns from 442 to 421. Consequently, the proportion of urban population in the total population was restored to the same level as before the Great Leap Forward.

2.1.1. Consolidation of a Binary Social Structure in Urban and Rural Areas

In terms of economic policy, the Great Leap Forward and the People's Commune Movement were contradictory. The policy of giving priority to the development of heavy industry effectively meant that the agricultural economy "paid tribute" to the industrial economy, requiring surpluses of agricultural production to be transferred to industrial development. Meanwhile, through administrative means and controlled consumption, urbanization in China lagged behind industrialization so as to guarantee that the resulting relatively high levels of social accumulations could be used to enlarge industrial reproduction, rather than to increase the wages and consumption of urban industrial workers.

During the First Five-Year Plan, this binary economic structure in urban and rural areas was basically transformed and, at the end of this period, in January, 1958, the CPC Central Committee and the State Council issued the "Regulations of the People's Republic of China on Household Registration," in order to consolidate the binary economic structure in urban and rural areas and to control urban population.[7] After that, China adopted strict administration of household registration. More specifically, the regulation specified that Chinese households must be divided into agricultural households and non-agricultural households, and that under normal conditions, peasants may not change their status to become permanent urban residents.[8] Compulsory transfer of agricultural surpluses reduced reinvestment in agriculture, and controlled urbanization stifled the urge to raise agricultural productivity. Hence the number of rural laborers became a decisive factor for agricultural production. During the Great Leap Forward, industries in the cities, when confronted with the task of constantly enlarging the scale of reproduction, required more capital accumulation and needed more resources to be transferred from the countryside, including a large amount of additional labor. Consequently, the large scale and rapidity of urbanization decreased the number of laborers in the countryside and weakened agricultural production, resulting in a decrease of agricultural surpluses and a short supply of grain. Meanwhile, cities were also confronted with more wages that needed to be paid, and more staff and workers who had to enjoy welfare. In summary, this program ran counter to basic economic law and the Great Leap Forward was doomed to failure.

When the restrictions on urbanization were broken during the Great Leap Forward, urban populations grew rapidly, putting even heavier burdens on the state. Therefore, one of the main objectives during the readjustment period was to reduce their size. After this objective was basically realized in 1964, the State Council endorsed the document of the Ministry of Public Security, specifying that China should further strictly restrain rural households from entering cities and towns, and stressed the need for strict administration of household registration. It was on this basis that the binary social structure in urban and rural areas, peculiar to China, was gradually formed for the purposes of guaranteeing the unity of the society and the economy, and for stabilizing state industrialization (Wang Sijun, 1996, 20). In addition, this binary social structure in urban and rural areas had several tangible by-products, and urban housing was one of the most important among them (Guo Shutian, 1990). In essence, urban residents were entitled to the allocation of state-owned houses and received housing subsidies in their wages, while people in the countryside had to pay for their own housing.

2.1.2. Development and Changes of City Form

In 1958, the number of China's industrial enterprises increased dramatically to 263,000 from 169,500 in 1957, and became the major way of absorbing newly added urban laborers. Along with the rapid growth of urban population and urban industries, more and more industrial areas and corresponding new residential areas appeared in cities. Moreover, some especially large cities, confronted with pressing daily problems of land development and population growth, began to seek new kinds of urbanization, resulting in the transformation of old urban areas and the development of satellite cities.

In the master plan of the City of Beijing in 1958, it was stated that the scale of the city should be placed under strict control, and that it should be defined by the city proper and the satellite towns. Also in 1958, Shanghai began to develop satellite towns so as to redistribute industrial enterprises and population. As mentioned, the idea of building residential areas was introduced into China at the end of the First Five-Year Plan, and was widely used in the urban property boom brought on by the development of urban industrial areas and satellite towns between 1958 and 1965. In essence, the master plan of the City of Beijing advocated the idea of "scattered development areas," weakening the old practice of dividing cities according to functions. Instead, cities like Beijing were to be composed of many subdivisions, each encompassing industries, residential areas and other facilities. This idea, to be described in detail later, came from the urban people's commune, which already combined industry with agriculture to form a new social structure, within which the small industries of the "Great Steel-making and Iron-making Movement" formed the background. Subsequently, implementation of this idea caused profound changes in urban residential areas, and the urban people's commune became a basic organizing and production unit in residents' lives.

2.2. Urban Housing Construction and Management

During the Great Leap Forward and the following period of economic readjustment, the proportion of China's total investment in urban housing decreased further. In the 8 years from 1958 to 1965, this investment made up only 4.82 percent of the total, much lower than the level of 9 percent recorded in the First Five-Year Plan. However, because of substantial increases in investment in capital construction during the Great Leap Forward, the actual housing area completed reached 153 million square meters, an increase of 62 percent over that of the First Five-Year Plan, only to be decreased by a large margin with the unfolding of economic readjustment in 1961. Specifically, by 1962, investment in capital construction had been reduced to 5,362 billion yuan, or one-seventh of the figure in 1960 (38,407 billion yuan), and investment in housing construction had

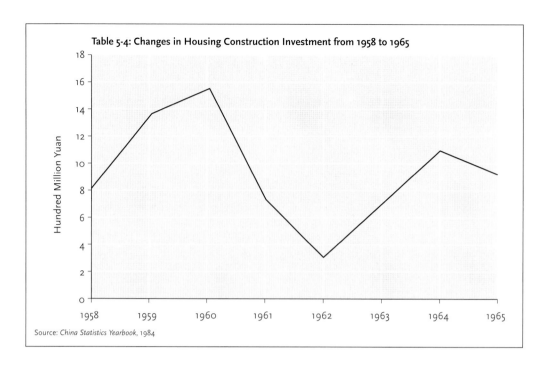

Table 5-4: Changes in Housing Construction Investment from 1958 to 1965

Source: *China Statistics Yearbook*, 1984

also dropped to the lowest level since 1953, with only 316 million yuan. Following this downturn, the gradual recovery of the national economy caused a rise in the investment in housing construction, which, by 1964, was close to the level recorded in 1957 (Table 5-4).

2.2.1. Changes in House Rents

In 1956, house rents were lowered throughout the country, and dropped further in 1958. In Beijing, for example, the housing rents of 80 percent of the households decreased, and in the remaining 20 percent who saw their rents raised, households only needed to pay 50 percent of the increase, in accordance with the "Standards for Civil Housing Rents" issued in July of 1958. However, although the housing administration saw its publicly owned houses increase by 5.21 million square meters in 1958 over 1957, the income from rents increased by less than 4 million yuan. Effectively, the average rent per square meter decreased from 2.206 yuan in 1957 to 1.236 yuan in 1958 (Sun Qinghua, 1991, 17).

As for state-owned houses, although the housing administration adopted the principle of "maintaining houses for rent," the Chinese government had constantly to reduce rents because of unforeseen contingencies encountered during the implementation of its policies. The national economy was plagued with serious disruptions and production decreases during the Great Leap Forward. These included a shortage of light industrial and agricultural products; the abolition of the wage system of distribution, with corresponding income decreases; and the rapid growth of urban population, resulting in a shortage of supply of basic goods (Sun Jian, 1992, 275). One obvious inference that can be drawn from these outcomes was that the important reason for the constant lowering of rents was the sheer drop in the actual living standards of urban residents.

2.2.2. Actual Living Conditions in Cities

As there was no broad-scale investigation of living conditions in cities at the time, it is impossible to give a direct description of this period. Nevertheless, through a comparatively detailed and complete housing investigation in some large cities, it is possible to catch a glimpse of the living conditions of the whole country. In Shanghai, for example, the existing area of dwellings in 1965 was 37,406 million square meters, and the living space per person remained around 3.8 square meters from 1958 to 1965. The housing stock there included apartments, garden-like houses, new workers' houses, new-style and old-style linong houses, and simple shacks, of which new workers' housing—mainly the "workers' new villages" built up by the state after the Liberation—made up 17 percent of the total. Between 1958 and 1965, some 442.3 square meters of housing were added, of which 60 percent was newly built housing and the rest were extensions to old houses. Those living in newly built housing occupied 4 to 4.5 square meters per capita on average, and those living in old houses had about 3.6 square meters on average. Under the low living conditions that prevailed, it was very common for several families to live in one house, or for several generations of a family to live under one roof.

3. The Major Development Stages of Housing Projects and Designs

Once again, socio-political and economic circumstances dictated the direction of housing design and planning in China, first under the influence of ultra-leftist policies and then under the period of adjustment to those policies. The advocacy of extreme economic measures led to experiments with alternative materials of construction and to the development of smaller dwelling units. During the ensuing period of social and economic readjustment, serious consideration was given to the actual housing conditions prevalent in China during the early 1960s, with the result that further new forms of housing and social organization were established, the chief among them being the people's commune. More conventional planning of residential areas also continued from the prior period, with a considerable amount of functional and spatial optimization of residential layouts.

3.1. One-sided Pursuit of the Economy Under the Influence of Ultra-leftist Ideology during the Great Leap Forward

Although investment in capital construction increased rapidly, the proportion of the investment in housing decreased during the Great Leap Forward, as mentioned earlier, because of the unchanging policy that regarded houses as non-productive construction. The average annual investment in housing over a three-year period had not yet reached the level of 1957, even though the rapid growth of urban population quickly increased the demand for urban housing.[9] Therefore, economic principle once again was stressed in ideological terms and became a determining factor in housing development. The basic premise was to provide the rapidly growing urban population with more houses without increasing the level of investment in housing construction.

3.1.1. Fluctuations in Housing Standards During the Great Leap Forward

An editorial, entitled "Our Slogan of Action—Combating Waste and Building the Country with Diligence and Thrift" printed in the *People's Daily* on February 2, 1958, criticized the phenomenon of "seeking perfection, novelty and large scale in construction"—especially in sectors that were regarded ideologically as being non-productive. On May 24 of the same year, the newspaper ran another editorial, entitled "Urban Construction Must be in Conformity with the Principle of Economy" and the political slogan of "opposing conservatism," put forward in the Anti-Rightist struggle of 1957, served as the motivation for various extreme actions. Cooperation with the Great Leap Forward on matters of economic construction, and the trend of one-sided economic pursuit regardless of the consequences, appeared again in urban housing design.

The main purpose of advocating frugality in the construction of houses during the Great Leap Forward was to reduce the cost of construction and to save steel products and other materials that were in short supply. Therefore, opposite to the exaggeration of output prevalent in the metallurgical industry and in agriculture, a totally different situation occurred in urban housing, where departments rivaled each other in lowering costs and standards. Houses were

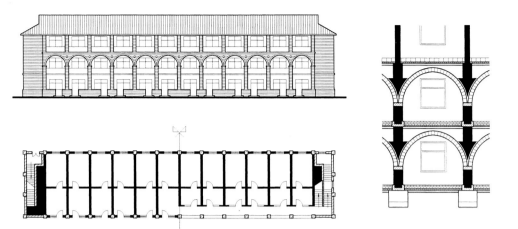

Fig. 5-1: Design for low-standard housing built of earthen bricks during the "Great Leap Forward"

even built with local raw materials and technology during this time, and a conference on local design work, held by the Constructional Engineering Department in April 1958, became a national exhibition of such housing, including houses made with bamboo-woven walls in Sichuan Province, and buildings constructed with materials other than steel, iron, cement, wood or brick in Harbin[10] (Fig. 5-1). Primarily due to the blind reduction of construction standards, housing, regardless of safety, could be generally referred to as being "low, small, narrow and thin." Needless to say, the resulting low-standard houses, without sufficient facilities, caused great inconvenience for their inhabitants, and later became dangerous forms of shelter.

With the progress of the Great Leap Forward, the widespread and over-optimistic estimation of economic development made people believe that a communist society would be realized soon. Consequently, housing designers were to be mentally prepared for substantial improvements in people's living standards, with the upshot that some high-standard housing designs emerged after 1959. One example was the standard design of the No. 9014 residential building in Beijing, on the Tsinghua University campus, where the area of a large room reached twenty square meters and a small room was over fifteen square meters in size (Fig. 5-2).

3.1.2. Development of Small-sized Apartments

The Forum on Housing Standards and Architecture was jointly held by the Ministry of Building Industry and Architectural Society of China in Shanghai from May 18 to June 4, 1958. The forum criticized previous practices of "combining short- and long-term goals

Fig. 5-2: The No. 9014 housing in Beijing

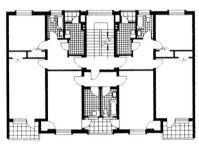

and putting emphasis on the latter," and decided to attach importance to short-term projects. Under the guidance of this principle, the issue of apartment division was raised, i.e., each family should have its own apartment, complete with kitchen and bathroom, and attention should also be paid to the sharing of rooms by several family members. Previously, as was mentioned, high standards in housing development and the pursuit of large amounts of space resulted in large rooms. Often different generations of one family had to live in one room, creating many inconveniences. The suggestion to increase the number of rooms in one apartment was accepted at the forum and the idea of the small apartment was popularized, although, in fact, the idea had surfaced at the end of the First Five-Year Plan. For example, small apartments were included in the Xingfucun neighborhood apartment buildings in Beijing.

The design standards proposed during the First Five-Year Plan of four square meters now, six square meters in the near future, and nine square meters in the long run, were replaced in 1957 by the actual standard of four square meters per person. This change, though small, was significant because it brought down the previously high design standard to reflect the real housing conditions in China. The change was also crucial because it emphasized citizens' present needs, without requiring them to sacrifice their present needs in exchange for a goal that was far away. (In fact, the goal of nine square meters per person was not achieved, even in 1978; the figure had dropped to 3.6 square meters, from 4.5 square meters in the early stages of the People's Republic.)

With the changes in design standards, rational improvements were made, as mentioned earlier, to the Russian-style inner-corridor flat, bringing it in line with China's climatic, economic and lifestyle conditions. For example, the Soviet-style flat of three two-bedroom units in a five-bay space (the plan of the 2-2-2 dwelling unit in the Russian residential design standard) was not reasonable. The rooms were so big that one flat was usually shared by two or more families, some of which ended up in rooms on the north side and received no sunshine at all. Meanwhile, the kitchen and toilet were placed on the south side in the middle of the unit. Based on such extensive observations, a design of four two-bedroom flats in a six-bay space resulted, whereby the rooms on the south side were either bedrooms or living rooms. The bedrooms of the two flats in the middle were also placed on the south side, and could be shared by two families. The two flats on the sides of a single apartment building each had one bedroom facing south and one bedroom facing north, and thus could be assigned to big families in a manner that would allow each family at least one room that received sunshine (Fig. 5-3). The design of the 2-2-2 flat configuration also underwent changes. For example, although the basic layout of the 2-2-2 flat was used in the configuration known as the 8014 Standard Housing Design in Beijing in 1958 (Fig. 5-4), the area of the rooms was smaller than before. The largest room would be from thirteen to fourteen square meters in area, while a small room was around nine square meters. Because of these design modifications, almost all families were able to get a flat for their exclusive use.

Fig. 5-3: Plan of an apartment building with a short, open corridor (left)

Fig. 5-4: Plan of the No. 8014 apartment building (right)

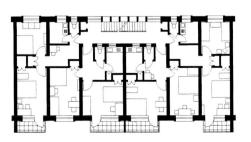

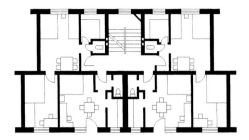

Fig. 5-5: Plan of the No. 8011
apartment building

Fig. 5-6: Plan of the apartment
building with open corridors on
Quzhenren Road in Shanghai

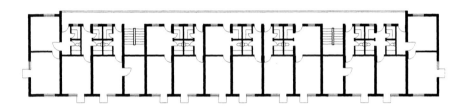

Meanwhile another configuration, the 8011 housing plan, also underwent marked changes. Under the influence of the idea of the small apartment, mostly one-bedroom and two-bedroom flats were created. Here, the advantages were obvious. Few families were required to share a flat with others and, because the rooms were smaller, the number of people living in one room was reduced (Fig. 5-5). This design also reduced the size of kitchens and toilets, therefore allowing provision of these facilities to each household. Furthermore, the 8016 Standard Design was a similar example. Based on the small outer-corridor apartment, architects in Shanghai conducted a careful study of this arrangement and the use of the kitchens and bathrooms. The final design they presented featured a two-square-meter kitchen and a two-square-meter bathroom for each unit, while not raising the average floor area per family (Fig. 5-6). In some small apartment designs, a modest livingroom was created as a link to all rooms, as well as a place for dining. Such designs were the precursor of the "small square hall" and "bright square hall" configurations that appeared later.

3.1.3. Standard Methods of Design and Industrialization

Starting from 1959, each province, city or autonomous region took over the responsibility of organizing standard housing designs from the State Construction Commission (Zhou Jinxiang, 1985, 348). This marked a shift from a unified standard design to paying more attention to local conditions, and various departments in charge of standard housing design were set up all over the country.

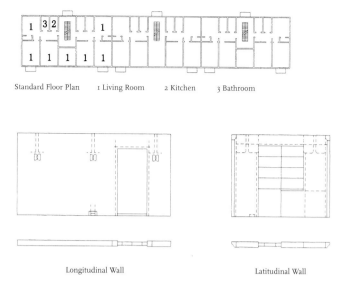

Fig. 5-7: An apartment building built with large haydite wall panels in Shanghai

Standard Floor Plan   1 Living Room   2 Kitchen   3 Bathroom

Longitudinal Wall   Latitudinal Wall

Emphasis on economy in housing development promoted research and development of industrialization. Houses made of large panels and wall panels of vibrated brick developed fastest in this period. This was because less reinforced concrete was needed in vibrated-brick wall panels, as they became denser after vibration and their strength and structural wholeness was greatly improved. Walls made of this material were thin, increasing the floor area of houses. In addition, this approach opened up another avenue for a more rational use of clay bricks.[11]

In 1958, Beijing began to build massive buildings with thin-webbed wall panels on a trial basis. By the 1960s, research had shifted to vibrated brick-wall panels, and extensive numbers of dwelling units made of this material were completed by 1965, with most of the units constructed according to the "64 panel type 1 housing standard" devised by the Beijing Architectural Design Institute, or with slight changes. Experimental houses with haydite concrete wall panels were also built in 1963, primarily in Shanghai and Tianjin, and houses made with wall panels built from industrial wastes, such as wet grinding slag, were constructed in Shenyang (Fig. 5-7). This period also saw the development of studies on other alternative building materials. In order to substitute for bricks and cement, industrial wastes such as sand, slag and stove ash were used to produce various bricks, blocks, wall panels and floors. In Shanghai, for instance, in 1961 some 300,000 square meters of housing were built with silicate blocks made from industrial wastes, saving more than 80 million bricks.

3.2. Housing Design During the Readjustment Period

Under the guidance of "readjustment, rectification, supplementation and improvement" in the Central Government, and in commemoration of the twentieth anniversary of the publication of Mao Zedong's "Preface to the Investigations in Rural Areas," the Ministry of Construction and Engineering issued an edict for conducting a survey of urban housing. Subsequently, an in-depth survey, particularly about housing standards, was conducted across the country, involving officials and experts from design institutes, housing management bureaus, architectural schools and colleges, and universities. Also, academic exchanges and free discussion of housing problems were a part of the Third Conference of the Chinese Architectural Society in November 1961, and in its annual meeting in December 1963.

3.2.1. Explorations and Enrichment of Housing Types

Influenced by a practical and realistic atmosphere, housing design entered an objective and pragmatic period. Reflections on previous design and construction problems, plus a renewed enthusiasm on the part of the architects, became the source of a stream of creative and varied investigations. Through these objective reflections, people realized that it would take a long time to improve housing standards. Although a large number of houses had been built since the founding of the People's Republic of China, the level of urban housing had not been improved greatly, primarily because of the initially poor conditions of cities, and a rapidly growing population. Clearly, housing standards did not reflect actual housing conditions and, as a result, newly built houses did not improve people's living conditions, but caused many of them to double-up on accommodations and share with others. From these deliberations, people developed a new understanding about urban housing standards and the inherent relationship between short-term and long-term goals. Furthermore, it was widely acknowledged that indices, such as per-square-meter costs of construction and area rations alone, were not sufficient to show whether housing construction was economical. Based upon careful investigation and research, the problem of the size of housing and its distribution was put forward. For example, if a house was too large and had a high area ratio and low unit construction cost, it was neither economical nor convenient. As mentioned earlier, a large house would almost surely be assigned to at least two families to share.

A debate broke out over small apartments. Those in opposition argued that because the lifespan of an apartment was comparatively

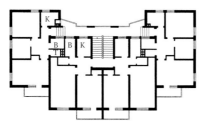

Fig. 5-8: Plan of experimental house 1 in 1964

Each flat was designed with a kitchen, a toilet and a bathroom. Thus the bathroom could be used as an additional kitchen when the flat accommodated two families, while the toilet was shared.

long, under the current housing standards, if one apartment was provided for one family to accommodate people's needs, the result would be too many one-bedroom apartments. When housing standards were raised in the future, these one-bedroom apartments would cause problems in distribution. Therefore, they suggested improving the actual living conditions of the families who shared one apartment (Fig. 5-8). By contrast, those who favored the one-apartment-for-one-family formula argued that "a house by definition is a building which gives shelter to the members of a family and that one-apartment-for-one-family should be the basic requirement" (Zhu Yaxin, 1962, 26). Considering the actual conditions at that time, they suggested building smaller apartments and increasing the number of rooms in each. Overall, it seemed important to design more small two-bedroom and three-bedroom apartments, as they also believed that one-bedroom dwellings were unsustainable. However, given the low per-capita living space and modest increases in household size, one-bedroom dwellings were in fact viable. Assigning a two-bedroom apartment to two families should not be the principal way to shelter one-bedroom families. Irrespective of the size of the family, married life is different from the life of a single person. Hence, the conclusion was that the one-apartment-for-one-family model best satisfied the needs of family life.

Based on investigations of local geographical conditions and climate, some designs with local features also appeared. Research on traditional construction skills also brought some changes to the practice of copying the Soviet experience. In fact, new attempts were made in the housing projects presented at the Zhangjiang Conference of 1961 and Wuxi Conference of 1963. Among them were houses with small internal yards suitable for hot areas, buildings with east-west orientations for cold areas, housing with considerable depth and internal yards which economized land, and independent flats and split-level houses suitable for complicated terrain. In the housing design of Shanghai's Fangunong, for example, architects increased the building depth and reduced the outer wall area facing the sun in order to decrease radiant heat gain. Small internal yards were used for ventilation and also to increase depth—and, therefore, to save land along streets (Fig. 5-9). Another example was the adoption of one-flight staircases in some low-rise houses, in

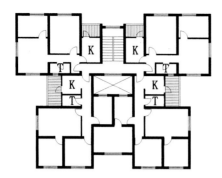

Fig. 5-9: Inner-yard apartments in
Fanguanong, Shanghai

order to make full use of the space under staircases and in attics
(Fig. 5-10).

After more than a decade of social and economic development
since 1949, urban residents enjoyed a better life in the 1960s than
in the 1950s, and new housing types also appeared. One example
was the apartment buildings with shops on the first floor; their
appearance met the urban residents' increasing need for commercial goods. It was also a sympathetic method for planning neighborhood environments after perimeter layouts were adopted. The first-
floor shops, for instance, could enliven the monotonous street scene
formed by the gable walls of buildings with a north-south orientation. Such apartment buildings not only helped solve the problem of
urban housing, but also reflected the period's emphasis on functional arrangement, circulation, organization and construction (Fig.
5-11).

Fig. 5-10: Housing for workers in Nanjing

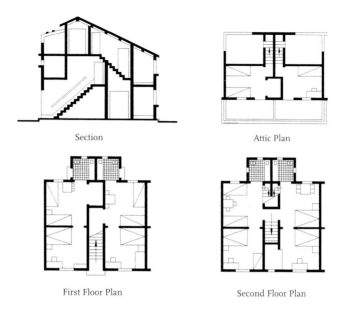

Section

Attic Plan

First Floor Plan

Second Floor Plan

3.2.3. Ultra-leftist Trends and Pressed Earth-wall Houses

The three years from 1959 to 1961 were difficult times for China. In order to withstand the pressure and economic blockade imposed by the Soviet Union, in 1960 the Chinese government began to exploit the Daqing oil field in northeast China. Under Premier Zhou Enlai's instruction of "combining cities with the countryside and workers with peasants, and creating conditions conducive to production and convenience for people's lives," the government decided quickly to turn Daqing into a new type of oil field with Chinese characteristics. Because of bad weather and difficulties with trans-

Fig. 5-11: First-floor commercial and residential buildings on Tianmu Road, Shanghai

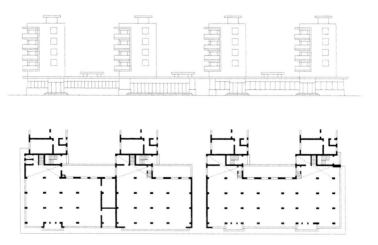

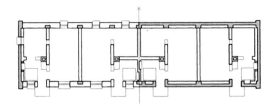

Figure 5-12: The plan of a residential area and houses with earthen walls in the Daqing oil field

Plan

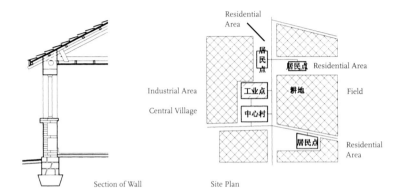

Section of Wall

Site Plan

Residential Area

Industrial Area

Central Village

居民点

居民点 Residential Area

工业点 耕地 Field

中心村

居民点 Residential Area

portation and in obtaining materials, an improved version of the local pressed earth-wall house was built. Each household had two rooms and an entrance through the kitchen. In this way, the housing needs of workers were solved in a short time and at low cost. From then on, lauded as a successful experience, simple, pressed earth-wall houses were built in other places in China, and the Daqing spirit of self-reliance became an example for others to follow. Consequently, under this influence, low-standard housing appeared all over the country, adding to the trend of reducing housing construction costs (Fig. 5-12). In November 1964, Mao Zedong called for a design revolution to promote technological innovation, and in line with the principle of "building the country through thrift and hard work," the design of "high-standard" houses was criticized. In 1965, the stress was once again put on learning from the spirit of Daqing in building simple, pressed earth-wall houses, and standards in house design were lowered further.

3.3. Planning of Residential Areas

The movement to establish people's communes in rural areas in 1958 soon spread to cities. It was believed that the People's Commune Movement was in conformity with the communist principle of combining cities with the countryside and workers with peasants, a transplantation that was accomplished without much difficulty.

Specifically, the Sixth Plenary Session of the Eighth National Congress of the Central Committee of the Communist Party of China, held from November to December 1958, put forward the idea that "the urban people's commune will be the tool for transforming old cities into new socialist cities and the organizer of production, exchange, distribution and welfare in people's lives, as well as the social organization which would combine industrial, agricultural, military, educational and trade circles and eventually merge government administration with commune management" (Jin Oupu, 1958, 34).

3.3.1. People's Communes in Cities

As mentioned, by July 1960, there were more than 1,000 people's communes in Chinese cities. Normally, they were established on the basis of existing social organizations, like large-scale state-owned enterprises, factories, institutions, schools or neighborhoods. Furthermore, the Master Plan for the City of Beijing in 1958 was heavily influenced by the notion of the people's commune, and became typical of planning in that period. It stressed the elimination of "the three differences" (differences between urban and rural areas, between workers and peasants and between mental and manual labor) and an eventual transition to a communist society. The plan stated clearly that urban residential areas should be organized according to the principle of the people's commune and, with this background, many new urban residential areas were designed and built and, although slightly different in some aspects, they all shared the following characteristics.[12] First, more functions were added to residential areas. For instance, because of the emphasis on the elimination of differences between urban and rural areas and integration of industrial, agricultural, military, educational and trade circles, as well as the combination of production and living, small factories were built in the residential areas. This allowed housewives, the elderly, the physically impaired and the disabled to participate in production. Meeting rooms were added for political activities and even drilling grounds were created, as every citizen was also a soldier.

Second, on the basis of public ownership of the socialist means of production, people's lives were organized collectively. Within the people's commune, members were required to work and live together. Things that would normally be done at home were now done collectively. For example, residents had their meals in a public dining hall and houses were built without kitchens. The washing and sewing activities of each family were also performed collectively.

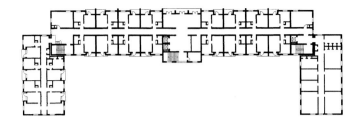

Fig. 5-13: Building of Chongwen People's Commune in Beijing

Street view

Apartment interior

Housewives were organized to work in neighborhood factories and children and elderly people were taken care of by the neighborhood. Organizationally, a people's commune was administered on three levels. Its basic unit consisted of some 2,000 people, an appropriate number for one public dining hall. Under the guidance of the idea of "integrating administration with the commune," the urban people's commune took the place of grassroots urban administration.

These communes were roughly of the same scale as urban districts or neighborhoods (Chen Zhaoyong, 1968, 31).

Third, the national principle of rectification also affected the planning and formation of urban people's communes. Following the popularization of the self-reliant spirit and experience of Daqing in 1964, new plans for building of residential areas in Daqing were worked out in order to put into practice some new ideas. Working areas were built next to the residential areas, making it convenient for workers to go to and from work. At the same time, each residential area had some farmland for family members of workers to grow grain and vegetables. In this manner, the city of Daqing was built from scratch, and the integration of industry and agriculture, as well as a self-sufficient lifestyle, made production convenient while meeting workers' basic needs. At the time, this model of self-sufficiency was considered a socialist ideal.

In hindsight, some ideas about the planning of urban people's communes are of significant interest. These included, for example, opposition to the divisions of a city according to function, the liberation of women and the socialization of housework. However, the fact that these ideas mirrored some of the trends of the later 1990s does not mean they were progressive or rational. Essentially, they were ideas originating from a self-sufficient, small-scale peasant economic ideology (Figs. 5-13 and 5-14).

3.2.2. Further Developments in Residential Area Planning

The planning of residential areas, first introduced into China at the end of the First Five-Year Plan, was widely applied during the Great Leap Forward, as many residential zones were built following the

Fig. 5-14: Building of the Hong-shunli Street People's Commune in Tianjin

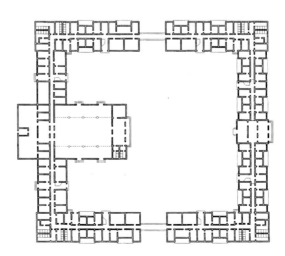

development of industrial areas in city suburbs and in satellite industrial towns. The financing, planning, design, construction, distribution and management of these residential areas were also unified. Furthermore, as city populations increased, more attention was paid to saving land and cutting costs in housing development. In Shanghai, for example, recommendations about increasing the density of residential buildings were put forward, and some are still active today. For instance, when a building is constructed between three to five storeys, one added storey will give an additional 800 to 1,000 square meters of floor space per hectare, but this effect is not obvious when the building is higher than six storeys. Also, when the depth of a room is less than 11 meters, an additional meter of depth will add 1,000 square meters of floor space in one hectare, whereas

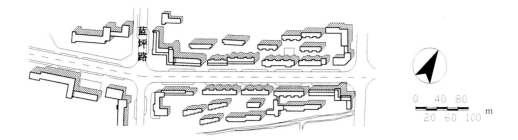

Fig. 5-15: Residential areas along Minhang Street in Shanghai

the floor space increase will be relatively small when the depth is above 11 meters. In addition, when the front distance between houses is reduced to 10 percent of its height, the floor space will increase 700 to 1,000 square meters in one hectare, and when the length of the house is between 30 to 50 meters, an additional 10 meters will produce an additional 800 square meters of floor space in one hectare, although the increasing margin will be noticeably smaller when the length of the house is more than 60 meters. Furthermore, a 10-centimeter reduction in the height of each storey will increase the floor space in one hectare by 500 square meters. Finally, an increase in the usable space of a plan does not affect the building density, but when the rise is small, at around 1 percent, then an additional 25 people can be accommodated in each 10,000 square meters of floor space (Wang Ye and others, 1960, 8).

The planning of residential areas, commonly called "new villages," in satellite towns had their own special features, incorporating a "street unit" or "neighborhood block" concept. In order to build the satellite towns quickly and to make full use of the service facilities of residential areas, the construction was carried out first with one street, then one block, then one more street, followed by one more block. The resulting criss-crossing of streets and lanes quickly came together to form a more or less complete urban landscape (Wang Dingzheng, 1959, 14). One other main characteristic of these residential areas was that the ground floors of the buildings along streets were used for stores or for other services. In this way there was little difference in access to stores and services for people living in the satellite towns from conditions they might encounter in cities (Fig. 5-15).

Notes

1. Put forward in a speech made by Mao Zedong at the Second Session of the Eighth National Congress of the CPC Central Committee. See Sun Jian, *The Economic History of the People's Republic of China (From 1949 to the Early 1990s)* (Beijing: Publishing House of the People's University of China, 1992) 229.
2. Sun Jian, 227. Take the steel industry as an example: in 1957, output was 5.5 million tons, and according to the final plan, steel output in 1958 would double the output of 1957 (i.e., 11 million tons).
3. "Under the Mao Zedong Banner," *Red Flag*, July 18, 1958. "Our direction should be to gradually organize a large commune in a planned way combining industry, agriculture, trade, education and military affairs, thus forming a basic unit in the society of our country."
4. The Resolution of the CPC Central Committee on the Establishing of the People's Commune in the Countryside, made on August 29, 1958. "Under the current situation, establishing the people's commune that develops agriculture, forestry, animal husbandry, side-line production and fisheries in an all-around way, and combines industry, agriculture, trade, education and military affairs, is the basic principle we must adopt to guide peasants to speed up the socialist construction, finish constructing socialism ahead of time and a step-by-step transition to Communism."
5. Sun Jian, The Draft for Trial Implementation by the CPC Committee of the Xushui County in China on the Adoption of Supply System by the People's Commune said: "The people's commune promised the '15 guarantees,' food, clothing, housing, shoes and socks, towels, soap, lamp oil, matches, heating expenses, bath, haircut, watching movie shows, medical care and funeral."
6. Sun Jian, 279. On September 30, 1960, "The Report Concerning the Controlled Figures in the National Economic Plan of 1961," endorsed by the CPC Central Committee, put forward the "Eight-Character Principle" for the first time. In January 1961, Vice-Premier Li Fuchun gave an explanation of the eight characters at the Ninth Plenary Session of the Eighth National Congress of the CPC: "readjusting the changed mutual relations among all sectors, consolidating the significant achievements made during the development and reform of productivity and relations of production, enriching the contents of some undertakings that have newly developed, and improving the quality of the new matters that need further improvement."
7. Reference to Section One, Chapter Four, "The Binary Economic Structure in Urban and Rural Areas."
8. The Regulations of the People's Republic of China on Household Registration adopted at the Ninety-first Meeting of the Standing Committee of the National People's Congress on January 9, 1958, specified: "if a resident moves

from the countryside to a city, he or she must bear the employment certificate issued by the city labor department, the enrollment certificate by a school, or an approval certificate by the city household registration organ."

9. *Statistical Yearbook of China,* (Beijing: China Statistics Publishing House, 1984) 194. The investment in housing development in 1957 totaled 1.274 billion yuan, while the average annual investment from 1958 to 1960 was 1.251 billion yuan. During the Great Leap Forward period, the investment in capital construction was 7.2 times that of 1957.

10. Li Jianhua, "Designs of the Building Built With 'the Materials Other Than the Four Materials' in Harbin," *Architectural Design*, vol. 4 (1958): 103.

11. "Development Trend of Housing Structures," by the Office of Industrial and Civil Construction of Institute of Building Science. *Journal of Architecture,* 32-35. 1960(1). Beijing.

12. *Journal of Architecture*, 9–12 (1958).

Chapter Six: The Cultural Revolution and Its Period of Influence (1966–1978)

The period from the 1960s to the mid-1970s formed a very special page in modern Chinese history. Influenced by the domestic and international political situation, Chinese society suffered through the calamity of the ten-year "Cultural Revolution," which began in 1966 and rapidly became a political storm that swept through the whole country, causing terrible social and political chaos. Not surprisingly, urban construction entered a stage of complete stagnation and urban housing development, controlled by an ultra-leftist ideology, once again emphasized extreme economy.

The chaos in the early Cultural Revolution caused common concerns in society and, in the early 1970s, the Central Committee of the Chinese Communist Party began to make adjustments to the development of the national economy, which, to some degree, had a reviving effect. Urban housing construction also moved forward somewhat in terms of standards, available types and degrees of industrialization. At the same time, the short supply of land in cities resulted in the emergence of high-rise apartment buildings and a general increase in the density of residential districts.

1. Social and Economic Background

Influenced by ultra-leftist ideology, the government during the Cultural Revolution did not change its strategy of giving priority to the development of heavy industry, even though the contradictions resulting from the longstanding implementation of this strategy began to emerge. The lack of effective demand created circumstances where urban industries were unable to expand, and, therefore, newly increased urban population could not be absorbed and unemployment began to rise. Throughout, an ultra-left political orientation was rampant, and the resulting social turbulence caused tremendous havoc in the national economy.

1.1. A Stress on Urban Development Shifting to Inland Areas

In 1964, before the Cultural Revolution, and based on the adjustment and rectification begun in 1961, Premier Zhou Enlai, on behalf of the Central Committee, put forward the major tasks of future national economic development. They were to build China into a strong socialist country with modern agriculture, industry, national defense, science and technology, and were soon to catch up with and surpass the world's advanced nations. In accordance with this strategy, the State Planning Commission put forward "Tentative Ideas for the Third Five-Year Plan (1966–1970)" in April of 1964, calling for an order of development beginning with agriculture followed by light industry and heavy industry. The basic task of the plan was to develop agriculture energetically to satisfy the essential needs of the people. Meanwhile, national defense and basic industry were to be strengthened and other fields like transportation, commerce, culture, education and scientific research were also to be developed. Moreover, according to the plan, the national economy would be further stabilized and coordinated and people's living standards would be improved, providing, in turn, an opportunity for urban housing development. However, due to incorrect estimations of the world situation in general and in surrounding countries in particular, the Party Central Committee revised the Third Five-Year Plan and put forward the strategic principle of "be prepared against war and natural disasters, and do everything for the people." In the draft of the Third Five-Year Plan, presented in September 1965, the orientation of work was changed from tackling people's problems with eating, clothing and daily essentials to war preparations. Emphasis was also put on inland construction, gradually changing industrial distribution and building the inland areas of the country into a strategic rear base. Consequently, by laying stress once more on capital construction of a productive nature, urban housing was deprived again of a chance for development. By contrast, the emphasis on urban construction shifted to the inland areas and investment in infrastructure was made far away from the cities.

1.2. Population, Land and Grain and the Pressure of Anti-urbanization Countermeasures

The government's erroneous criticism of the family planning policy of the late 1950s caused a subsequent uncontrolled population explosion. The enormous population base, a high natural growth rate and improvements in medical care all resulted in a rapid increase in China's population. Although the government began to carry out family planning policies in cities as early as 1964, problems with overpopulation emerged in the Cultural Revolution, of which feeding the large population was foremost. Because of an emphasis on industry to the neglect of agriculture, agricultural productivity failed to increase for a long time, and the output of grain was directly connected with available areas of arable land. Consequently, the government began to advocate frugality in utilizing land, avoiding occupation of arable land and increasing building density in urban areas. In cities, overpopulation made it difficult for people to find jobs, and the "heavy-industry-first" policy not only slowed down the development of light industry, but also resulted in a shrinkage of the urban area's tertiary sector. The artificial restraint on consumption deprived industries of the impetus to expand further and they therefore failed to provide more jobs. As a result, cities began to face substantial employment pressures. The government organized some political anti-urbanization movements, including moving city residents to border areas to support their development and settling high-school graduates in the countryside. Over time, these measures eased the mounting pressure on urban population and employment. However, the government did not recognize, for a long time, the deeper problems existing in the economic structure, such as the imbalance between industrial sectors and uncontrolled population development.

2. Relevant Policies and the Situation of Urban Housing Development

The serious economic and social disruption caused by the Cultural Revolution placed serious demands on housing. Many of the administrative bodies formerly responsible for housing provision were closed and coping with acute shortages became the order of the day. Housing standards deteriorated appreciably and overcrowding, always a prevalent condition, became even more serious.

2.1. Urban Planning and Housing Management Bodies in the Cultural Revolution

Starting from the middle of the 1960s, the urban planning and housing management system suffered serious damage. Offices at various levels were either paralyzed or closed. In November 1960, at the Third Conference for National Planning, it was proposed that there would be "no urban planning in the next three years," and in 1967, the State Housing Administration was terminated. As urban housing management departments lost their functions, funds for urban maintenance were badly misappropriated and urban housing—as well as municipal and public utility facilities—fell into disrepair, and the number of dangerous buildings increased. In the early 1970s, after Deng Xiaoping took charge of the Party Central Committee, the government began to pay attention to some of the serious problems in urban development and started to resume urban planning.[1] Together with a resumption of project approval and a strengthening of construction management, these measures improved urban circumstances to a certain degree.

2.2. Acute Land Shortage, High-rise Buildings and Uncontrolled Infill Developments

Overpopulation and a shortage of available urban land caused people to attach importance to economizing land in urban construction. The state leaders began to reiterate on various occasions the importance of saving land and, in order to increase building density, high-rise apartments were built in some large cities. At the same time, the comprehensive utilization of land was emphasized. With the focus of urban construction shifting to the inland and remote areas, housing investment in cities shrunk. Most housing development was done on small land parcels that were usually only available in the old city proper.

2.3. The Stagnation of Urban Housing Development

In the early stage of the Cultural Revolution, the society and life in general fell into great disorder, resulting in a stagnation of urban housing development. In fact, the floor space of urban housing that

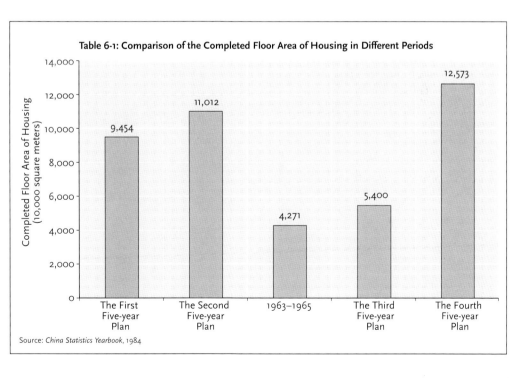

Table 6-1: Comparison of the Completed Floor Area of Housing in Different Periods

Source: *China Statistics Yearbook*, 1984

was completed in the Third Five-Year Plan was less than half of that in the Second Five-Year Plan (Table 6-1). In the early 1970s, as the government made another readjustment to the economy, housing investment and construction were resumed. However, the percentage of housing investment in overall capital construction never reached the 9 percent of the First Five-Year Plan and, instead, fluctuated around 5 percent and even dropped to 2.6 percent in 1970, the lowest since the founding of the People's Republic of China.

2.4. Housing Conditions in Cities

Due to the slow development of housing supply, the housing conditions of urban dwellers became worse, even though the amount of floor space per person remained at four square meters. Before 1978, however, no survey of housing conditions was conducted nationwide, and it was not until 1985 that a general survey of housing conditions occurred in China. Nevertheless, this survey took place close enough to the end of the Cultural Revolution to reflect some of the problems of that period.

According to the survey, more than a quarter of the dwellers in cities and towns, nationwide, had housing difficulties. Among them, over 1.2 million families had no house, and nearly 10 million families lived in very simple and crowded apartments. Furthermore, the housing shortage was particularly pressing in large cities like Shanghai and Beijing (Chen Huaning, 1994, 16).

In the 1970s, the floor area per family in cities was usually 27–35 square meters, with a living space of 3.5 to 4 square meters per person. Kitchens were usually shared, with an average area of 2.5 to 3.5 square meters per household. Water supply and sewerage systems, together with toilets, were provided outside the building, or on each floor, or on every two floors, inside residential buildings. Indeed, housing standards were low, even though in the later period of the Cultural Revolution, standards were raised and the situation improved.[2]

3. The Main Stages of Planning and Design

The main stages of planning and design for housing can be divided into two episodes. The first coincided with the early period of the Cultural Revolution and deliberately emphasized a decline in housing standards down to a most basic level of building conditions. The second, corresponding with the later period of the Cultural Revolution, represented another readjustment and the reinstitution of concerted efforts efficiently to improve housing quality in relation to scarcity in land and other resources. It was during this latter stage that high-rise buildings began to appear again in several major cities.

3.1. The Continual Decline of Housing Standards in The Early Period of the Cultural Revolution: The Pressed Earth-wall Houses

Before the beginning of the Cultural Revolution, there was a trend toward lowering the standard of housing in cities; the pressed earth-wall houses in Daqing, described earlier, marked the start of a low standard of housing. In 1965, Mao Zedong issued an appeal to carry out a housing design revolution, and began to break through the existing standards by politically supporting the practice of lowering them, regardless of the consequences. From March 21 to 31, 1966, the fourth conference and academic meeting of the Architectural Society of China was held in Yan'an, Shaanxi Province. The summary of the conference states that "this conference stressed politics and has broken with the old practice of discussing the academy for the sake of the academy. It has carried forward the Yan'an Spirit [the spirit of self-reliance and hard struggle] as well as the spirit of *gandalei* [pressed earth-wall houses] in civil architectural design, and seriously exchanged the experience of designing low-standard apartments and dormitories."[3] Consequently, the gandalei apartment buildings continued to be constructed in the early period of the Cultural Revolution, as represented by Jianyilou, or simply constructed buildings (Fig. 6-1). Basically, these were of two kinds: one with inner corridors

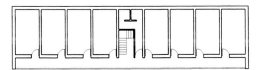

Fig. 6-1: Simple housing in Jianchang Hutong in Beijing

and the other with open corridors. In both cases, the corridors linked every room, none of which included a kitchen or toilet. The inhabitants cooked their meals in the corridor and there were public toilets and public washing rooms located separately inside the building. Materially speaking, such apartments were very similar to dormitories.

The continued decline of housing was also reflected in the drawing up of housing standards. In 1966, the Ministry of Building Industry issued its "Opinions on the Architectural Standards of Apartments and Dormitories," according to which the living space per person should be no larger than four square meters and that per family it should be no larger than eighteen square meters. In cities, low-standard apartment buildings were built, with per-square-meter costs of no more than thirty-five yuan in the south, no more than forty-five yuan in the north, and no more than fifty yuan in extremely cold areas. On the basis of those costs, each region made their own specific standards, further cutting the overall construction cost and lowering levels of quality. Public latrines without cisterns or other flushing devices even appeared in some buildings.

3.2. Urban Housing Development in the Late Cultural Revolution

In 1973, the State Construction Commission issued "Proposals for Revising the Building Standards of Apartments and Dormitories," stipulating that: 1) the floor space per family was to be thirty-four to thirty-seven square meters and thirty-six to thirty-nine square meters in extremely cold areas, and 2) multi-storey buildings should be the major type of dormitory. In large and medium-sized cities, buildings should have from four to five storeys, with per-square-meter costs of no more than fifty-five, sixty-five and eighty yuan in the south, north and extremely cold areas, respectively. Nevertheless, as can be seen, these standards were much higher than those of 1966, and floor space, instead of living area, was used as the criterion to limit the area of an apartment.

3.2.1. Changes in Housing Standards and the Evolution of Different Apartment Types

With respect to housing standards, the one-apartment-for-one-family idea and small apartments were widely accepted. Since the per-family area was small, the most common dwelling units were those with short, open corridors. In such a unit, one staircase served four two-bedroom apartments and families shared toilets, although they had separate kitchens. Resembling the 2-2-2 standard design (three two-bedroom apartments sharing a staircase) of the Soviet Union,

 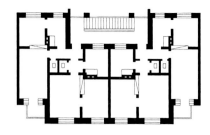

described earlier, such dwelling units adopted the 2-2-2-2 form (four two-room apartments sharing a staircase) within six bays. The 2-2-2-2 form not only ensured the orientation and ventilation of each apartment, but also economized on constructed land area (Fig. 6-2).

China covers a vast territory, with different parts of it varying greatly in climate and in the habits and customs of people. Unified standard design, therefore, could not meet the needs of such different regions simultaneously and, since local governments established their standard design institutions in 1959, as mentioned earlier, localization became an important aspect in the promotion and implementation of standard design. Governed by certain fixed indices, localities made revisions and adjustments to the standard design according to their specific conditions and requirements. Throughout, it was required that the actual housing needs of the local people were satisfied, while also conforming to the state's residential and building standards, as well as to methods of industrialization. For instance, in northeast China and other bitterly cold areas where there was no central heating, a fire wall—a wall with flues for space heating—was included in many housing designs (Fig. 6-3). However, in the south, with a hot and humid climate, the most important task was to keep every apartment well ventilated and dry, as well as to reduce the radiant heat from the kitchen to other rooms. Thus, some special forms of dwelling units appeared, including the type with every family having two doors opening off the open corridor (Fig. 6-4). In addition, out of consideration for national defense during the Cultural Revolution, the state shifted its construction emphasis to inland areas, and therefore many cities began to build their new industrial, mining and residential districts in mountainous areas. As a result, attention was paid to the special form of houses and apartments built on mountain slopes, and these forms were developed and applied (Fig. 6-5).

After the concept of the standard design was introduced in the 1950s, there had been fluctuations in how the standard was controlled. However, the level of living space per capita basically

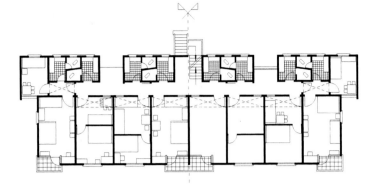

Fig. 6-4: Plan of a residential building in the Wenchong Shipyard, Guangdong Province

Fig. 6-5: The Standard Apartment Building of 1974–75 in Sichuan Province

remained at 4 to 4.5 square meters in cities, and, therefore, neither the design standard, nor related service standards, reflected the efforts made by architects to improve urban residential conditions. Under rigid space standard controls, only a limited influence could be produced, proceeding along the lines of some very specific techniques and details of housing design. A case in point was the above-mentioned localization of the standard design. In addition, there was a shift away from passageways to a small lighted livingroom inside an apartment, as noted earlier. Effectively, the passageway connecting rooms in the earlier standard design merely served as a passage. However, in the late 1950s and early 1960s, the width of the passageway was expanded to make a small square room used for dining or as a temporary bedroom, but, because it was too small and

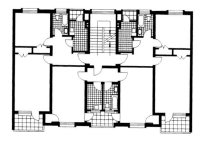

Fig. 6-6a: Plan of the No. 9014 apartment Building in Beijing

Fig. 6-6b: An apartment building with a small-lighted living room

Fig. 6-6c: A Type-B Apartment Building in Beijing, 1973

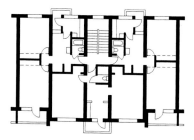

Changes in design from hallway to a small-lighted living room: from design No. 301, 9014 (6-6a) to an apartment building with a small-lighted living room (6-6b). Later, the hallway was enlarged to function as a dining room.

received no natural light, it was seldom adopted in later housing design (Wang Shouju, 1978). Later, influenced by the concept of increasing the depth of an apartment, the same square room was placed in the middle of the apartment and received light indirectly from elsewhere in the dwelling unit. Such apartments were called "the small, lighted livingroom type" (Fig. 6-6). Besides this innovation, a new apartment type, with a livingroom of some fifteen square meters, began appearing in Guangzhou, in order to meet the needs of returned overseas Chinese (Tomokiyo, 1995). Moreover, both "the small, square livingroom type" and "the larger livingroom type" proved to be valuable contributions for later housing design in China. At the same time, it can be seen that architects, while complying with the strict control of housing standards, made improvements to dwelling functions and made the apartment as efficient as possible.

In addition, changes took place in the facade and design details of urban apartment buildings. After the traditional big roof was criticized in the 1950s, the form of urban apartments became a secondary issue, as noted earlier, and attention was paid to function rather than to facade decoration. The practice of providing a balcony for the sake of its effect on the facade, without considering internal function, had basically been abandoned. Instead, the facade was mostly a simple brick wall or concrete frame, with some simple ornaments on window frames, eave ends and parapets, and the layout of balconies basically ensured that every family had its own out-door space.

3.2.2. Land Shortages and the Appearance of High-rise Apartments

The increasingly serious conflict between rising population and scarce land resources in cities made the problem of economizing on land use more important. In the early 1970s, the leaders of the central government made it a policy to protect arable land and to promote high-rise urban housing. Consequently, some large cities, such as Beijing and Shanghai, began to construct high-rise apartment buildings and, in order to save land, most were divided into two zones (Fig. 6-7). Usually the first floor was for commercial purposes and other floors above were for living. The depth of the buildings was usually small and most had open corridors, allowing the utilization rate of elevators to be raised and service extended to more families. Meanwhile, the rooms of each small apartment were placed on the south side of the corridor in order to guarantee that the main rooms faced south (Fig. 6-8). Industrialized methods of construction, first introduced in the 1960s, were commonly used, such as the sliding moulded-panel technique commonly employed in Shanghai. Furthermore, a concrete-frame structure was used in

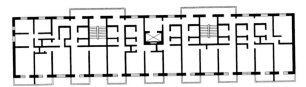

Fig. 6-7: High-rise apartment buildings on Qiansanmen Street, Beijing

Source: *Editorial Committee of the Construction History of Beijing*, 1958, 178

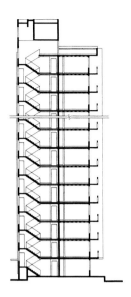

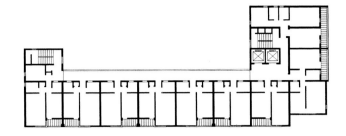

Fig. 6-8: A 13-storey high-rise apartment on North Caoxi Road, Shanghai

some high-rise apartment buildings in order to avoid the interference of load-bearing walls at ground level.

Because of the high cost and high construction requirements for high-rise apartment buildings, there was much controversy over their viability in helping to resolve the housing problem. Some people pointed out that the major advantages of high-rise apartment buildings were the concentrated open space that could be created among them, as well as the shortening of outside infrastructure, such as pipelines. They also believed that by making improvements to multi-storey apartment buildings, the goal of economizing on land use could be achieved. Their proposals—such as increasing building depth, reducing the ceiling height of each floor, increasing the number of apartments facing the east or the west, and the design of setbacks to the northern side—produced major influences on urban housing in China, and continues even today.

3.2.3. Development of an Industrialized Housing System

Since 1949, housing industrialization had always been a goal of Chinese urban housing development. In fact, as already noted, the introduction of standard architectural designs was an attempt to establish a complete industrialized system comprising architectural design, the manufacture of components and the construction of housing. However, because of low productivity and the government's general neglect of housing development, the industrialization process was still at an imperfect stage, despite nearly twenty years of practice.

Primarily, industrialization included three aspects: the standardized design, factory-made components and mechanized construction. During the First Five-Year Plan, China started to learn from the Soviet Union about the practice of creating a standard design, including the establishment of floor area standards, the making of standard drawings and the selection of basic construction systems. As discussed earlier, in 1955, the State Construction Commission authorized the Urban Construction Department to take charge of the standard design of housing, at which time the department drew up specific standard designs for six parts of the country; in 1959, the standard design of housing became the responsibility of provinces, municipalities and autonomous regions. In addition, the Construction Engineering Department established the Institute of Standard Design in Beijing, with branches in other parts of China, in order to take charge of both national and local interests. However, during the economic period of adjustment in 1961, it was terminated. In the mid-1960s, the Construction Engineering Department then set up the Management Bureau of Standard Design in Housing to take charge of all work and, before 1970, two levels of standard design management were implemented at the national and local levels. In 1970, however, the Institute of National General Standard Design was also terminated and all work on standard design was carried out locally (Zhou Jinxiang, 1985).

Before 1978, a mixed structure in brick and concrete was popular in housing, and when general design drawings first appeared during the First Five-Year Plan, the level of standardization started to rise. After the 1960s, floors, staircases, balconies, air ducts, garbage shafts and lintels gradually came to be prefabricated, and some construction machinery, such as the tower crane, was manufactured especially for brick and concrete apartment buildings. After the earthquake struck Tangshan in 1976, structural pillars and ring beams began to be added to brick and concrete apartment buildings and, except for the brick laying, which needed to be completed by hand, other parts of apartment buildings were mainly constructed using machinery in what amounted to a partly industrialized housing system (Hu Shide, 1993, 21).

Besides the brick and concrete apartment buildings, other building systems developed by China included block systems, prefabricated large concrete panels, large-scale moulded panels, sliding moulded panels, concrete frames, concrete tunnels and pre-cast concrete box buildings. Of these, large concrete panel, large moulded panel, block and framed lightweight panel systems were commonly adopted for housing construction.

Pilot projects of large panel structures were launched in 1958 and began to catch on after 1966. According to incomplete statistics, by the end of 1977, a total of 1 million square meters of large concrete panel structures had been constructed in Beijing, Nanjing, Kunming, Xi'an and Shenyang. The advantages of such a technique were a high degree of prefabrication, earthquake resistance, fast construction and high operating efficiency. It was also a construction system subject to the influence of seasons and capable of using

Fig. 6-9: A construction site using the large concrete panel system, 1964

industrial waste. Its major disadvantage was its high cost, primarily because the large concrete panel structure used more steel and cement in order to make buildings earthquake resistant and thermally efficient in cold northern areas (Fig.6-9).

Large-scale moulded panel housing began to develop rapidly after 1974, and by the early 1980s, over 8 million square meters of apartments had been completed. Essentially, they were of two types: one with both inner and outer walls cast *in situ*, and the other with the inner wall cast *in situ* and the outer wall prefabricated. The advantages were earthquake resistance, fast construction and easy mastery of the technique. The disadvantages were consumption of large quantities of cement and that construction proved difficult during winter in cold areas. Also, in the construction of multi-storey buildings, much steel was used in both the cast *in situ* internal structures and in prefabricated external concrete components (Fig. 6-10). The cost was also rather high.

In 1957, a block system of housing began to be developed. It was commonly adopted in the south and promoted in some parts of the north. According to incomplete statistics, the nation's annual production capacity of blocks was over 1 million cubic meters and, by the beginning of the 1980s, over 6 million square meters of hous-

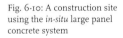

Fig. 6-10: A construction site using the *in-situ* large panel concrete system

Fig. 6-11: A construction site using the block structure system

Fig. 6-12: A construction site using the lightweight panel system

ing had been completed using this system, of which nearly 1.4 million square meters were constructed in 1977 alone. The advantages of this system were that it was easy to construct, had a low cost and was very adaptable. At the same time, it could employ substantial amounts of industrial waste and other local materials. Also, the plan and spatial arrangement of these block structures was both convenient and flexible. Furthermore, the construction period was from a quarter to a third shorter than other approaches and 10 percent lower in cost than conventional brick and concrete structures. The major problems lay in the block itself. Often it was deficient in compressive strength, tensile strength and thermal insulation properties (Fig. 6-11).

Fig. 6-13: The residential area of
high-rise apartment buildings on
North Caoxi Road, Shanghai

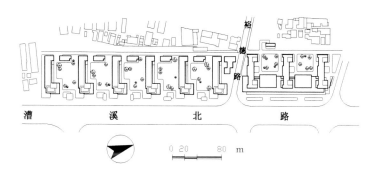

漕   溪   北   路

0 20   80   m

Pilot projects in framed lightweight-panel housing started in 1975, using a reinforced-concrete frame bearing structure. The advantages were lightness, economy of materials, a reduction in the amount of shipping required and simplified design and construction, as well as earthquake resistance. In addition, it made the arrangement of rooms flexible and adaptable to different requirements and could easily be used for housing as well as for public buildings. Construction speed was fast and, when compared with other building systems, each square meter was 40 to 60 percent lighter and cement savings were on the order of 15 to 50 percent. However, before 1978, the framed lightweight panel technique was at an experimental stage and was not adopted on a large scale[4] (Fig. 6-12).

3.3. Planning of Residential Areas: Increases of Density

During the Cultural Revolution, as the emphasis of industrial construction shifted to inland areas, a group of new industrial districts,
with attached living quarters, were constructed. Meanwhile, in the
large coastal cities, because there were few new industrial projects,
housing development stressed reconstruction of older areas and the
extension of existing areas. These two circumstances had a common
result, namely, a sharp rise in the building density of residential
areas, reflecting both pressures from urban population and land
shortage.

In Shanghai, for instance, the scale of building in residential
areas shrank drastically during the Cultural Revolution, and there
were almost no new construction projects. Of those that were completed, some were to adjust and extend existing living quarters, and
others involved renovation of old houses and the provision of housing for those who were relocated as a result of other large-scale public works (although, in fact, few municipal public facilities or services were constructed at that time). The appearance of high-rise
apartment buildings in Qiansanmen Street, Beijing, and in Caoxi
Road, Shanghai, also reflected the trend of developing high-density
apartment buildings in this period and, with them, corresponding
increases in urban density (Fig. 6-13).

Notes

1. "Some Opinions on Strengthening Basic Construction Management,"
   endorsed by the State Council, June 1973; and the "Notice on Strengthening
   the Management of Urban Maintenance Expenses," issued by the State Planning Commission, the State Construction Commission and the Ministry of
   Finance, December 22, 1973.
2. "The Trial Building Standards of Apartments and Dormitories for Workers
   and Staff Members in Sichuan Province," issued by the Construction Commission of Sichuan Province, 1972.
3. Conference proceedings (Beijing: Architectural Society of China, 1966) 2.
4. Institute of Architectural Design under the Institute of Building Science, State
   Construction Commission, "Appraisal of Four Building Systems of Housing,"
   Journal of Architecture 2 (1979): 4–5.

Part Three: Housing Development from 1978 to 2000 after China Adopted Reform and Opening-up Policies

by
Lü Junhua and Shao Lei

Introduction

There was no lack of ups and downs in housing development during the period of reform and opening-up. But compared with the period prior to the Cultural Revolution, the general development was more continuous and steady, which largely could be attributed to stable policies in social and economic development. Although the development of housing itself did not display clear-cut stages during this period, this exposition is based on the time-frame of social, economic and political change, in order to reveal better internal relations with housing policy and production.

Beginning in 1979, China entered a period of sustained and rapid development, with reform and opening-up to the outside world as the guiding policy. Indeed, in the twenty-two years from 1978 to 2000, China made great progress in its understanding of socialism and a socialist economy, and this progress can be divided into three phases. First, the Third Plenary Session of the Eleventh Party Central Committee, held in December 1978, guided by the policy of emancipating the mind and seeking truth from facts, produced a shift in the party and state focus from class struggle to socialist modernization. Against this political background, people began to re-examine the numerous problems in the planned economy—established under the strong influence of the former Soviet Union—and began to explore an economic system suitable for China's national conditions. Second, at the end of 1984, the Third Plenary Session of the Twelfth Party Central Committee made clear the policy of building a planned commodity economy based on public ownership. This represented a new understanding by the Communist Party about the issue of commodity and changed the ideology toward establishing a planned economy with a commodity economy, even though the ideological issues involved remained a focal point of discussion and controversy. Third, in 1992, the late Chinese leader Deng Xiaoping made a creative ideological breakthrough regarding issues that had long been disputed, and began to affect economic development. Essentially, Deng defined the nature of socialism as "to unfetter and develop the productive forces," and later on, the Fourteenth National Congress of the CPC explicitly advocated building a socialist market economy with Chinese characteristics.

Since then, great changes have taken place in China's social and economic structure. Economic operations were transformed from the dominance of mandatory planning to the dominance of market forces. In terms of ownership, singular public ownership gave way to the co-existence of multiple economic sectors, although still dominated by public ownership. With regard to investment, singular budgetary allocation was replaced by diversified channels including budgetary allocation, financing, self-fundraising and foreign capital investment. Over a twenty-year period, China's national economy grew at an average rate of close to 10 percent per annum, and the gross domestic product (GDP) increased 5.92 times. More important here, this substantial economic growth provided a solid foundation and motivation for housing construction.

Compared with economic restructuring, however, political reform lagged behind. In 1980, political reform was proposed as a relatively independent task to deal with the malady of over-centralized power in the traditional political structure. Nevertheless, due to both domestic and international political turbulence, the goal of political reform changed in content and speed, focusing on the improvement of the People's Congress, with the result that the political structure remained basically intact. Following economic reform, in the process of transferring and re-distributing interests, power combined with capital, not only increasing transaction costs, but also disturbing the prior optimized allocation of resources. The combination of power and capital also prompted social segregation. Naturally, with the deepening of the economic restructuring, contradictions rooted in non-economic realms became more severe, and the diminishing marginal utility of economic restructuring became more conspicuous.

Housing development reflects both social progress and economic growth, as well as changes and contradictions caused by the redistribution of social interests during reform and the period of opening-up. Over the intervening years, housing reform in urban areas completed the transition from a welfare housing system to a socialized housing security system. Housing construction made unprecedented progress, both qualitatively and quantitatively, and modernization of the housing industry became the general goal of China's housing development.

At the early stages of the reform and opening-up, housing construction was characterized by efforts to build more in order to alleviate the shortage of supply. Measures were adopted to mobilize the initiatives of governments, both at the central and local levels, as well as among enterprises and individuals, so as to lighten the state's burden and to increase investment in housing. Accordingly, several parts of the country launched experiments in the selling of publicly owned housing. Widespread discussions and practices centering around saving land and increasing residential density were also carried out. By the mid-1980s, the per-capita living area of urban population rose from 3.6 square meters to 6 square meters, the fastest per-capita increase since the founding of the People's Republic in 1949. Large-scale housing construction also promoted research on improving the living environment and diversifying building types. In particular, active theoretical explorations and practices in some architectural institutes greatly helped raise the overall standard of housing design.

In the mid- and late 1980s, the establishment of the theory of a socialist market economy accelerated the commercialization of housing. People came to realize that it was impossible to establish a real housing market if the rent of publicly owned housing remained excessively low. Some cities took the lead in launching experiments to raise rents. But these efforts were eventually aborted, due to general fluctuations in political and economic development.

A better understanding of commercialized housing and increasing living standards set higher functional requirements for housing and the development of residential areas. China's "Blue Paper on Technical Policies," promulgated in 1985, made explicit stipulations about the spread of dwelling-unit standards, representing a breakthrough in improving living conditions. The reform pertinent to land use promoted real estate development; thereafter, comprehensive housing development was carried out, mainly by realty developers, and gradually became the principal component of housing construction in urban areas. Against this background, experiments in the development of urban residential areas were launched in 1986. Centering around human needs, these experiments successfully aimed to enhance the functional, environmental and service quality of residential quarters through elaborate planning, better design, higher-quality construction, comprehensive development, supportive facilities and scientific management.

Under a socialist market economy, the early 1990s witnessed an unprecedented growth in the real estate industry. However, due to an incomplete system of clearing prices, an overheated real estate business also resulted in a bubble economy. By improving the economic environment and rectifying the economic order in the mid-1990s, the Chinese economy then entered a period of steady development. Unfortunately, the eruption of the Southeast Asian financial crisis also posed a new challenge, and prompted China to adopt measures to enable the housing industry to become a new consumption focus and point of economic growth. In short, by hoping that housing consumption could pull along general economic growth, housing reform was allowed to proceed more forcibly. It was even stipulated that 1999 would be the final deadline for housing distribution under the old welfare system.

Deepening economic reform further diversified the social structure. The resulting polarization of the rich and the poor led to varying levels of housing affordability among different families. While the supply of some expensive high-quality housing fell short of demand, several generations of many families also found themselves crowded into one room. Therefore, it became a top priority to establish a complete social-security system while also developing the housing market. Housing construction, primarily in the hands of real estate developers, gradually became enriched, and architectural style, residential-area planning, real estate management, community construction and lifestyle ideas all became "selling points." In line with its general policy of modernizing the housing industry, the state initiated the pilot project of better-off urban and rural housing and the so-called little-better-off housing project, followed by experiments in various urban residential areas. Today, modernization of the housing industry has become an inevitable trend in China's housing development.

Chapter Seven: Housing Development at the Beginning of Reform

1. The Social, Political and Economic Background at the Beginning of Reform

The Third Plenary Session of the Eleventh National Congress of the CPC, convened at the end of 1978, put an end to the Cultural Revolution and the 'leftist' political line of policy-making. After ten years of damage and in order to rapidly restore normal order, state reform and development of the national economy became central tasks. Along with this reform and development, China's urban construction returned to a rational path and the number of cities and levels of urbanization constantly increased.

In 1980, with the introduction in rural areas of the "household-based system of contracted responsibility linking remuneration to output," China announced its economic reform and immediately achieved unprecedented success. This laid the foundation for the application of economic reform in urban areas. At the same time, urban enterprises, owned by the people as a whole, began to carry out reforms and focus on expanding their power. Although individual's initial understanding of the characteristics of the social economy did not transcend the planned economy, the evolving practices in rural and urban areas challenged traditional theories and concepts.

1.1. The Convention of the Third Plenary Session of the CPC Eleventh National Congress and the End of the "Ultra-leftist" Political Line

The Third Plenary Session of the CPC Eleventh National Congress, which was convened in December 1978, marked a brand-new starting point for China's economic reconstruction. In view of the leftist ideology that ran rampant after the founding of the People's Republic of China, and especially the ultra-leftist errors of the Cultural Revolution, the session's historic contributions were the guiding principle of emancipating the mind, seeking truth from facts and uniting the people as one. Use of the slogan "taking class struggle as the key link" was stopped, and a decision was made to shift the emphasis of work toward socialist modernization and to adopt the policy of reform and opening to the outside world. Under the guidance of the principles approved at the Third Plenary Session of the CPC Eleventh National Congress, a series of policies and principles aimed at restoring and strengthening the national economy were promulgated. As a result, the economy began to come back to life after having been on the verge of collapse, and urban people's livelihoods rapidly improved.

1.2. Decentralization of Power and Changes in the Distribution Pattern of National Income

As described in some detail earlier, after the Communists came to power in 1949, China set up a highly centralized economic system by imitating the Soviet model. The central planning departments made economic decisions in a unified manner, keeping strict control over all local economic activities, enterprises and even individuals. The centralized distribution of national income meant that state accumulation was the principle means of accruing capital under China's traditional economic system; state financial income made up a very high proportion of the national income, while the income of individuals was very low. Ordinary Chinese relied, to a great extent, on welfare-in-kind and on the rationing of basic consumer goods.

The Third Plenary Session of the CPC Eleventh National Congress clearly pointed out the shortcomings of the old system. To lighten the state's burden, mobilize local enthusiasm, motivate enterprises and improve economic results, the government began to give back to enterprises some power and the profits they were entitled to. Within the traditional planned system, the relations between the central and local financial authorities were the guiding link of the distribution pattern. Under the central authorities, the government at all levels played the role of a cashier in implementing the local revenue and expenditure plan worked out by state financial authorities. Reform of the financial system—the main aspect of which was to delegate power to lower levels—divided the scope of revenue and expenditure for central authorities and localities. It also divided the financial revenue into three categories: 1) a fixed income for governments at all levels; 2) a fixed proportional income for central authorities and localities; and 3) a situational income. In this way, localities began to gain a certain financial power, the power of local governments was expanded and their enthusiasm for invigorating the economy was mobilized. All this laid the foundation for further reform of the financial and taxation systems. Starting in 1978, state-owned enterprises, which were accessories of the government, gradually turned themselves into relatively independent commodity producing and managing entities. The government adopted a series of measures to expand enterprises' autonomy over their operations and to transform them into entities that assumed sole responsibility for their profits and losses. As for government departments and institutions, the central authorities decided on a fixed annual allocation of funds for each unit. If it was not enough, it was up to the unit to make up the difference (Deng Qing, 1995, 31). The government readjusted significantly its policy on individuals' income and, as a consequence, the gross income of workers and staff increased by 16.6 percent annually and financial subsidies grew by 63.2 percent annually on average. Other welfare in kind also expanded (Yang Lu and Wang Yukun, 1992, 5).

Decentralization resulted in drastic changes in the distribution pattern of the national income. At the end of the 1970s, the proportions of government, enterprise and individuals' income were 33.5, 19.3 and 47.2 percent, respectively. In the mid-1980s, the proportions changed to 18.7, 28 and 53.3 percent, respectively. However, after payment transfers, the final proportions of the distribution in the same period were 22.6, 10.6 and 66.8 percent, respectively, meaning, on the one hand, that an ever-increasing proportion of the national income went directly to residents. On the other hand, enterprises were the key link in transferring expenditures, and the welfare from enterprises became the main source of welfare for residents. In this scheme of things, the main problem facing China's urban housing system was the process of assigning low-rent housing provided by all enterprises for their employees; thus, residents' dependence on enterprises for housing became the largest obstacle to housing reform (Yang Lu and Wang Yukun, 1992, 21–24).

1.3. Increasing Levels of Urbanization

From 1949 to the end of the Cultural Revolution, urban planning was often disrupted because of changes in political philosophy. At the end of this period, in March of 1978, the Third National Conference of Urban Work was convened. Since then, the Chinese government has attached importance to urban planning, as the conference stressed the significance of urban planning and the prominence of urban construction in the national economy. China decided to increase investments in urban construction by collecting urban maintenance fees, and worked out many other significant policies, such as strengthening housing development and increasing investments to solve the problem of housing shortages. Since then, China's urban construction has returned to a healthy position and housing construction has gradually increased.

The policy of reform and opening to the outside world provided favorable conditions for urban development. Rural economic restructuring touched off a reform in agricultural production, enabling surplus rural laborers to move to cities. On the other hand, along with the development of the national economy, the so-called convergence effect of cities became stronger and stronger, thus attracting more and more rural immigrants. Improvements in urban construction strengthened the cities' ability to accommodate more people. In the five years after the Third Plenary Session of the CPC Eleventh National Congress, the level of urbanization increased from 17.92 percent in 1978 to 21.62 percent in 1983, or an average annual growth rate of 1.54 percent, the fastest rate after the founding of the People's Republic. At the end of 1983, China had 20 cities with a population of over 1 million and the total population of cities had reached 42.05 million, four times greater than in the early days of New China. Rapid progress in urbanization also increased demands for urban housing.

2. Housing Policy at the Early Stage of Reform: Initiation and Experimentation

In the first thirty years after the founding of the People's Republic of China, the general level of housing for urban residents declined, as discussed earlier, due to various errors in the development of the national economy and in housing policies. When the Cultural Revolution was brought to an end, the amount of per-capita floor space was at its lowest point, and serious housing shortages became a prominent social problem and gained people's attention. According to 1978 statistics released by the Ministry of Construction on 182 cities throughout the country, per-capita floor space had declined from 4.5 square meters in 1952 to 3.6 square meters. In the same 182 cities, 6.89 million families hardly had a place to live, making up 35.8 percent of total city households. Obviously, with this situation, housing reform was the only way for the government to solve the problem of housing shortages.

Before these reforms, however, the funds allocated by the state for capital construction were the only investments in urban housing, and its development depended very much on the favor of decision-makers. Under the leftist orientation, it was natural for the government not to attach importance to such non-productive investment and, during the Cultural Revolution, housing development was in a stagnant state, so much so that the housing shortage became a pressing social problem that could explode at any time.

The damage done to social productivity generally during this time was also substantiated; per-capita GDP in 1978 was only 379 yuan.

After initiation of reform, significant changes took place in the structure of distribution within the national income, and the government was no longer able to solve the housing problem simply through allocating funds for capital construction. The only way to ease the housing shortage was to change the old housing system established under the planned economy, wherein the state was responsible for all housing development, and enthusiasm for this change among various sectors was mobilized. However, to achieve this, the Chinese government was confronted with three important issues. They were: 1) how to understand the nature of home ownership; 2) where to obtain funds for housing construction; and 3) how to increase the government's financial revenue.

2.1. Controversy Over the Nature of Home Ownership: Commodity or Welfare?

Under the socialist ideology, the matter of what should be regarded as economic commodities was always an important and sensitive question. Before 1978, when the leftist ideology ran rampant, the functions of commodity production and the law of value were denied. It was believed that all exchanges that occurred within the collective ownership of the people did not result in a transfer of ownership and were not commodities. Some people even maintained that, under socialism, the means of subsistence were not commodities. Principally, this was because consumer goods were provided to laborers in exchange for production, and, under socialism, laborers were not commodities. Therefore, the distribution of consumer goods should be a distribution in kind and, under the guidance of this ideology and as noted earlier, many consumer goods, including urban housing, were not regarded as commodities, but were distributed as welfare.

Soon after the Third Plenary Session of the CPC Eleventh National Congress, the government announced its housing reform policies. People in theoretical circles began discussions on issues such as welfare and commodities, means of production and means of subsistence, as well as on the first distribution sphere and the second distribution sphere, in an effort to understand the true nature of home ownership. The key was how to understand the judgement and design of socialism by the founders of Marxism, and widely different viewpoints were expressed in this discussion. Some insisted on the welfare nature of home ownership. Some denied it completely. Others maintained that housing had the nature of being both welfare and a commodity. In short, disputes helped people deepen their understanding of housing and to achieve substantive progress. Gradually, people began to understand that houses were commodities and, under housing commercialization, assignment of housing as welfare would be discarded and people's salaries would be raised so that they could afford to buy houses.

In 1984, the Chinese government said that there should be more experiments in the commercialization of urban housing. Encouragement was given to the real estate business in order to provide more funds for housing and to ease housing shortages.[1] In October 1984, the Third Plenary Session of the CPC Twelfth National Congress decided that the socialist economy was a planned commodity economy under public ownership, and since then discussions on housing commercialization have deepened still further.

2.2. Changes in Housing Investment and Construction: Reducing the State's Burden

As described in Part Two of this book, during the socialist transformation after 1949, the Chinese government controlled existing housing properties through the gradual change of real estate rights and centralized management, while it controlled newly built housing through the monopoly of capital and land. The allocation of urban land resources was a highly administrative process, and the government at all levels controlled all land allocation. Moreover, housing investment was a fixed proportion of the funds allocated by the state to each enterprise and institution for capital construction. Therefore, the government had the ability directly to control and restrict urban housing construction. Growth in the total amount of housing resources depended completely on a government department's decisions on investments, and those that could obtain state-planned projects were almost all enterprises and institutions with ownership by the people as a whole, or large collective enterprises (Deng Qing, 1995, 22).

In the 1970s, the Office for Unified Housing Development (OUHD) was established. This office was in charge of land requisition, planning, construction and unified management. As the state requisitioned land, the land requisition fee was very low, and the capital for requisitioning land was paid from the state budget. Furthermore, the construction of supporting urban infrastructure was also undertaken by the government. Starting from 1979, in order to find funds for housing development and to reduce its burden, the state began to motivate central authorities, localities, enterprises and individuals to solve the housing problem. Apart from the traditional manner of fund allocation, many other methods were used, such as enterprises collecting funds, credit capital and individual investment. Of these, the funds raised by enterprises themselves gradually became the main component of total urban housing investment, making up 60 to 70 percent. In large cities, well-off individuals bought commodity housing offered by their work units or real estate companies, while in small cities, employees made investments in housing development. In 1980, the investment by individuals accounted for only 1.6 percent of the total. But in the following years, the annual growth rate was 13 percent, and by 1983, individual investment made up 7 percent of the total investment in housing development (Table 7-1).

Table 7-1: Changes in private investment in housing construction

Source: *China Statistics Yearbook*, 1984 and 1985

Year	Private Investment in Housing (100 million yuan)	Percentage in Total Investment in Housing of the Year (%)	Completed Floor Area of Privately-invested Housing (10 million sqm)	Percentage in Total Completed Floor Area by Year (%)
80	2.0	1.6	0.65	6.4
81	5.5	3.8	1.3	11.7
82	8.0	4.3	1.3625	10.4
83	10.1	5.4	1.3803	10.7
84	13.6	7.0	1.672	13.5

After the initiation of reform, changes among the major investors in housing development also brought forth changes in housing construction. The traditional method of organizing housing construction by administrative fiat was basically discarded, and a policy that favored work units developing their own housing was successful, greatly easing housing shortages in the 1980s. However, this type of housing development had its own problems. For instance, plans for housing development were approved by different departments and construction was done on the basis of individual projects. As a result, they did not conform well to a city's overall plan, nor with public service and infrastructure provision.

Land-use policies were also changed. The adoption of reform and opening to the outside world made Chinese-foreign joint ventures and Sino-foreign cooperative enterprises possible, although also giving rise to the problem of using land with payment. Therefore, on July 8, 1979, the Law on Chinese-Foreign Joint Ventures was promulgated, specifying that "the investment of the Chinese partner in the joint venture may include the right to use of a site, provided for the joint venture, during the period of its operation. If the right to use of the site does not constitute a part of the Chinese partner's investment in the joint venture, the joint venture shall pay the Chinese government a fee for such use." From then on, using land with payment laid the foundation for the creation, development and prosperity of a real estate market and, in 1980, the National Urban Planning Work Meeting decided that urban construction should consider comprehensive development and advocated the founding of comprehensive urban construction and development companies. Consequently, OUHDs—the capital construction organs under the Construction Committee of the Bank of Construction and the capital construction organs of each city—became real estate development companies with the characteristics of administrative institutions. Following this, in 1984, the State Planning Commission and the Ministry of Urban and Rural Construction and Environmental Protection promoted a reform of considerable significance. They promulgated the "Interim Provisions of the Comprehensive Urban Development Companies," specifying that a comprehensive urban construction and development company is an enterprise with independent legal qualification and is an independent accounting unit responsible for its own operations. The document also urged administrative development companies to become enterprises. From then on, real estate development companies began to participate in the allocation of urban real estate resources as a relatively independent economic factor.

2.3. Reform of Housing Distribution Experiments With Selling Houses on Favorable Terms

Under the old system, it was the types of ownership of an enterprise or institution that decided their accessibility to land and other investments. Basically, there were two types. The first were state-owned enterprises and institutions that could obtain capital construction funds from the state. The others were non-state-owned enterprises that had no hope of obtaining funds for housing development from the state. Of the state-owned enterprises and institutions, those that were larger and of a higher administrative level could obtain housing investment more easily than those at smaller and lower levels.

After 1979, within the state-owned system, houses were still distributed among employees as welfare. However, as the state reduced the funds allocated to enterprises, the proportion of the funds raised by enterprises themselves became larger and larger, and the construction and distribution of houses were mainly under their control. In some enterprises and institutions with great power and financial resources, their investments in housing construction exceeded their actuarial level. By contrast, those enterprises without profits or income built a small number of houses, or none at all, and the living conditions of their staff and workers became worse.[2] According to statistics, in 1982 the floor space per urban resident increased by 0.8 square meters from 1978, and the year saw the addition of some 600,000 more families without sufficient living space, bringing the total number to 7.49 million, or one-third of the total number of households. Compared with 1978, families without houses also increased by 680,000, reaching 1.99 million households.[3]

Selling state-owned houses on favorable terms was the first brave attempt to resolve the matter of ownership after the adoption of the housing reform policy in the early 1980s.[4] At that time, as noted earlier, great changes took place in the distribution of the national income. Residents' cash income increased greatly and as a result, financial revenue was reduced, placing state finances under great pressure. Thus, how to let residents use their money became a key point in macro-economic policy and paved the way for the selling of state-owned houses on favorable terms. More specifically, selling state-owned houses with subsidies was the main approach. In 1982, the state decided to conduct experiments in Changzhou, Zhengzhou, Shashi and Siping,[5] where residents were encouraged to buy and repair houses by themselves and where the People's Bank of China began to handle deposits for purchasing and repairing houses.[6] In Changzhou, for example, when a person bought a dwelling, he or she would pay one-third of the total price, and the local government, or his or her enterprise, would pay the remaining two-thirds. The person might also make a lump-sum payment or pay by installments. If the person made a lump-sum payment, he or she would enjoy favorable treatment with a 20 percent discount. However, if the person paid by installments, the first payment could not be lower than 50 percent of the total, with the balance to be paid in full within five years. As for the housing bought by individuals with subsidies, the buyer owned the property rights and the housing administration department would issue that buyer with a house property certificate. Positively influenced by these experiments, many cities throughout the country then began to sell houses on favorable terms.

In short, selling state-owned houses on favorable terms was welcomed by broad masses of people. Changzhou planned to sell 158 single dwellings for the first time and, within 10 days, over 1,000 households had registered to purchase them. By January 1984, the above-mentioned four cities sold 2,140 single dwellings to individuals, with a total investment of 16.4 million yuan, and the capital that was recovered, plus the capital that would be recovered by installments, accounted for 30 percent.[7] However, during this experiment, some problems appeared. First, in the enterprises and institutions with good economic returns, selling state-owned houses was subject to resistance, ranging from leaders to staff and workers, who preferred the traditional way of obtaining welfare dwellings from their enterprises and institutions—i.e., those with vested interests under the traditional system were now obstacles to housing reform. Second, the average price per square meter for old houses in China was only 20 yuan and, due to such a low price, some people in power, most of whom already had substantial houses, used their position to buy additional houses. Needless to say, such eventualities were subject to various criticisms, and the selling of state-owned houses at low prices gradually stopped in the mid-1980s (Yang Lu and Wang Yukun, 1992, 6).

3. Planning of Residential Areas and Housing Design: A Solution to the Housing Shortage

When the Cultural Revolution came to an end, housing development, stimulated by the new housing reforms, grew by leaps and bounds within a short period of time. New residential areas mushroomed, and from 1979 to 1982, some 310 million square meters of housing was completed in cities and towns across the country, accounting for 37 percent of the housing built since the founding of the People's Republic of China. Living space per-person in urban areas rose from 3.6 square meters in 1978 to 4.6 square meters at the end of 1983.[8] Given such large-scale development, more research was required for the planning of residential areas and for housing design, involving issues such as land saving, housing function, environment design and the construction of public facilities. As a result, planning research, which had been dormant for more than a decade, started again, beginning with practical problems.

3.1. Emphasis on Land Saving and Raising Residential Density

Rises in the level of urbanization and the explosion of urban population strained land already in short supply for construction purposes. Therefore, the key issue in housing development became one of providing living space for an ever-increasing population on an already limited supply of land. The architectural community conducted comprehensive research on the matter. They studied, for instance, the impact on density of changing the number of floors and the depth of housing blocks. They also examined the way a building was deployed on a site, including lining up slab blocks in a row; the combination of high-rise and low-rise housing; the combination of long, narrow buildings and buildings with square footprints, as well as east and west orientations, corner apartments and oblique compositions. They also discussed how to raise density by cleverly placing public buildings and rationally deciding upon the land use of each parcel within a residential area. Particular topics that drew heated discussion and became influential included the use of high-rise buildings, the housing depth of residential buildings and the setbacks allowed on the north side on the top floor.

The construction of high-rise buildings was proposed mainly to save land and to raise population density. The high-rise developments completed in China in the 1970s were all in the form of slab blocks, and most had long corridors on each floor to make full use of elevators. By the end of the 1970s, Beijing saw rapid development of high-rise apartments, where large numbers were erected along Qiansanmen Avenue in the old city. By the end of 1981, 416 high-rises apartments had been built all over China, with three-fourths of them located in Beijing.[9] To the Chinese, high-rise structures were something new, although in foreign countries there had already been extensive studies of their advantages and disadvantages. Lacking a unitary policy, Chinese architects and scholars embarked on a heated discussion of the prospects for high-rise dwellings. The main argument against high-rise housing was that it cost more. Its plan also had a lower rate of usable space, needed a long construction period, was costly to maintain and had high power consumption in addition to poor environmental and social effects. Moreover, in an ancient capital like Beijing, the predominant feature of the city landscape, in the form of low-rise courtyard compounds, would be seriously damaged by high-rise developments. Furthermore, high-rise construction was not the only means of saving land, as land saving not only depended on how many storeys a building had, but also related to its depth. Calculations, for instance, indicated that a high-rise building with a ten-meter depth occupied the same amount of land as a lower multi-storey building with a twelve-meter depth. In summary, the opponents of high-rise construction believed that efforts should be made to improve multi-storey buildings, make full use of small yards, move kitchens and bathrooms further inside to increase depth and to reduce the width of each housing unit. This, they claimed, could save cost as well as land (Zhang Kaiji, 1978).

By contrast, arguments for high-rise housing stressed that the economic benefits should be measured by taking the whole scope of city development into consideration. It was true that for the time being, the quality of elevators could not meet the functional requirements of high-rises dwellings. But this could also be a motivation for elevator producers to improve their technology and reduce costs. As productivity progressed, the quality of elevators would eventually be increased. There were many ways to save land, but, whatever approach was taken, to increase the number of storeys of a building was undoubtedly the most fundamental method. What's more, this did not hinder the increase of depth. To increase living space and provide housing in a country like China, with its large population and comparatively scarce land, seeking a fundamentally three-dimensional approach would be the only viable solution (Zheng Naigui and Hu Huiyuan, 1981).

Later development proved that, whatever the arguments were, high-rise building quickly increased due to its advantage in saving land. By the mid-1980s, the proportion of high-rise housing development in Beijing, for instance, had risen from the original 10 percent to 45 percent, and in an attempt to reduce the costly use of elevators, some eight, nine and ten-storey buildings were constructed without elevators in Guangzhou, Wuhan and Chongqing. This naturally created great inconvenience for their inhabitants, although there were some successful examples. The Donghu apartment building in Guangzhou, for example, had eight storeys, with the seventh and eighth floors in a duplex arrangement. Not equipped with elevators, the building adopted a double-deck horizontal access system. People living on the first floor entered their apartment from the ground floor. Those who lived on the second floor and above entered the building from a second-floor outdoor public corridor, thus enabling inhabitants to climb no more than six floors (Fig. 7-1).

In addition to adding more storeys to housing, another important method in saving land was to increase the depth of the complex. At the end of the 1970s, standard housing depth in China was between 8 and 10 meters. The reason for such a small depth was that China had a low standard in terms of useable floor space per unit. Rooms were small and increasing the depth would reduce the width of each dwelling, adversely affecting the daylighting of rooms. Second, traditionally the direction of a dwelling was of importance to the inhabitants. At the time, few families had air-conditioners and the key factors that affected a unit's micro-climate was its orientation. The room that faced south would be warm in winter and cool in summer, so it was always popular. On the other hand, the room

Fig. 7-1: Donghuxicun in
Guangdong

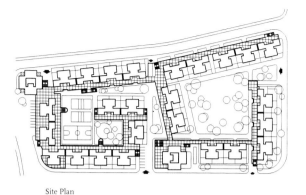

Site Plan

Plan of   Plan of the
the Seventh Floor   Eighth Floor

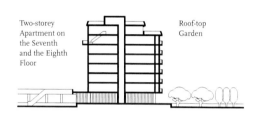

Two-storey
Apartment on
the Seventh
and the Eighth
Floor

Roof-top
Garden

The Second Floor Traffic Platform

that faced west would be extremely hot in the afternoon in summer-time and, therefore, was always avoided. These ideas limited the plan. Third, China's general low living standard meant that the kitchens and bathrooms of ordinary families were poorly equipped and, as Chinese cooking was greasy, people liked to have windows in their kitchens and bathrooms that opened outward for better ventilation. The upshot was that these facilities occupied many outer wall areas, and increasing the width of the units made it difficult to enlarge the depth of a house.

Creating small yards in an apartment building could also enlarge the depth of the building. A nationwide housing design competition was held in 1978, with one design featuring an inner yard in an attempt to save land. A comparison of the depth of the prize-winning schemes revealed that the depth of the first-prize scheme was 10.14 meters, the second-prize winner was 9.18 meters, and a design with three small yards had a depth of 12.4 meters. If other conditions were equal, the design with the small yards had a 27 percent higher density than the first two, indicating that an increase in the depth of the building had obvious effects in saving land. Therefore, some opponents of high-rise housing did every-

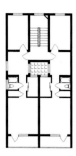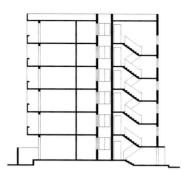

Fig. 7-2: Small patio house project

thing in their power to popularize small-yard buildings as a viable substitute (Fig. 7-2). However, an apartment building with an inner yard was not very convenient in actual usage. Take ventilation, for example: many such designs placed the kitchen and the inner yard close to each other, and smoke and steam from the cooking blew into the inner yard so that people could smell what was cooking in their neighbors' kitchens. Another problem was lighting. As the number of floors rose, families on lower floors normally received poor lighting because of the small yard. In addition, inner yards were public areas seldom frequented by families. The result was poor sanitation and, generally, this type of housing design was not very popular.

Whether a housing project could save land or not usually depended on two factors. The first was the design of the house; its depth, number of floors and the height of each storey. The second was the layout of the house, and architects would make every effort to raise the holding capacity of a building when they were sure that all other necessary requirements, including adequate sunlighting, were met. In the reconstruction of the old city area in Huolan Street in the Yangpu District of Shanghai, for instance, in order to raise the density of the multi-storey apartment building, architects from the Department of Architecture of Tongji University made the setback on the north side, effectively needing only to consider the sunlight distance of three storeys at the back. Meanwhile, the depth of the building was increased and a small yard was constructed to improve conditions of sunlight. The receding steps lowered the depth of the small yard and increased the amount of sunlight for families living on the lower floors. Calculations showed that such a building could accommodate 24.6 percent more floor space than a normal six-storey apartment building (Zhu Yaxin, 1979, 43-48) (Fig. 7-3). Moreover, the "Interim Regulations on the Standards of City Planning," issued in 1980, stipulated that the distance between each apartment

Fig. 7-3: Huolanxincun in
Shanghai

0   50   m

Site Plan of Huolanxincun

Floor Plan

Plan of the Second and Third Floor   Plan of the Fourth Floor   Plan of the Fifth Floor

A Terrace House Design and the
Space Saving Design

Experimental Housing

Design No.2 of Shanghai Housing

building within a residential area "for inhabitants on the first floor,
should receive no less than one hour of full-window sunshine on
the day of winter solstice in the place in question," and this became
an essential factor affecting residential planning. As a result, the
receding stepping of floors on the north side of a building, which
made it possible for buildings to have more frequent sunshine,
became widely accepted and used, and remains very popular today.

3.2. Improvement of the Environment of Residential Areas: Strengthening Services and the Search for Non Row-housing Forms

The Cultural Revolution caused serious damage to public service facilities. Urban residents found it difficult to bathe, get vegetables, find a place for breakfast, have a haircut or send their children to kindergarten. At the time, cities could not even meet the most fundamental needs of their inhabitants. For instance, before 1978, there was an extreme shortage of outlets providing commercial services (Table 7-2). Consequently, the "Interim Regulation on the Standards of City Planning" stipulated the requirements for public facilities—including the size of facilities and their specific service targets per thousand people—in both big and small residential areas, and provided a guideline for the construction of public facili-

Year	National Commercial Service Centers in Urban Area		
	Total (10 thousand)	number/ 10 thousand people	total of People Served Per Center
1957	100	10.1	99
1978	21.8	1.8	556
1979	33.9	2.6	385
1980	80.1	5.9	169
1981	105.7	7.5	133
1982	149	10.3	97

Table 7-2: Statistics of National Commercial Service Centers in urban areas from 1957 to 1982

Source: China Planning Research Institute, "Residential Area Planning," 1984

ties as a necessary part of the planning of all residential areas. Subsequently, service outlets mushroomed from 1980 to 1982, reflecting development of public facilities near residential areas.

As mentioned, urban planning was abolished during the Cultural Revolution. The ultra-leftist ideology simplified the planning of housing and this resulted in the rise of parallel building slabs everywhere. All residential areas in China looked very much alike, disregarding local conditions and differences between the north and the south. The outdoor living environment was monotonous and dull, and the aesthetic aspects of architecture were completely discounted (Fig. 7-4). As the Cultural Revolution came to an end and large-scale housing development got underway, an attempt was made to give residential areas a new look, with an emphasis on diversified planning and design.

In the planning of residential areas in this later period, the three levels of consideration that had first appeared in the 1960s were adopted. They were: housing *per se*, the neighborhood cluster, and the residential area. After meeting the requirements for a residen-

Fig. 7-4: Monotonous rows of houses

tial area, sunlight and housing density, diversified planning was achieved through the grouping of differently shaped housing units, and special features were attained through the manipulation of height and length in order to shape the outdoor space. Emphasis was put on the layout of residential areas, and general planning and the road system were worked out by considering particular aspects, such as typography and climate. On this basis, houses were grouped and public facilities were organized to form a characteristic environment for residential use. In Beijing, for example, in a competition for residential area planning held in 1980, enriching the outdoor space of the residential area became the principle guideline. The prizewinner emphasized a simple but clear road system, upon which diversification of the building form was achieved through a combination of rectangular buildings and towers (Fig. 7-5). The planning of *Fuziangxili* at Huangcun, also in Beijing, conducted in 1983 and 1984, gave strong consideration to the combination of social, economic and environmental effects, and was representative of the planning of residential areas and housing design at various levels during that time (Fig. 7-6).

Fig. 7-5: Site plan of the Tayuan neighborhood in Beijing

0   60
30   90   m

Fig. 7-6: Site plan of the West Fuziangxili neighborhood in Beijing

1. Middle School
2. Day care and Kindergarten
3. Elementary School
4. Housing Office
5. Electric Room
6. Boiler Room
7. Stores
8. Public W.C.

3.3. Strict Control Over Housing Floor-area Standards and Housing Design

For a long time after the founding of the People's Republic of China, as described in Part Two, a welfare housing allocation method was adopted. With a large population and limited investment in housing, the government's strict control over housing area standards became central to the problem of easing housing shortages. Given the low standard in available floor space, housing design had to focus on higher rates of usable space, resulting in long outer corridors, one staircase serving four or even eight families, pass-through kitchens, shared toilets, etc. As the Cultural Revolution was brought to an end, the national economy recovered and people's living expectations were raised, calling for higher floor-area standards. According to the standards set by the state in 1977, "for inhabitants of walk-up apartments associated with newly built factories or mines, twenty-eight to thirty-four square meters per household (thirty-six to forty square meters in cold areas) were required on average. For employees of old factories or mines, the average construction area per household was thirty-nine to forty-two square meters, because the size of families was normally larger, although the average housing area per family for the whole of the factory or mine was kept at no more than forty square meters (forty-two square meters in cold areas)." The state then raised the standards in 1978 by saying that "normally the construction area per household should not exceed forty-two square meters, but if new materials like prefabricated or *in situ* large-panel systems were used, then forty-five square meters was permissible. For colleges and universities, as well as scientific research institutes directly belonging to a province or higher authority, their housing could enjoy a higher standard, but not exceeding fifty square meters."[10] In 1981, the state raised the standard once again, this time setting four standards for differently targeted populations. Housing Grade 1 allowed forty-two to forty-five square meters for employees of factories and mines. Housing Grade 2 allowed forty-five to fifty square meters for ordinary cadres. Housing Grade 3 allowed sixty to seventy square meters for intellectuals with intermediate academic titles and for principal heads and deputy heads at a county level, and Housing Grade 4 allowed eighty to ninety square meters for high-ranking intellectuals and bureau-level cadres.[11] In addition to these specific standards, the state emphasized that they were just standards for design and construction, not for housing assignment, indicating the government's concern about the construction of higher-standard housing in a period of housing shortage. Moreover, these concerns were not without reason. As local governments and enterprises became a major force in housing investment and construction, some of them built increasingly larger apartments, and the trend toward higher-standard housing seemed to be out of control. In 1983, the State Council distributed the "Stipulation on the Strict Control of Housing Standards in Cities and Towns," reiterating that, given the limited economic capabilities and dire housing shortage, housing standards had to be kept at a low level. To effectively keep housing standards under control and guarantee the number of apartments required, the government further stipulated that the volume of housing development would not only be measured by the total area of housing completed, but also by the actual number of apartments completed, and both were prerequisites when applying to carry out housing development.

In the early period of China's reform and opening up to the outside world, when housing was a part of an enterprise's welfare system, standards of housing were still under strict control, but demands for higher standards of living required that utilization functions be improved. Changes in family structure also had profound effects on housing design. For a long time after the founding of the People's Republic, housing shortages, rapidly increasing population and a simple way of life did not require architects to pay much attention to the influence of family structure on housing design. Usually, a house or apartment was distinguished by the number of bedrooms it had. The criterion used to divide a house or apartment was a general consideration, but not a legal criteron,[12] and, when people's standard of living was low, such a simplified division did not cause many problems.

After China adopted the policy of reform and opening to the outside world, people demanded a higher quality of life. They became more aware of the problems existing in housing design and its usage. Moreover, research and surveys on family structure were conducted that provided the basis for housing design and assignment, and most research pointed to a trend of reduced family size. This was also the predicted result of the government's family planning program.

As people's standard of living rose, they exhibited higher demands for the more and more sophisticated functions in housing. For instance, a survey was conducted in nine cities, including Shenyang, Shanghai, Fuzhou and Wuhan, asking people for their opinions about their housing built after 1980. The majority said that their houses were too crowded, the privacy of a personal realm was not guaranteed and they lacked necessary storage space. They felt that many inconveniences existed at home that did not provide them with a sense of stability and safety. In the 1960s, rooms in a house were measured by the bed, and whether the quality of a house was good was decided by the rate of usable space in the plan. This was the so-called "sleep-type" housing, and it lasted until the end of the 1970s, when the marked economic changes of the 1980s caused family consumption to grow considerably. In the 1970s the three most sought-after consumer goods were radios, watches and bicycles. The sought-after goods became black-and-white TVs, one-vat washing machines and one-door refrigerators in the mid-1980s. Soon these changed to color TVs, two-vat washing machines and two-door refrigerators in the late-1980s. The increase of household appliances, such as refrigerators, electric fans, TVs, washing machines and air-conditioners also required more space in the house and so more constraints were imposed on housing design. Architects had to take into consideration the use of appliances without affecting the flexible use of the internal space of a house. Furthermore, the rising quality of life brought a broader range of family activities. Home was where people held parties and enjoyed other recreational activities, as well as a place for study, work and receiving friends. An architect who considered only how to provide a place for the family to stay in would not be able to meet people's needs. The state raised a slogan that was roughly translated as "housing design should not only give people shelter; rather it should be a comfortable home with separate rooms for different functions." This meant that, while the living space for each family would remain comparatively small, arrangement of rooms within a house must be appropriate and flexible, and many attempts were made by architects in this respect (Fig. 7-7).

3.4. Efforts at the Standardization and Diversification of Housing Design

Conflicts between standardization and diversification of housing design were inevitable in Chinese housing development. When the system of standardization was not elaborated upon, the result was simplified rather than varied designs. After studying some foreign theories, such as the SAR (Foundation for Architectural Research) in The Netherlands, architects conducted fruitful research and application on this topic, and some colleges of architecture involved in housing design and construction produced noteworthy designs. These also had considerable influence on later housing design.

Fig. 7-7: Plans for small but space-saving units

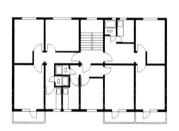

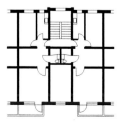

However, because of their advanced nature, most were not adopted for broader applications after limited trials.

In brief, standardization and diversification of housing development meant, first, standardized and diversified manufacture of components. Second, it meant standardized and diversified design of units, and the combination of the two resulted in a systematic design, with an assembly or configuration of parts that could realize both qualities. Architects first decided on architectural modules and then the way they were to be arranged. Commonly used methods of arrangement included fixed-unit configurations, allowing for a flexible division of interior space by each household. In fixed-unit configurations, architects decided on plan parameters, which

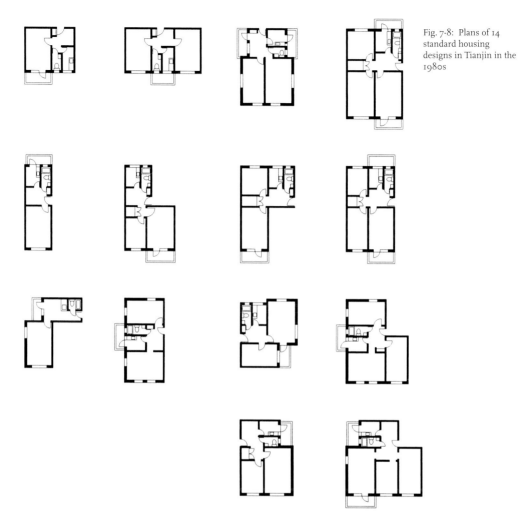

were used to form a basic room. Then, basic rooms were formed into unit arrangements, which would further form apartments and apartment buildings. As China had strict stipulations on floor-area standards and apartment types were limited, it was economical to adopt this method, and apartment buildings designed in this manner developed appreciably.

Standard housing design in Tianjin in the 1980s featured the household as its fundamental target, and design proceeded in the following manner. First, typical rooms were laid out and then a typical apartment unit was designed as an expression of the standard design and, finally, a housing block was formed. After making a comprehensive analysis of apartment types, family size, plan parameters and other spatial considerations, architects decided on fourteen basic apartment layouts. With floor space ranging from 31.8 square meters to 66.52 square meters, these apartments became the basic units in what amounted to a standard design. Configuration of these fourteen apartment layouts would form twelve units, which were then arranged to form different apartment buildings according to site and tenant requirements (Fig. 7-8).

In the 1984 national competition for brick-and-concrete housing, the series of terrace garden houses, designed by the School of Architecture of Tsinghua University, drew everyone's attention. Unified modules and prototype rooms were cleverly arranged to form varied five- and six-storey buildings. Use of the rooms was flexible and every family had a ten-square-meter balcony. Furthermore, the design also made it possible for varied site planning to be realized. Careful arrangement produced a pleasant space and environment. Space inside and outside the house was mixed seamlessly, creating rich and varied layers and a living space full of human touches. Moreover, after being put into practice, this design was welcomed by inhabitants in Beijing, Tianjin and Yantai (Fig. 7-9). However, the ability to raise construction density through terraced garden houses was limited and, given housing shortages at the time, construction in large quantities was out of the question.

Starting in 1984, the Nanjing Architecture and Building College (now called Southeast University) had been involved in the research and practice of SAR housing in Wuxi. Emphasizing the participation of inhabitants in the design process, parts of the house were divided into two categories known as "sustaining parts" and "separable parts" respectively. The former included bearing walls, floor panels and roofs, while the latter included lightweight partitions for internal use and furniture combinations. The design and manufacture of the two categories were done separately, making it possible for the inhabitants to get involved. With the policy that both the state and individuals bear some cost of housing development, the state invested in the production of the parts in the first category and individuals invested in the second category. Supportive parts then became the responsibilities of investors, management and design departments, and inhabitants chose and decided on the type, standard, specification and arrangement of the separable parts (Fig. 7-10).

In 1979, the Department of Architecture of Tianjin University made a design proposal for a low-rise, high-density integral living environment, and a trial construction of 30,000 square meters was completed in Changjiang Street in the Nankai District of Tianjin. In light of new trends, such as smaller families and the commercial-

Fig. 7-9a: Terraced garden houses

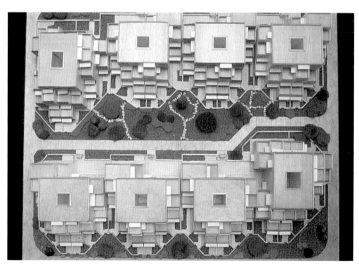

Fig. 7-9b: Terraced garden houses

First Floor Plan

Second Floor Plan

Third Floor Plan

Fourth Floor Plan

Fifth Floor Plan

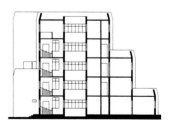

Section B-B

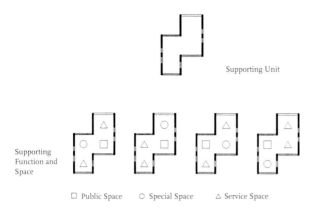

Fig. 7-10: The SAR housing system

Supporting Unit

Supporting Function and Space

☐ Public Space   ○ Special Space   △ Service Space

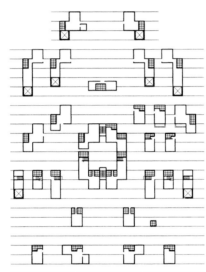

Combinations

218 Reform and Opening-up Policies

Fig. 7-11: Low-rise, high-density
apartment buildings in Tianjin

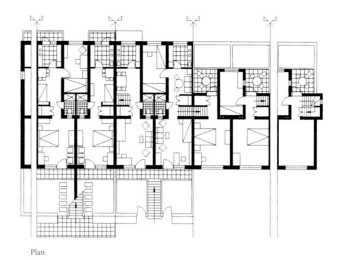

Plan

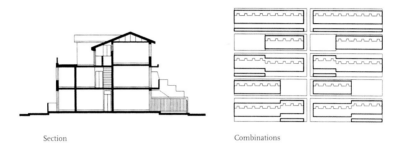

Section

Combinations

ization and diversification of housing, they improved the original plan in 1984. Each household was guaranteed at least one room facing south and one big room that received sufficient sunshine in winter. Many three-storey apartments and some six-storey apartments were used to form groups of apartments, producing an overall density equivalent to six-storey buildings (Fig. 7-11).

Notes

1. Government Work Report, delivered at the Second Session of the Sixth National People's Congress on May 15, 1984.
2. Reference to the Blue Paper on Technological Policies of China, 2, (1985): 13.
3. State Commission for Restructuring Economy, "The Existing Problems of the Urban Housing Economic System of and the Opinions on Reform," report of November 3, 1983.
4. In 1980, State leader Deng Xiaoping clearly pointed out that the "construction industry can make money...urban residents may purchase dwellings, and may also build houses.... Both new and old houses can be sold...after houses are sold, I think the rent should be readjusted, and subsidies should be offered to staff and workers with low wages."
5. "The Report on the Forum for Selling Dwellings in the Cities on a Trial Basis" submitted by the State Construction Commission and the Urban Construction Administration, and approved by the State Council on April 17, 1982.
6. From a speech of a leader of the People's Bank of China. *Economic Daily*, February 22, 1983.
7. *Construction Yearbook of China*, 1984–1985, 127.
8. Blue Paper on Technological Policies of China, 2, (1985): 13.
9. Blue Paper on Technological Policies of China, 2, (1985): 16.
10. Reference to the No. 222 Document of the State Council, issued in October 1978, which carried the report by the State Construction Commission, "Report on Speeding up Urban Housing Development."
11. Reference to "Regulations on the Design Standards of Workers' Housing" and "Supplementary Regulations," 1981.
12. Generally, "with the exception of couples, people of the opposite sex, 12 years or older, should live in different rooms (but elderly women can live with older boys). No more than four people should live in one room, and each person is entitled to a floor space of 4 to 6 square meters."

Chapter Eight: Housing Construction in the Planned Commodity Economy (1985–1991)

1. Socio-Economic Development and Fluctuation in the Course of Reform

In October 1984, the Third Plenary Session of the Twelfth Central Committee of the Communist Party of China (CPC) clarified guidelines for establishing a planned commodity economy based on public ownership, marking the arrival of consensus about the nature of a socialist economy. Prior to 1984, reform was carried out mainly in rural areas where many heartening changes took place, including a substantial increase in agricultural output and a significant rise in farmer's incomes. Beginning in 1984, the focus of reform was shifted to cities. While deepening the reform of enterprises, China introduced a wide range of operations, based primarily on a system of contracted responsibility. Multiple forms of ownership, multiple forms of distribution and a market system, featuring the transaction of various production factors, began to emerge, vigorously promoting industrial development and urban construction. However, due to the long-standing practices of the prior planned economy, the subsequent process of simplifying administrative procedures and delegating powers to lower levels made a corresponding mechanism of supply and demand hard to form. Drastic fluctuations accompanied economic growth and often adversely affected reform of the housing system.

1.1. Establishment of the Socialist Planned Commodity Economy

The Third Plenary Session of the Twelfth CPC Central Committee on October 12, 1984, summed up both the positive and negative experiences in China's socialist economic construction since the Third Plenary Session of the Eleventh CPC Central Committee, especially with regard to experiences in rural and urban economic restructuring. It proposed to further implement the policy of invigorating the domestic economy and opening China's economy to the outside world, as well as accelerating reform of the entire economy by focusing on urban areas. It made clear that the fundamental task of the reform was basically to change the economic system that hampered the development of productivity into a socialist economy full of life and vitality and with Chinese characteristics. In essence, by breaking through the conventional wisdom that had set the planned economy against a commodity economy, it pointed out that China's socialist economy was to become a planned commodity economy based on public ownership. The resolution was passed at the session, and thus became the programmatic document guiding all-around economic reform in China, further improving the economic reforms in urban areas started as early as 1981 by the State Council. The session required cities to give further play to their leading role in order to create open, network-like economic zones at different scales, especially around large- and medium-sized cities.

1.2. Unfolding of Urban Economic Restructuring

As mentioned earlier, a planned economy had been practiced in Chinese cities for several decades. Its powerful centralized control of resources helped China establish a basic modern industrial system, as well as an urban economic system, in the relatively short time since the founding of the People's Republic. However, at the end of the Cultural Revolution the national economy was badly out of balance, with a low efficiency in resource allocation and utilization, as well as inadequate momentum for further development. Consequently, the reform of the urban economic system unfolded by concentrating primarily on the concepts of dynamics and balance. Specifically, more autonomy was to be granted to enterprises. The fiscal system was to be reformed further in order to expand the autonomy of local government in financial expenditures, and price controls were to be relaxed.

Economic development in cities also changed the structure of industry and population. In April 1986, China adjusted the criteria for establishing a city and the number of cities rose dramatically to reach 353 at the end of 1986, an increase of 160 over 1978, while the population in cities jumped from 79.55 million to 122.634 million.[1] In October of the same year, regulations concerning the establishment of towns were also revised. The number of towns reached 8,463 at the end f 1986, an increase of 196 percent over 1978, while the population in towns increased from 40.39 million to 59.477 million. The total urban population thus rose from 119.94 million in 1978 to 182.11 million in 1986 (Cao Hongtao, Chu Chuanhen et. al., 1990, 126).[2]

1.3. A Brief Analysis of Economic Fluctuations

Reform of the economic system required the state rapidly to expand residents' consumption, while continuing to maintain a relatively high level of accumulation, and clearly these two aims were contradictory within the framework of a planned economy. In the mid- and late-1980s, when the demand-supply mechanism was yet to be fully formulated, market-oriented reform was still a simplification, inevitably leading to economic fluctuations.

Briefly, there occurred three economic contractions between 1984 and 1991, the first in 1985. During the first three years of reform and opening-up, the national economy developed in a healthy and coordinated manner. As a result, an impatience for quick results occurred. At the end of 1984, financial expenditures, money supply, investment in fixed assets and resident's income all rose substantially, leading to inflation in 1985. As a result, the government had to limit the growth of the money supply, and although inflation was brought under control, economic development slowed down.

The second economic contraction happened in 1987. To alleviate the negative effects of economic austerity, the government implemented macro-readjustments in 1986. But the economy soon got overheated and the conflict between total supply and total demand intensified. Having no other alternative, the government adopted a policy of double contraction aimed at tight fiscal and financial management. Finally, the third economic contraction occurred in 1988, and proved to be the worst economic fluctuation in the ten years since the adoption of the policies of reform and opening-up. For several successive years consumer confidence was impaired, which, together with the increased money supply in 1988, led to a nationwide purchasing panic and an increased outlay by banks as high as 23.3 percent. The expansion and relief of consumption accumulated over the prior ten years threw the durable consumer goods sector into steep decline and eventually led, in 1989, to political turmoil. It was in such a grim economic situation that the Third Plenary Session of the Thirteenth CPC Central Committee was held at the end of 1988, where it was decided to improve the economic environment and rectify the economic order. Subsequently the consumer market entered a sluggish period, which lasted until early 1992.

As one might imagine, these economic fluctuations affected housing construction. Newly constructed housing in urban and rural areas was 188 million square meters in 1985, 193 million square meters in 1986 and 1987, 203 million square meters in 1988, 156 million square meters in 1989, and 173 million square meters in 1990 (Table 7). Consequently, the line graph in Table 7 shows a low annual growth in newly constructed housing in urban areas between 1985 to 1991. As indicated, 1989 witnessed the only declining trend since the reform and opening-up and, overall, improvement and rectification of the national economy was having an obvious positive impact on housing construction.

2. Housing Reform: Fluctuation and Development

Through reform in the early 1980s, the Chinese economy grew relatively rapidly and significant changes took place in its macro-economic structure. Problems and contradictions emerging from the transformation of the traditional planned economy also became more acute. The change in the distribution of national income, the revelation of real labor costs, the rationalization of industry and the financial strains placed on the government all simultaneously affected housing. In the early 1980s, housing reform focused mainly on housing investment, while in the mid- and late 1980s, it became more involved in the flow of funds within the macro-economy and fluctuated accordingly.

2.1. Ups and Downs in Housing Reform

Under the system whereby housing was distributed as welfare, it was assigned to workers almost free of charge. As described earlier, rents were extremely low and inadequate for housing maintenance, let alone for housing production. Thus, the first problem in the commercialization of housing was how to deal with existing publicly owned dwellings where residents were beneficiaries of vested interests (as well as resistant to the raising of rents). The second problem stemmed from the fact that commercialization of housing was impossible to accomplish overnight. People's low incomes, resulting from the long period of the planned economy, could hardly be reversed in a short time. In the 1980s, only a tiny minority of people could afford to purchase housing. Therefore, large amounts of residential building had to be constructed for lease. If the rents were high, it placed considerable pressure on people with low incomes, incurring discontent and creating unstable factors in the national economy, such as financial strains on banks. But if rents remained low, people did not want to purchase houses, effectively disabling housing reform. In addition, under the system of welfare distribution in kind, a considerable amount of newly completed urban housing was allotted to workers and staff each year, either directly or indirectly. This increased both the difficulty and the cost of housing reform and adversely affected the development of a housing market. Consequently, rent actually became a focus as well as a difficulty among the numerous problems facing housing reform.

In the mid-1980s, when the development of the national economy was in an upward trajectory, experiments were carried out in cities such as Yantai, Tangshan and Bengbu to raise rents through financial subsidies. Yantai was the first city to implement a general reform of housing. Basically, it raised rent for publicly owned housing and demanded more money for more housing. At the same time, publicly owned housing was put on sale for either the entire property right or for a limited property right. Preferential treatment was granted to the former, and the latter cost 70 percent of the former, although the use right and inheritance right could not be transferred, leased, given as a gift or traded. Many similar experiences were accumulated from experiments in housing reform in these cities, but they failed to be spread in time. Although there were several reasons accounting for the failure, the most fundamental cause was the relationship between demand and supply, as well as distribution, which still existed under the system of a planned economy. Since the two systems were difficult to form into a benign cycle, it was impossible to establish a sound price mechanism and, as a result, the rent reform lacked a driving force.

As mentioned, the year 1988 witnessed a purchasing panic throughout China with declining bank savings. National finances were in such dire straits that the initial funds for raising rents could not be afforded. Raising funds among residents and stabilizing the overall financial structure thus became the focal point of economic policy and, as a result, withdrawal of funds through selling old houses became the hot spot of housing reform. However, the sale of housing at low prices was only an expedient measure aimed at alleviating economic problems and, like the attempt in the early 1980s, it had many flaws and quickly came to an end.

After the fluctuations in the mid- and late 1980s, as well as the sluggish market between 1989 and 1990, the Chinese economy began to improve. Moreover, a better understanding of housing reform was obtained after these fluctuations. In 1991, the government issued "Suggestions on Promoting All-round Reform of the Urban Housing System," making it clear that reform should be based on the transformation of transfer mechanisms. The suggestions also set, as an essential goal, reform of the housing system in urban areas, as well as the objective of commercializing housing. In the meantime, institutional formation, such as the establishment of firms specialized in house financing and social operations, was also proposed.

2.2. Rapid Development of the Real Estate Industry

Another decisive factor in housing development in this period was the emergence of a real estate industry with the motivation of reforming land policy. Under the existing economic system, land was used free of charge in the form of an administrative allotment, resulting in a serious waste and a loss of state-owned assets. With tight finances and a heavy burden of investment in urban construction, the state decided to reform the land-use system. The key to this reform was the adoption of a monetary, market-oriented land-use system, and explorations and trials in urban areas provided an opportunity for the development of real estate businesses. Specifically, in May 1984, the Sixth National People's Congress decided that commercialization should be promoted further in urban housing construction and that a real estate sector should be established. Furthermore, fees and taxes should be collected for the use of land according to its location and value in a city.[3] In 1987, by taking advantage of its preferential treatment as a special economic zone, Shenzhen took the lead by leasing, for the first time, land under Chinese sovereignty, whereby a paid transfer of land-use rights was effected, although land ownership remained unchanged. Later on, another two pieces of land in the zone were sold through bidding and auction, marking the inception of a genuine real estate industry in China. Under the influence of Shenzhen, coastal provinces and municipalities became enthusiastic about the real estate business and, when amendments were made to the Constitution in 1988, it was stipulated that "a land-use right can be transferred in accordance with the provisions of law."

Generally speaking, the system of housing allotment basically remained intact in the 1980s, although the real estate business, driven by market demand, also experienced rapid development and yielded huge profits. This eventuality further underlined the problem with the macro-economic structure and with the real estate business at that time. Essentially, the impetus for the real estate business came from the economic returns of enterprises, but a considerable portion of those economic returns were acquired through increasing costs. Also, the purchase of market housing mainly involved institutional purchases and, in the short-term, resulted in an incomplete reform of other enterprises. Essentially, they allotted purchased market housing to workers and staff as a form of in-kind welfare. In this way, workers and staff obtained housing and the real estate business accumulated prodigious funds, but the relationship between supply and demand in the national economy was further distorted.

3. Planning and Designing of Housing: Functional Improvements

In the 1980s, the annual completed housing construction of residential buildings averaged 150.32 million square meters, or about 10 times that prior to 1979. In terms of either quality or quantity, residential buildings were much better than those constructed during the Cultural Revolution, even though some problems could not be solved in such a short period of time. For instance, the planning of residential areas often suffered from poor infrastructure, incomplete supporting facilities, unpleasant environments and inconvenient lifestyles. The design of individual dwelling units was afflicted with problems such as poor functional layout, overly simple exterior appearance, cheap kitchen and toilet equipment and neglected detailing. In addition, low technological involvement, poor construction quality and inferior realty management characterized residential areas constructed during this period.

Under the guideline of commercializing housing, the planning of residential areas and housing design were no longer restricted by the set forms of the former planned economy. The concept of an "apartment unit" was introduced, advocating more civilized living conditions; the gross floor area of a housing unit was no longer taken as the only controlling indicator. Indeed, planning put more emphasis on environmental quality and the complete functioning of a community, and housing design began to take on broader technological considerations. In short, although housing construction still conformed to the traditional, supply-driven planned economy, housing planning and design improved significantly through constant exploration and practice.

3.1. Overall Progress: Technical Guidelines for Housing Construction

In 1983, China launched the first large-scale technical and policy-making initiative for housing since the founding of the People's Republic. In 1985, the "Blue Paper on Technological Policies of China" was put forward, embracing technical policies concerning urban and rural construction and housing construction. Relevant provisions set forth standards and directions for the planning and design of housing, in addition to drawing on the achievements of theoretical research and practice, as well as lessons learned from foreign experiences and technologies in the 1980s. The guidelines established the general goal of housing construction to attain a moderately high standard of living by the end of the century. Specifically, each urban household should have a unit that was inexpensive but practical, with a per-capita living area reaching eight square meters. Further technical guidelines made detailed provisions in the planning and design of housing, including the control of housing standards, improvement of environmental quality, the introduction of comprehensive modes of development, the strengthening of standardization and diversification, as well as energy conservancy. Of these, the understanding of standards of residential development was of great significance. More specifically, the technical guidelines continued to emphasize the strict control of residential and land-use standards in new developments. The concept of the apartment unit was introduced, which, together with a measure of construction area, was taken as the major controlling construction criterion, and the usable floor area became the major standard of distribution. Throughout, the purpose was to improve the quality of family living. Besides necessary separate rooms, a unit of housing should have an independent kitchen, a toilet with corresponding facilities, such as a shower, as well as gas service and a heating system. Therefore, residential buildings were to be designed with apartments that, small as they were, had a complete complement of functions suitable for one household.

A general nationwide housing survey was conducted during 1985 and 1986. Among 39.77 million urban households, 62.56 percent had independent kitchens, 6.48 percent had shared kitchens, and the remaining built their own kitchen or used makeshift kitchens located in corridors. About 24.23 percent had independent toilets, 9.85 percent had shared toilets, and the rest used public toilets on the street. About 57.34 percent of the units had their own tap water and 15.85 percent shared tap water. About 96.72 percent of the households had electric light, 8.4 percent had coal gas and 6.23 percent had shower facilities. Altogether there were only 9.662 million (24.29 percent of the total) complete units of housing in urban areas, where a complete unit accommodating one household comprised a sitting room, a bedroom, a kitchen, a toilet and an aisle or porch (Ye Rutang, 1987). From these results it can readily be seen how important the introduction of the concept of an apartment unit was in housing design and, in the mid- and late 1980s, the improvement of dwelling functions in a small area constituted the main thrust of theoretical research and practice.

3.2. General Change: Comprehensive Development

Housing construction in urban areas had long relied on state investment and usually featured scattered uncoordinated construction.

Although a more progressive method of raising funds for unified construction was adopted, the lack of a business perspective made accumulation impossible. This also handicapped the construction of auxiliary facilities in residential areas and limited their social, economic and environmental benefits.

As early as 1980, the State Council proposed that "real estate companies should be organized to try comprehensive development in small cities and satellite cities, a city's new districts and areas, and the redevelopment of old cities." Here, "comprehensive development" referred to complete arrangement and unified management, ranging from surveying, planning and design to land allotment, demolition, site preparation and infrastructure construction, including road building, water supply, sewage, power supply, gas supply, heating and communications. Consequently, in the mid-1980s, along with the development of the real estate business, a comprehensive mode of development became the major ingredient of housing construction. Effectively, through comprehensive arrangement and unified management of planning, design and infrastructure construction, an attempt was made to change the prior crude and scattered forms of construction and to coordinate the relationship between housing construction and urban development, thereby linking the economic and social benefits with environmental benefits. In the meantime, the introduction of business operations and competition also provided a foundation for the improvement of comprehensive benefits.

The comprehensive mode of development also promoted the real estate industry. In practice, however, it was hard to fully maximize the comprehensive economic, social and environmental benefits initially sought. Driven by real estate profit, the single-minded pursuit of an advantageous plot ratio occurred in housing construction. Housing designed in this frame of thinking often sacrificed function in order to attain higher densities. Some housing was too deep and rooms at the center of the floor plan were poorly lighted. Some residential buildings had nine or ten floors without elevators and with no provision of private outdoor living space. Some buildings used perimeter-block layouts with no special design consideration for east-west orientations, resulting in a poor micro-environment. In some high-rise buildings, there were eight or ten apartments on each floor and a considerable number of the apartments had poor lighting and orientation. Many housing projects were the result of exploiting a special connection with, or bargaining with, planning and administrative departments, and the pursuit of profits was the most important factor.

3.3. Urban Residential Area Experiments: Launching and Leading Role

Recognizing that the accomplishment of strategic goals in urban housing construction must rely on technological progress, China launched an experiment in the construction of urban residential developments in the mid-1980s. The slogan for the pilot projects was "high standards with relatively low cost, high quality with relatively low space standards, complete functions in small areas, and a pleasant environment despite limited land coverage." In all, planning and design embodied a human-centered philosophy. Through elaborate planning, as well as more meticulous design and construction, comprehensive development improved substantially. Also, with an emphasis on the diffusion of scientific and technological knowledge, mature new technologies, new materials, new techniques and new equipment were employed. Moreover, the pilot urban-residential development projects marked a milestone in housing construction in China, and the State Economic and Trade Commission listed experiments in the development of residential areas as one of the fifty key technological development projects during the Seventh Five-Year Plan period (1986 to 1990). With these experiments entrusted to the Ministry of Construction for implementation, three cities—Wuxi, Tianjiu and Jinan—were selected to represent the south, north and middle regions, respectively. The construction area of the three pilot residential projects totaled 500,000 square meters, involving a total infrastructure investment of 300 million yuan. The overall experiment was carried out in 1986 and 1987 and completed in 1989. However, although the number of residential areas in the trial was trivial compared with the numerous urban residential areas completed each year at that time, they played an influential and exemplary role in the planning and design of residential buildings.

3.3.1. Improvement of Outdoor Environments

Inherited from the design legacy of the previous thirty years, the planning of residential areas was characterized by three levels of consideration, as mentioned earlier. They were the residential building, the neighborhood cluster, and the residential area as such. Outdoor living environments were made pleasant through skillful utilization of landforms, landscape planting, elaborate division of space and inheritance of local traditions. Various methods were followed to enrich the living space by organizing individual buildings according to rhythm and contrast. In Wuxi's Qinyuanxincun, for example, which was among the first batch of trial residential areas, the arrangement of neighborhood clusters was dominated by slab blocks. The combination of towers with the long buildings created an interlocking spatial configuration that formed different types of neighborhoods and courtyards at the southern and northern entrances. Meanwhile, attention was paid to the height change of buildings so that a rich skyline profile was formed (Fig. 8-1). In another example, Tianjin's Chuanfuxincun was divided into four neighborhood clusters around a central greenbelt, with each cluster having its own character. One cluster, for instance, mainly comprised terraced garden housing, while another was arranged in an interesting composition of apartment units. Another had connected freestanding buildings with platforms forming elevated streets, and still another combined units of considerable depth with land-saving tower blocks (Fig. 8-2).

Among the second batch of experimental urban residential developments was Changzhou's Hongmeixicun—the epitome of architecture in the region of streams and lakes lying south of the Yangtze River. The buildings had white walls with black tiles and different bridge galleries at the entrance of each group, as well as landscaping along the stream running through the residential area. The overall appearance reproduced an indigenous image of small bridges, flowing streams and cottages typical of a region of waters and lakes (Fig. 8-3). Qingdao's Sifang neighborhood was also a successful example of a residential area, with a strong character developed on the natural lay of the land. It was located on a hilly site with a sloping land area of twenty-five meters difference in elevation, in addition to a natural gully running north-south and two natural water bodies in the central section. The planning of the residential areas maintained the natural landscape as much as possible, with

Fig. 8-1: Master plan of
Qinyuanxincun Village

1. Stores
2. Central Park
3. Kindergarten
4. Activity Centers for Seniors
   and Youths
5. Middle School
6. Neighborhood Committee
   and Day care
7. Bicycle Garage
8. Water Pump and Tower
9. Police and Security
10. Clinic
11. Electric Station
12. Village Sign
13. Water Treatment Plant
14. Market
15. Sculpture

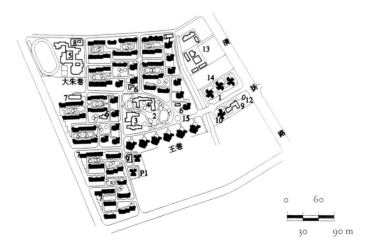

Fig. 8-2: Master plan of
Chuanfuxincun

1. Restaurants
2. Culture and Activity Center
3. Village Park
4. Commercial Areas on
   the First Floor
5. Elementary School
6. Kindergarten
7. Boiler Room
8. Public Transportation Station
9. Green Areas
10. Public Facilities
    (Neighborhood Committee,
    and Garage)

▬▬ Residential Building

☐ Public Facility

⬭ Green Area

the housing blocks sprawling in an orderly way on the rolling hill-side. In line with the shape and orientation of the gully, the northern portion maintained the original green slope and the open central portion of the site was constructed in a stepped square that served as the community center. In the south lay open green land composed of the entrance and water bodies (Fig. 8-4).

Beside these experimental residential area developments, the overall improvement of planning and design in housing could also be seen in many other remarkable new residential areas. For

instance, Beijing's Fangzhuang New Residential District, mainly composed of high-rise residential buildings, had a high plot ratio but a low building density. Inside, Fangchengyuan was divided into three residential groups. In the north was situated a group of tower buildings, together with courtyard-like playing grounds, and their curvilinear distribution produced a graceful dynamic spacial effect. In the south, the other two groups of residential buildings were mixed together with tower buildings, low stepped structures, large playing grounds and green spaces (Fig. 8-5).

In Shenzhen, the Baishaling residential area departed from the usual horizontal or vertical patterns of building. Its design was high-lighted by a dynamic overall form, with several dozen tower build-

Fig. 8-3: West Hongmeixicun in Changzhou

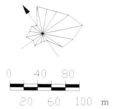

ings radiating from a large open space that served as the center of the residential area. Outside, there was a diamond-shaped framework of roads, with another fifteen high-rise buildings stretching out in a radial manner (Fig. 8-6).

3.3.2. Improved Services in Residential Areas

Through the developments of the early 1980s, housing made substantial progress in qualitative terms. Many designers made explorations into improving living environments and the quality of life.

Fig. 8-4a: Sifang neighborhood in Qingdao

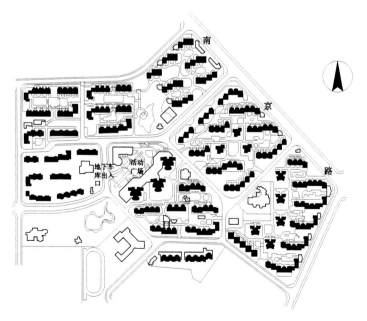

Fig. 8-4b: Sifang neighborhood in Qingdao

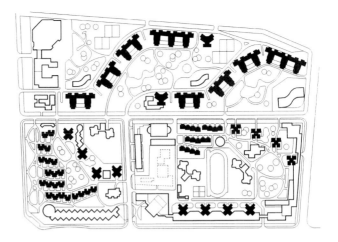

State regulations regarding supporting facilities also helped to
remove many inconveniences in the daily life of residents. In addition, planning and design in the experimental residential areas
made further inroads into perfecting available services, giving them
full play and fitting designs closer to the needs of residents. In short,
human-centered design made another big stride.

In some residential areas, free trade developed along the roads
outside, and even extended onto the main road within the residential areas themselves. Although these retail stands facilitated residents' shopping convenience, they also adversely affected traffic and
environmental quality, necessitating reconsideration of residents'
behavioral habits in the layout of supporting service facilities. Some
residential areas, such as Wuxi's Qinyuanxincun and Changzhou's
Hongmeixincun, were successful in this respect. Both provided sup-

Fig. 8-6: The Baishaling high-rise
residential district in Shenzhen

porting shopping facilities on main sections outside the residential areas, and other service facilities, such as cultural centers and banks, were provided at the center according to their service radius. The outlying commercial layout enabled residents to buy daily necessities on their way home from work, on the one hand, and the business expansion of such facilities brought about more economic returns on the other. Meanwhile, facilities oriented to the community at the center of the residential areas could combine with open-space areas in a flexible way to ensure a pleasant environment and, overall, residents were happy with such a rational layout.

3.3.3. Traffic and Bicycle Parking

Roads in residential areas both help organize and provide a safe external space for people to use, as well as guiding the flow of vehicles and other traffic. Therefore, a quiet and safe road system is important to ensure a high quality of life and a safe environment. In the experimental residential areas, the main streets were designed with bends and turns aimed at forcing vehicles to slow down. In the building clusters, one or two entrances were provided and dead-end roads were incorporated to reduce the possibility of through-traffic. Some residential areas tried to separate people and vehicles. For example, Shenzhen's Binheh housing district was noted for its corridors, which combined the housing tower blocks into an organic whole. More specifically, the corridors, specially designed for walking, connected buildings of more than two floors and, by the use of these corridors, pedestrians and vehicles were separated. Decorated with small objects and plants, the corridors also served as places of rest and amusement. Under the corridors, facilities for commercial services, together with parking lots for cars and bicycles, were placed conveniently for residents (Fig. 8-7).

China is a "kingdom of bicycles" and every urban household has at least one bicycle. Moreover, for a considerably long time, the bicycle will remain a major means of transportation and its number will continue to rise. Naturally, the parking of bicycles is an inevitable issue in residential areas, although in the past inadequate consideration and limited investment has largely excluded parking for bicycles from design considerations. Sometimes a makeshift shelter was put up in front of a residential building. Otherwise residents had to put bicycles out of doors or place them in public corridors, staircases or even within their homes. The resulting disorder spoiled the look of the environment and offered opportunities for theft, thus reducing the sense of security in residential areas. More recently, elaborately designed outdoor facilities have been provided for the

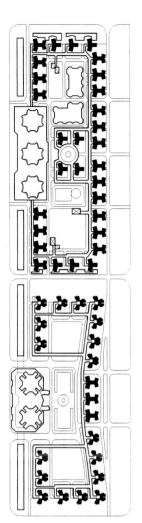

Fig. 8-7: The Binheh residential district in Shenzhen

parking of bicycles. Wuxi's Qinyuanxincun, for instance, provided various bicycle storage areas. Besides a centralized area with comparatively large space, each building complex was designed with semibasement storage areas in some tower blocks, or had the storage built up at the back of the buildings. Subsequently, residents found much convenience in parking their bicycles in these scattered small locations. In Beijing's Enjilixiaoqu, built in the 1990s, each building complex has an independent semibasement storage area, the entrance to which adjoins the entrance of the building complex, while the roof of the storage area connects with the adjacent landscaped open space, forming a platform (Fig. 8-8). In Zongbeixiaoqu, the experimental housing district in Chengdu in Sichuan Province, the storage areas were directly connected with the basements of buildings to enhance their convenience for residents (Fig. 8-9).

3.4. Further Diversification of Housing Design

With deepening reform in housing commercialization, many valuable investigations were made regarding housing design and, as commercialization relaxed the restriction on housing standards, the design focus shifted to housing functions. On the one hand, designs tried to match, in a reasonable way, residents' lifestyles and living standards. On the other, designs tried to give more flexibility to housing as a special consumer good. For instance, the concept of the apartment unit was an affirmation of the different functions in housing and an indication of a higher demand for different spaces in people's daily lives. Moreover, different families had different needs for the division of their space (Fig. 8-10). Following the tech-

Fig. 8-8a: The Enjili neighborhood in Beijing

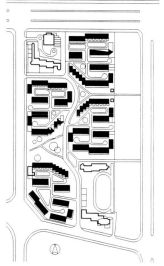

Fig. 8-8b: Master plan of the
Enjili neighborhood in Beijing

Fig. 8-8c: Neighborhood Committee and Bicycle Parking Area of
Enjili neighborhood in Beijing

Entrance to
the Cluster

Mail Boxes for
Residents

Entrance and Exit

Wall

Mail Boxes
for Residents

Mail Delivery

Mail Room/Office
of Neighborhood
Committee

Office of Neighborhood
Committee

Fig. 8-9: Layout of bicycle garages
in Zongbei neighborhood, Chengdu

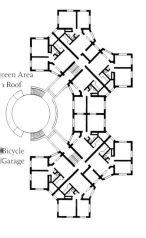

reen Area
1 Roof

Bicycle
Garage

nical provisions put forth in 1985 about housing construction that
required housing to be designed according to the apartment unit,
China promulgated standards for housing designs in 1987, stipulating that "housing should be designed by unit and that each unit
must be a single house not sharing an entrance with others. It
should [also] have a bedroom(s), a kitchen, a bathroom and a storeroom." In addition, units were classified as small, medium or large
according to different uses and family compositions. The usable
floor area was to be no less than "eighteen square meters for a small
unit, thirty square meters for a medium-sized unit and forty-five
square meters for a large unit." With limited floor areas, adaptability and flexibility became crucial factors for improving the functional aspects of housing design.

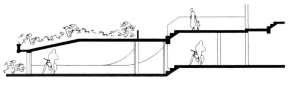

Bicycle Garage of Zongbei Neighborhood

Fig. 8-10: Space division by residents

Couple + Daughter (15)
Couple with a teenage daughter

Couple + Son (20) + Daughter (18)
Couple with grownup children

Two Grownup Sons

Couple with a young daughter

Couple + Son (18)
Couple with a teenage son

Couple with a young son

3.4.1. High-rise Housing Development

Due to its advantages in land saving and development efficiency, high-rise housing developed rapidly. As already noted, in 1987 the proportion of high-rise buildings in housing construction in Beijing rose to 45 percent from the earlier proportion of 10 percent. However, as in the early 1980s, high-rise buildings were also seen to have intrinsic disadvantages. Especially in a city with a long history, the construction of high-rise buildings constituted a major contradiction to the protection of the traditional cityscape. Beijing, for instance, imposed strict control on the height of buildings, and the city consequently looked like a wok—low at the center but high around its periphery—even though some projects, surpassing the height limit, kept emerging to spoil the historic environments of the inner city.

Overall, the government adopted a cautious attitude toward the construction of high-rise buildings. The 1985 technical provision on housing construction clearly stipulated that urban housing should primarily be multiple-storey and the construction of high-rise resi-

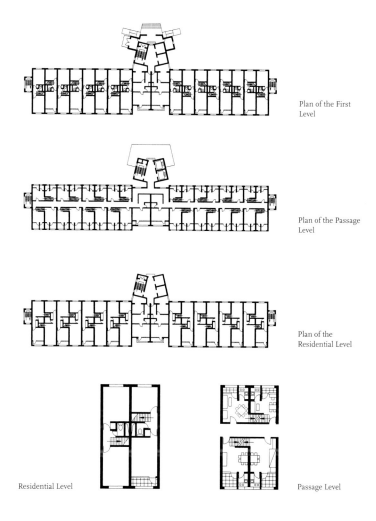

Fig. 8-11: Duplex high-rise apartment building in Quyangxincun, Shanghai

Plan of the First Level

Plan of the Passage Level

Plan of the Residential Level

Residential Level

Passage Level

dential buildings should be maintained under strict control. At designated sites in a city, when there was an evident land savings to be gained from the construction of high-rise residential buildings as well as adequate provision of technical equipment, an appropriate number of high-rise residential buildings could be built. At the end of 1987, the Ministry of Construction issued another document requiring all cities to exert strict control on the construction of high-rise residential buildings. In 1990, the Beijing municipal government proclaimed regulations governing "the strict control on high-rise housing construction," and in the same year, Shanghai adopted measures to control high-rise housing projects (Zhang Kaiji, 1990).

Formally, the development of high-rise housing during this period displayed a trend towards variation. First of all, the types of plan being developed were enriched. High-rise residential buildings in

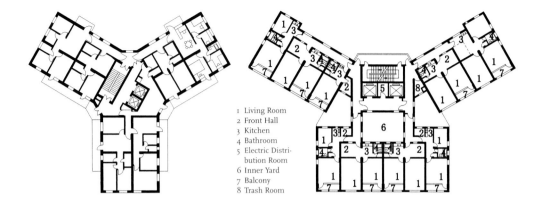

1 Living Room
2 Front Hall
3 Kitchen
4 Bathroom
5 Electric Distri-
  bution Room
6 Inner Yard
7 Balcony
8 Trash Room

the late 1970s were mainly built according to basic floor plans. In the mid-1980s, slab and tower high-rise buildings experienced substantial development, including the inclusion of duplex apartments, cross-shaped plans, frog-shaped plans, etc. (Figs. 8-11 to 8-17). At the same time, the standard of high-rise housing varied considerably according to the living standards of residents. Shanghai's Yandang Building, for instance, was the first high-rise apartment building constructed by a Chinese-foreign joint venture. Each apartment had two bathrooms and a spacious and well-lit kitchen, both of which were rare in the mid-1980s (Fig. 8-14). Also in Shanghai, the Aijian Building was designed for returned overseas Chinese. Each apartment had two bedrooms and a sitting room, with an overall floor area reaching ninety-five square meters (Fig. 8-15). Nevertheless, the standard of housing projects in most urban redevelopments could not be mentioned in the same breath with such buildings (Fig. 8-16).

Along with further research in high-rise housing design, there appeared some brilliantly devised layouts with better functional qualities and lower cost. For instance, the butterfly-shaped plan was a result of optimizing all other plan forms of high-rise residential buildings in relation to light, the amount of usable space available in the plan, building structure and land savings (Fig. 8-17).

During this period, research on the adaptability and flexibility of housing was also widely conducted as a further development of the housing standardization and diversification begun earlier. Generally speaking, the basic technique was to provide space flexibility in apartments, within the framework of a systematic design. Usually, it was applied to systems with large bays, with little change in the area of each apartment. Flexible partitions were used to create different types of apartments so that the housing could change in accordance

Fig. 8-12: Plan of the Y-shaped high-rise residential building of Xibahe, Beijing

Fig. 8-13: Plan of the Y-shaped 20-storey residential buildings on South Zhongshan Road, Shanghai

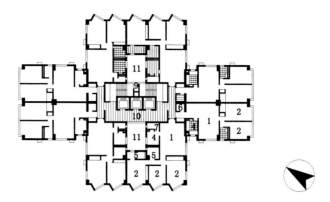

Fig. 8-14: Cross-shaped plan of the Yandang Residential Building, Shanghai

1 Living Room
2 Bedroom
3 Closet
4 Kitchen
5 Bathroom
6 Half Bath
7 Storage Room
8 Air Conditioning Room
9 Trash Room
10 Elevator
11 Light Well

with varying needs. The Xiaokang well-to-do residential area projects in Shijiazhuang, Hebei Province, were good examples of this large-bay flexible arrangement (Fig. 8-18). The stepped garden residential buildings in the Xishawang neighborhood in Yantai, Shandong Province, however, were a demonstration of a brick-concrete, small-bay flexible arrangement. Such designs made the plan layout more flexible, and residents could do the partitioning themselves (Fig. 8-19). The SAR housing project in Wuxi, described earlier, not only attained the goal of diversification, but also emphasized the stress on housing adaptability and flexibility by allowing residents to participate in the housing design.

In the design of multiple-storey housing, arrangements with concave-convex plans emerged to tackle the weakness of the small-sized, inner-light well, while ensuring adequate depth in housing to increase density. With appropriate geometry in the resulting external recesses, the lighting and depth of units were easily made acceptable. Consequently, such housing developed rapidly during

Fig. 8-15: Frog-shaped plan of the Aijian high-rise residential building, Shanghai

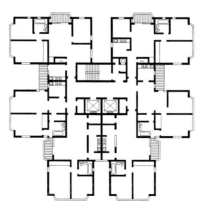

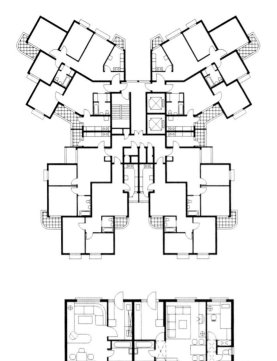

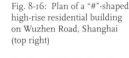

Fig. 8-16: Plan of a "#"-shaped high-rise residential building on Wuzhen Road, Shanghai (top right)

Fig. 8-17: Butterfly-shaped plan of a high-rise residential building (top left)

Fig. 8-18: Plan of well-to-do housing in Shijiazhuang (bottom)

the mid- and late 1980s and was massively applied to multiple-floor residential buildings with low- and middle-range space standards (Fig. 8-20).

3.4.2. Pursuit of Local Architectural Style

To borrow the form of traditional dwellings is often an important way to improve the architectural quality of the external space and can be easily identified with by residents. For instance, the horsehead wall in the traditional dwelling in the southern region along the Yangtze River was refined and integrated with the gable of residential buildings in Suzhou's Sanyuanxincun, providing a unique flavor. In Wuxi's Qinyuanxincun, Hefei's Amber Mountain Villa and Changzhou's Hongmeixicun, some exposed walls were rendered in a quietly elegant manner, while some were bold and bright. Some windows on the eastern and western gables were decorated with lintels that not only provided a sunshade but also presented a

Fig. 8-19: Plans of terraced
garden houses in Yantai

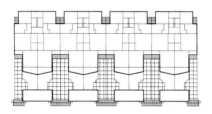

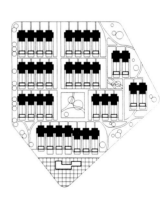

Fig. 8-20: Plans of multi-storied
recessed housing

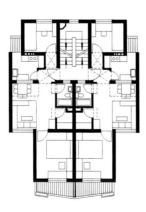

Fig. 8-21: The Hupo neighborhood in Hefei

Fig. 8-22: The Sanyuan neighborhood in Suzhou

Fig. 8-23: The Kangle neighborhood in Shanghai

unique profile to the building's elevation. Still others had the gable constructed in the manner of traditional framing (Figs. 8-1, 8-3, 8-21 to 23). Some housing design even employed the city's cultural and historical tradition. For instance, Qingdao's Sifang neighborhood areas used local materials, and some other housing adopted dormers and other devices characteristic of the colonial period. As a result, the warm red-colored roofs, the blue sky and the emerald plants set each other off beautifully (Fig. 8-4).

Notes

1. See the approval of the State Council of the "Report of the Ministry of Civil Affairs on Adjusting Standards for City Establishment and on the Leading Role of Cities over Counties," April 1986.
2. Data about urban population are controversial due to differing statistical measures. The first *Exploration of China's Urbanization*, authored by Ye Weijun and others, published by China Prospect Publishing House in 1988, used the same data as this book. The fourth census in 1990 made an adjustment in population data after 1982. According to the 1996 *Statistical Yearbook of Chinese Population*, the urban population was 172.45 million in 1978 and 233.84 million in 1986. Due to the complexity of statistics on urban population, this chapter bases its analysis on the trend rather than on specific figures.
3. Government Work Report of the Sixth National People's Congress, 1984.

Chapter Nine: Urban Housing in the Early Period of the Socialist Market Economy (1992–2000)

1. General Socio-economic Development and Urban Construction

After three years of improving economic conditions between the end of 1988 and the end of 1991, the real estate industry boomed, particularly following Deng Xiaoping's speech during his southern China tour. Rapid development of the real estate industry also boosted macro-economic growth, quickly leading to an overheated economy and so-called bubble prosperity. The state had to intensify its macro-economic regulation in 1993 in order to reverse these abnormal developments and, after a "soft landing" in 1997, the Chinese economy entered into a new period of stability.

1.1. Construction of a Socialist Market Economy With Chinese Characteristics

In the spring of 1992, Deng Xiaoping delivered a series of important speeches on his inspection tour in southern China. Deng made a brilliant exposition on ideologically related issues, such as the relation between planning and market forces, which had long been a topic of debate in China's economic reform. In essence, the speeches relieved the ideological constraint that included the planned economy and the market economy as two parts of the same system. October 1992 saw the holding of the fourteenth CPC National Congress, which clearly stated the objective of establishing a socialist market economy. It proposed to modify the Eighth Five-Year Plan and the Ten-Year Plan and raised the projected annual economic growth rate from 6 percent to 8 or 9 percent. Guided by this policy, the gross national product (GNP) in 1993 increased by 13 percent over that of 1992. Together with this economic growth, reform continued to both deepen and widen, centering on the establishment of a market system. New "hot spots" kept emerging, however, including price reforms, the development of a securities market, experiments in a shareholding system, the development of a futures market, development of the real estate market, and changes in the operation of state-owned enterprises.

1.2. The Overheated Economy and Macro Regulation During the Period of Transition

Following Deng's southern China tour, the Chinese economy experienced unprecedented growth. In particular, there was considerable enthusiasm for the real estate industry. In 1988, there were 3,124 realty developers in China and, from 1988 to the end of 1991, the number remained steady at around 3,000. In May 1992, the number was still less than 4,000, but jumped to 12,000 by the end of 1992. Of these, over 2,000 were solely foreign-funded, or Chinese-foreign joint ventures. At the end of the following year, the number of concerns reached 30,000, or 10 times the number from two years before. In 1992, a total of 73.2 billion yuan was put into real estate development, with an increase of 117 percent over 1991. Developed land reached 233.4 square kilometers, up by 175 percent; the construction of market housing, at 190 million square meters, was up by 57.8 percent; completed market housing, at 4,288.9 square meters, was up by 36 percent; and the business volume of realty developers, at 52.9 billion yuan, was up by 87 percent.[1]

In 1992, it was planned to lease 2 million mu (133,400 hectares) of land for development, but the actual figure reached 3.6 million mu (240,120 hectares), an increase of 80 percent, causing significant loss of cultivated land. In Shanghai, for instance, 112 tracts of land were leased during the period between January and August of 1992, more than 9 times the amount leased in the prior 4 years. However, owing to the lack of a fully developed market mechanism, the real estate business was very speculative and became the most fashionable way of making money. In 1992, the balance of real estate loans exceeded 50 billion yuan, as people, in a "bearish" stock market, tried to seek other means of investment. Fundraising in various forms and for various purposes was conducted and, by April 1993, funds raised by various means surpassed 100 billion yuan, to be spent mostly for real estate speculation in eastern coastal areas.

Illusory demand and speculation resulted in bubbles in the real estate market and many problems were exposed. The large land supply, for instance, exceeded the capability of development and construction, leaving large areas of land idle and further intensifying speculation. Trading in real estate became chaotic, and speculators obtained huge profits from land that had been allocated through administrative means, causing a considerable loss of state-owned assets. Real estate prices skyrocketed and, while investment in real estate development kept increasing, the sale of market housing lagged behind in a lopsided manner. The supply of luxury apartments and villas, for example, substantially exceeded demand.

The overheated economy represented by the real estate industry was also a demonstration of disorderly supply and demand at a deeper level and, before long, accelerated the encroachment of inflation. Funding shortages for economic growth resulted in indiscriminant loans and fundraising, creating disarray in the financial sector. The expansion of the demand for domestic investment resulted in an imbalance of international payments and depreciation of the renminbi. In the latter half of 1993, the central government tightened macro-economic regulation and revoked part of the loans by cleaning up the development zones. With enhanced land management and an improved trading market, the real estate market cooled down.

Thanks to the macro-regulatory policies adopted by the central government, the real estate industry took on a new look. One-third of the development zones were suspended, one-third of real estate developers closed down, and another third reduced the scale of their operations. More than 20 million mu (1,334 hectares) of land that failed to be developed as scheduled was taken back, and inland provinces withdrew huge amounts of funding from coastal areas. The real estate trading volume also declined, with prices falling by 15 to 20 percent, and the momentum of real estate investment slowed down. For instance, the investment during January to June of 1993 increased by 143.5 percent over the same period in 1992, but the increase in the whole year stood at 124.6 percent, falling by 18.6 percent when compared with the first six months. Against this economic background, in 1994 China intensified its housing reform.

1.3. Troubles With the New Round of Economic Growth

Beginning in 1993, after three years of macro-economic regulation, the Chinese economy entered a relatively stable and orderly period. Prices began to fall and inflation was brought under control. However, the new round of economic growth exposed many deep-seated problems in the economic restructuring that was occurring. Inflation, for example, had always been a principal impediment that restrained economic growth, and price controls were usually achieved at the cost of slowing economic growth. Rational orientation of investment and consumption was regarded as the key to economic growth and the state made a transition from extensive to intensive economic growth. Usually, traditional economic growth was based on extensive financial inputs, yet, because of administrative interference, huge inputs failed to yield commensurate outputs. By contrast, intensive economic growth was a highly efficient means of accumulation and production which optimized resource allocation. As a result of economic restructuring, beginning in the 1980s, the national income began to tilt toward individuals, and means to transform income into effective investment depended to a large degree on a sound financial system and on a rational orientation towards consumption. This was also the key to realizing more fully intensive economic growth.

Meanwhile, the reform of state-owned enterprises entered a substantive period of engagement, centering around "relinquishing part of the power and profits to enterprises" and using a system of "contracting-out" to provide a driving force for enterprise development. Nevertheless, problems relating to enterprise efficiency remained fundamentally unsolved as relinquishing part of the power and profits to enterprises further weakened constraints on property rights under the planned economy. Moreover, as substantive reform was not carried out in relation to the multiple identity of enterprises in political, economic and social terms it was, therefore, difficult for enterprises to achieve maximum efficiency. Further, under the circumstances of a weakened property right, the system of contracting-out resulted in deleterious short-term behavior by contractors. In the face of these problems, the Third Plenary Session of the Fourteenth CPC Central Committee proposed to establish a system of modern enterprises by forming economic groups, through amalgamation and centralization, and to exact further economic improvement. However, because of the incomplete system of property rights and the underdeveloped capital market, the reform of state-owned enterprises proved difficult, and the trend toward declining efficiency continued.

The industrial structure, formed in the traditional planned economy, was also hard to improve. Problems such as the orientation of local interests, weak mechanisms of investment constraint and a lack of supporting services made it difficult to achieve an optimal organization for economic improvement. As a consequence, duplication and overstocking of commodities were common phenomena and improvements in this sector became a key for maintaining economic growth.

In 1997, Southeast Asia was stricken by a financial crisis, which produced a major impact upon the global economy, especially in Asia. China was no exception. First, investment in Southeast Asia was reduced drastically, inevitably affecting China. Second, as Southeast Asian countries spurred on growth in their exports through currency depreciation, China faced fiercer competition, making it extremely hard to maintain high rates of economic growth. If the renminbi did not devalue, China could hardly compete with other Asian countries. If the renminbi did devalue, it would have further aggravated the entire Asian economy, while triggering domestic instability. The only way out was to stimulate domestic demand and increase consumption and investment, while also avoiding duplication in construction activities. Therefore, China put an emphasis on development in three areas: 1) infrastructure, such as highways and railways; 2) high-tech industries; and 3) building trades, mainly in housing construction. Furthermore, it was under these socio-economic pressures that China adopted policies, in the mid- and late 1990s, to industrialize housing construction, deepen the reform of housing and enable the housing industry to become an active component of economic consumption and growth.

2. Housing Reform in the Market Economy

By the mid-1990s, China's reform of housing was over ten years old, and the dire shortage of housing in the early 1980s had been greatly relieved. But housing was still in short supply, not only in terms of throughput but also in terms of distribution. While demand for housing increased with the increase of urban population and rises in residents' income, 66 million square meters of market housing remained idle, representing over 100 billion yuan in rent. While the state spent 200 billion yuan each year in constructing, repairing and managing urban housing, the per capita living area of 4 million urban households was less than 4 square meters. More specifically, in 1985, the per-capita living area of 75 percent of urban households was 4.4 square meters, while the per-capita living area of the remaining 25 percent was over 14.8 square meters. At the same time, the difference in income between low- and middle-income and high-income households was less than two-fold. By contrast, in 1996, the per-capita living area of urban residents had reached 8.4 square meters, with about 75 percent of urban families living in multi-storey buildings. Of them, close to 30 percent lived in housing with one bedroom and one sitting room, or with only one bedroom, while 30 percent lived in housing with three bedrooms and one sitting room, or with a larger amount of space. For the same period, the difference of family income between low- and middle-income households and high-income households was less than three-fold, and, obviously, the difference in housing standard was much larger than the income difference. Therefore, in some sense, the intrinsic shortage of housing in the 1990s was largely a result of excessive housing consumption. The ten-year reform had swung between raised rents and housing sales, but the fundamental problem remained unsolved, and the reform in the mid-to-late 1990s was widely divergent from that originally intended in the early 1980s.

2.1. A New Trend in Housing Reform: A Stress on Institutional Aspects

Under the guideline of establishing a socialist market economy, reform was accelerated in all fields and the direction became clearer. The state issued its "Suggestions on Promoting All-Round Reform of the Housing System in Urban Areas" in 1991, and set out to deepen the institutional aspects of housing reform in 1994, further clarifying the basic goals. More specifically, the state resolved to establish a new housing system in urban areas, in line with a socialist market economy, and to commercialize and socialize housing. In addition, it set out to accelerate housing construction, improve living conditions and meet the increasing demands of urban residents.

Basically, the deepening of the urban housing reform covered the following aspects. First, the state, individuals and an individual's work unit should all contribute to investment in housing construction. This was different from past practice, wherein only the state and the work unit were responsible. Second, the system wherein the work unit took responsibility for construction, distribution, maintenance and management of housing was to be changed into one featuring a socialized and professional operation. Third, the distribution of housing as welfare-in-kind was to be changed into a new mode that involved monetary wages. Fourth, a method of supplying economic and practical housing to low- and middle-income families in the form of social security was to be established, along with a system of supplying market-rate housing to high-income families. Fifth, public reserve funds for housing were to be established. Sixth, housing finance and housing insurance were to be developed and a housing loan system was to be established, featuring simultaneous consideration of political and commercial benefits. Finally, a standard real estate trading market and a socialized housing maintenance and management market were to be developed.

However, clarification of the line of thinking in housing reform was one matter, but smooth operation was another. The difficulty encountered had nothing to do with the policy itself, but embodied the numerous contradictions involved in the country's overall economic restructuring. In 1991, the policy of "the parallel practice of renting and selling" was adopted, which raised the annual house rent to 30 yuan per square meter and set the lower limit for a house sale at 120 yuan per square meter. This led to another round of sales of publicly owned housing at low prices across the country, as all areas tried to set their prices close to the state-stipulated minimum. Subsequently, in 1994, the state made explicit regulations forbidding such practices, bringing the sale of housing to a standstill. In the same year, new measures were taken to deepen housing reform, quickly prompting house sales in 1995. At this stage, however, the problem emerged of different departments vying with each other for the management of funds from house sales. According to the Ministry of Finance, the majority of the money from selling publicly owned housing should be turned over to the state, with enterprises or institutions retaining only 10 to 15 percent. This provision clearly dampened the initiative of work units in house sales, and, at the end of 1995, the sale of publicly owned housing became stagnant once more.

In 1997, efforts to raise rents failed to achieve the expected results. The goal set in 1994 for the year 2000 was that house rent should be roughly equivalent to 15 percent of the income of an average household. Actually, statistics in 1996 about rents in 35 large- and medium-sized cities throughout the country showed that rents only accounted for 3.64 percent of the income of a family with two incomes (Zhu Jianhong, 1997), which was far below the goal of 15 percent (Table 9-1). With the eruption of the Southeast Asia finan-

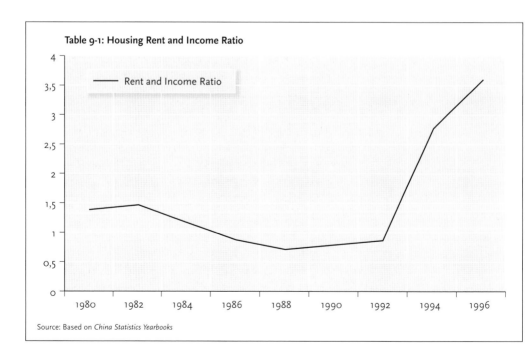

Source: Based on *China Statistics Yearbooks*

cial crisis in 1997, China quickly set forth the policy of expanding economic growth through the housing industry and, with this, reform was accelerated.

2.2. Rationalization of Housing Investment Mechanisms

The sale of market-rate housing had been a main contradiction in the housing reform. Great fluctuations existed in the sales volume of market-rate housing since the mid- and late 1980s. In fact, the sale of market-rate housing increased by 33.72 percent in 1988 over 1987, but decreased by 22.49 percent in 1989 over 1988. Similarly, sales increased by 12.03 percent in 1990 over 1989, but decreased again by 5.41 percent in 1992. The most dramatic fluctuation occurred around 1993, when the increase in 1993 over 1991 reached 84.81 percent, but dropped to 84.54 percent in 1994. At the end of 1996, idle market-rate housing throughout the country totaled 66 million square meters, involving over 100 billion yuan in stagnant funds.

The substantial fluctuation in the sale of market-rate housing revealed one fact: namely, that the purchase of commodity housing did not represent genuine housing demand. On one hand, large amounts of market-rate housing remained idle and, on the other, housing was still in short supply. The solution to this impasse was to establish an effective supply-and-demand system and to form a sound market, from production to circulation and through to consumption. Clearly, it was impossible to rely solely on state subsidies, and rationalization of investment in housing construction became absolutely necessary.

2.2.1. Reserve Funds

A system of public reserve funds was launched following many successful practices in other countries, such as Singapore, in order to meet immediate funding needs. Here, public reserve funds refer to a certain sum of money discounted monthly, in a certain proportion, from the wage of each worker and from the gross wages of a work unit. Further, the staff and workers can use the money for purchasing or building housing and, usually, the proportion was 5 percent (Miao Leru, 1996).

Essentially, public reserve funds have four characteristics. First, the funds are collected on the principle of "individual saving and unit support," whereby the in-service staff worker and his or her work unit turn over funds to a housing reserve account each month, in accordance with a certain proportion of the worker's wage and the work unit's total wages. Also, the worker has a right to all the money that is saved in the individual reserve account. Second, the housing reserve funds are managed in a unified manner, based on the principle of "combined responsibility, authority and benefit." Third, the housing reserve funds are earmarked for housing. Accordingly, the staff worker can only use the funds for purchasing, building and repairing housing. Fourth, in order to guarantee the staff worker's rights and interests, the principal and interest of the reserve fund are returned to the worker upon retirement.

From a market point of view, the largest barrier in the benign cycle of funds involved in housing reform had been the simultaneous insufficiency of effective demand and effective supply. The insufficiency of effective demand was attributed to low incomes and sluggish housing consumption, resulting from the long practice of distributing housing as welfare. This could only be changed with deepened reform in all regards. The insufficiency of effective supply, by contrast, was because the state could not shoulder the responsibility for housing construction alone. Therefore, the adoption of a public reserve fund was aimed primarily at expanding sources of funding and increasing their effective supply for housing.

From May 1991 to March 1995, a total 534 million yuan in reserve funds were raised across the country. During this period, 3.07 billion yuan of special housing loans were extended to work units from the reserve fund, which were used to construct 2 million square meters of housing for staff workers. In addition, loans of 250 million yuan were made to work units in dire housing situations, and 150 million yuan in loans were provided for the renovation of old and dangerous housing, as well as 360 million yuan of direct investment in simply constructed housing. In 1995, one-fourth of the funds for housing construction in Shanghai came from the public reserve fund, and at the end of 1997, public reserve funds in 31 provinces totaled 80 billion yuan (Zhu Jianhong, 1988, 1995).

2.2.2. Reform of Income in the Form of Welfare-In-Kind

From the very beginning of national reform and opening-up to the outside world, the state tried to initiate housing reform. However, house rents up until 1996 among thirty-five large- and medium-sized cities throughout China indicated that the rent of publicly owned housing accounted for only 3.64 percent of family income, while the per capita rent for publicly owned housing in urban areas accounted for only about 1 percent.[2] From an economic point of view, rent reform was clearly related to the entire national economy. For instance, when price controls conflicted with rises in rent, the focus was usually shifted to price control. In 1996, Chongqing, for instance, raised housing rents to 0.8 yuan per square meter. But the new rate was implemented for just three months and then dropped to 0.5 yuan per square meter, due to the high price index. In the same year, although the proportion of rent in the expenditure of two-job families rose to 5 percent in major cities, it began to decline soon after.

In 1997, housing reform ushered in a new opportunity. Considering the possible impact of the Southeast Asian financial crisis and especially the prospect of currency depreciation upon China, as well as problems emerging in domestic economic restructuring, the central government chose to make housing a new source of economic growth. Specifically, it was decided to expand housing construction while simultaneously increasing the effective demand of residents for housing by discontinuing its distribution as welfare and adjusting the expenditure structure. Essentially, this move was aimed at meeting the housing needs of residents, on the one hand, and boosting the national economy on the other. Effectively, it also meant that work units should no longer construct, purchase or distribute housing; instead, they should transform the various funds available to them for housing into subsidies for staff and workers, either as a one-time payment or in multiple installments (e.g., once a month). With this money, workers should then purchase or rent housing on the housing market and not rely on the work unit. Needless to say, raising rents and distributing housing by monetary means impinged on the vested interests of many groups in society. Housing distribution under the traditional system was closely connected with power, and so it was impossible to adopt a simple monetary method that did not affect the strong entrenchment of power. Consequently, how the state would make compensation for the change in distribution became a key issue in overall efforts to restructure the economy.

With respect to raising the income levels of residents, a benign cycle of housing investment depended on housing consumption. However, increases in residents' income came from the money derived from the former distribution of housing as welfare, and yet the distribution of housing in kind within the traditional enterprise welfare system was not based on the rational circulation of funds. Therefore, a considerable amount of funding could not be given to staff and workers and, inevitably, increases in their wages contracted significantly. In addition, because welfare varied among different enterprises, housing conditions of workers could also be drastically different. Along with the existence of some private residential property, this made it extremely hard to find a reasonable and fair solution to issues of rent and compensation. Housing distribution through monetary transactions encountered similar problems. For instance, plans that had already been implemented, or were to be implemented, were quite different in various areas. In particular, questions arose about how housing subsidies should be paid to workers. Should it be paid all at once, or should they be paid on a monthly basis? Should they be paid directly, or be vested in housing reserve funds? Should all workers, whether they had housing or not, and whether they had bought housing or not, be eligible for housing subsidies, or should there be some difference? Other aspects, such as what percentage individuals should pay, were also involved. Ultimately, these and other questions justified the state countermeasure of "focusing on efficiency while giving consideration to fairness."

With the reform of housing distribution through monetary transactions, and Shanghai's initial success with putting publicly owned housing on the market, all areas in the country began a progressive opening of markets for re-trading purchased public housing, as well as for economic and practical housing. In the meantime, Tianjin, Shanghai, Wuhan and other cities started exploring the transfer of the right to use public housing on the market. Subsequently, the linkage of secondary and tertiary real estate markets greatly facilitated the use of housing resources, promoted market circulation, spurred on housing consumption and generally boosted the real estate industry. For instance, in Shanghai, real estate trading reached 31.5 million square meters in 1998, with more that one-sixth being publicly owned housing, an increase of 94 percent over the previous year, and the transaction volume stood at 6.33 billion yuan, an increase of 118 percent. After selling the purchased publicly owned housing, fully 90 percent of the residents made another purchase of housing. This, together with the purchasing of market-rate housing—using the price difference from the right to use publicly owned housing—enabled the sale of 1.11 million square meters of market-rate housing, accounting for over 10 percent of the total area sold and for 1.44 billion yuan in housing investment.

2.2.3. Personal Credit for Housing

In the early 1980s, four cities, including Guangzhou, experimented with the sale of publicly owned housing. To support this reform, the People's Bank of China provided housing savings-and-loan services, whereby staff and workers could participate in saving, or apply for loans to purchase, build or repair their dwellings. However, these services were small in scale for two reasons. The first was related to housing policy. For instance, work units provided flexible conditions for subsidizing housing payments so that staff and workers need not apply for loans. The second related to bank policy, under which there were no preferential loans to attract customers, a problem plaguing the entire financial sector.

In the mid- and late 1990s, reform of the financial system became the core issue in China's economic restructuring. Fiscal subsidies for housing reform were limited, and yet a long-term benign cycle must rely on a complete financial system. Lacking a complete system of personal credit—and in order to avoid risk— banks provided short-term housing loans that demanded complicated procedures. Furthermore, loans from public reserve funds were even more difficult to secure. In Beijing, for example, only one in three hundred staff members and workers who enjoyed the rights to public reserve loans could successfully secure a loan. Therefore, it remained an arduous task to improve lending for housing further.

2.3. Establishment of a Multi-layered Social-security Housing System

The housing of low- and middle-income residents is a key issue in any housing reform. Most countries, including some with market economies, have tried to resolve this issue through aid policies and social security measures, and many have accumulated successful experiences. In essence, a social security system, instead of being a contradiction to market-oriented processes, is an important means to deal with the issue of social fairness in the marketplace; while conducting its housing reform, China should also establish such a multi-layered system.

2.3.1. High-priced Market-rate Housing

The price of market-rate housing in China comprises several components. They are: construction cost, profit, tax, various fees for supporting urban facilities and price differentials in the land being developed. The cost of market-rate housing, in turn, includes land-use fees, expenses for the resettlement of residents and the removal of obstacles, expenses for the prior period of engineering and design, building and installation expenses, management fees and interest on loans.

Limited land resources in urban areas and the implementation of a land-assignment system has led to a rapid rise in land prices. Also, adoption of a one-time land price has had a similar effect, i.e., real estate developers pay a single seventy-year price for the transfer of a land-use right. According to provisions stipulated in the "Regu-

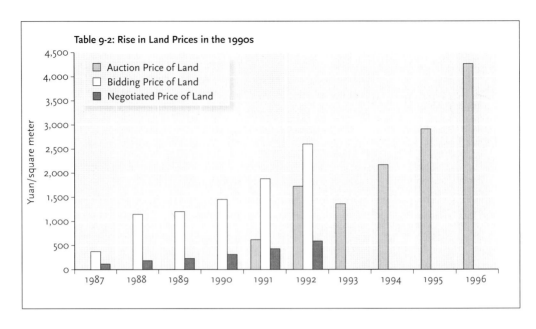

Table 9-2: Rise in Land Prices in the 1990s

lations on Assignment and Transfer of State-owned Land in Urban Areas," the maximum term for the transfer of land for residential purpose is seventy years and, considering the rapid rise of land prices, realty developers deemed it worthwhile to pay for this right at one time. The resulting soaring land prices, however, made the price of housing skyrocket in turn (Table 9-2).

Excess taxes and fees also constituted an important reason for the persistently high price of market-rate housing. Typically, the collection of taxes and fees accompanied the whole process of real estate development and included eleven payments during site clearance, eighteen payments during application for development approval, six payments during construction and a further eighteen payments during the actual sale of property. In 1997, an investigation in 7 cities revealed that taxes and fees increased from 10 or so payments to from 60 to 180, and averaged about 80 payments. From 1985 to 1993, the price of market-rate housing in Guangzhou increased 2.87 times, while the cost of construction increased only 1.19 times. Land-use price increased 1.32 times and taxes and fees increased by 5.7 times. In Beijing, expenses for the 4 major supportive urban facilities and utilities, including roads, electricity, water and gas supply, accounted for 16.2 percent of the development costs and 11.6 percent of the price of market-rate housing.

In the planned economy, urban land was used free of charge and the government had no financial wherewithal to build supporting facilities. To guarantee supporting facilities and to make people's lives easier, various utility and infrastructure fees, as well as construction fees for supporting facilities, were apportioned to the housing price. Consequently, the increased financial burden was obscured when the housing purchase was made by a work unit. But when individual staff and workers purchased housing, the mode of fee collection added the increased burden to the purchase, resulting in a reduced sale of regular market-rate housing. Moreover, as relocation became more difficult and compensation for resettlement rose to even higher levels, expenses kept increasing. Worse still, the substandard real estate market and an incomplete legal system let realty developers go too far in enlarging their profit margins (Ye Yonglie, 1997, 195-208). All these factors contributed to the high price of market-rate housing in China, and it was only really accessible to high-income earners and for institutional purchases. As shown in Table 9-3, it was impossible for ordinary staff and workers to buy such housing directly, especially given the ratio of housing price to family income in some parts of China.

	Average Living Area (sqm)	Housing Price (Yuan/sqm)	Average Income Per household (Yuan)	Ratio of Housing Price and Income
National	74.75	1,194.12	9,076	9.84
Beijing	63.92	2,740.30	13,046	13.42
Tianjin	62.62	1,681.20	10,728	9.82
Liaoning	66.73	1,312.50	8,538	10.26
Shanghai	57.18	1,921.34	14,810	7.42
Shandong	80.56	855.74	8,676	7.95
Guangdong	88.25	2,140.45	14,234	13.27
Sichuan	74.23	734.33	8,056	6.77

2.3.2. Social Security Applied to Market Housing

Application of a social security system to market housing in urban areas means that the government makes policies concerning the production, exchange, distribution, consumption and financing of affordable and practical housing provided to low- and middle-income earners (Lu Youjie, 1996). Essentially, it is the opposite of a market system that supplies market-rate housing to high-income earners, although the two together constitute a complete housing supply system and represent the present direction of China's housing reform.

The material outcome of a social security system applied to market housing is economical and functional housing. On one hand, the government grants various forms of support, such as tax reductions and exemptions during construction, so that housing can be used as compensation for a displaced family, for instance, or for relocation and for resettlement. On the other hand, it remains market housing, only that its costs are relatively low and profits limited to a point where people with low and middle incomes can afford it.

The term "economical and functional housing" can be traced back to 1985 in the "Key Points of Technical Policies Concerning Housing Construction in Urban and Rural Areas." In that document, it was proposed that "by 2000, every urban household should have a unit of economical and practical housing." Further, in 1991, the state decided to devote considerable effort to the development of economical and functional market housing and gave priority to households with small housing or no housing at all. Then, in July 1994, the State Council made the "Decision on Deepening the Reform of Housing in Urban Areas" as a further guideline for housing reform. The Decision stressed "accelerating the construction of economical and functional housing and establishing a new housing system in urban areas at the end of the century, so that urban residents can live in moderately comfortable housing."

2.3.3. Nonprofit "Live-in-Peace" Social Housing Projects

The "live-in-peace" social housing projects refer to the construction of housing sold at state-set prices, and was primarily aimed to solve the housing problem of urban residents, as well as staff and workers in large- and medium-sized state-owned enterprises. Such housing was sold to urban households with poor housing conditions at the middle and low levels of income; here, a household with poor housing conditions referred to one whose per-capita living area was less than or equal to four square meters. Local governments determined the levels of low and middle income according to their various levels of economic development. As housing constructed in the live-in-peace social housing projects was not for making profit, it was not viewed as market housing and had further differences with "economical and practical" housing.

Implementation of the live-in-peace social housing projects followed the road of the planned economy. First, a leading group of housing reformers, under the State Council, determined the list of cities to implement the housing projects, as well as the corresponding scale of construction. Then the State Development Planning Commission communicated to the cities the plans for each project, the scale of loans involved and the amount of self-funding expected in the same mode of management as investments in fixed assets. Further, the State Development Planning Commission and the People's Bank of China then arranged loans, and land for construction was assigned through administrative means by the local government, with relevant expenses either being reduced or exempted. The city government was responsible for urban infrastructure construction, and expenses for supporting public facilities at the residential-area level were equally divided between the city government and the assigned building budget.[3] In all, live-in-peace social housing projects made up 10 percent of the annual housing construction in urban areas. The housing constructed was to be neither high-standard luxurious housing nor simply equipped buildings. Further, the average construction area per unit was to be no more than fifty-five square meters and mainly composed of two-bedroom units. The one-time acceptance rate of engineering quality was to reach 95 percent or above, and the finished quality rate 25 percent or above.[4]

To sum up, the guiding principle of the live-in-peace social housing projects was to combine with other aspects of housing reform in order to promote overall success. Accordingly, the live-in-peace social housing was to be sold and managed as regular real estate, so as to set an example. At no time were the live-in-peace social housing projects to substitute for civil housing construction. According to the "Plan for Implementing the State 'Live-in-Peace' Project," the project began in 1995, was due for completion in five years, and has increased the expected level of construction area by 150 million square meters.

2.3.4. Low-rent Housing for the Lowest-income Earners

In May 1999, China adopted "Methods of Managing Low-rent Housing in Urban Areas." The purpose was to establish and improve a multi-layered system of housing supply and to solve the urban housing problem of families with the lowest income. Here, low-rent housing referred to ordinary housing provided to permanent urban residents with a family income at the lowest level; it formed part of the social security provisions of the government and work unit. There were several sources of such housing, including vacated former publicly owned housing that conformed to the standards of low-rent housing stipulated by the local government; existing publicly owned housing that conformed to standards stipulated by the local government regarding the construction area and usable area or fixtures; and housing for low rent constructed with funds provided by the government and work unit. It also included housing for low rent purchased with funds provided by the government and work unit; donated housing that conformed to the standards of housing for low rent; and housing acquired by the city or county government, through other channels, in accordance with the local conditions that conformed to the standards of housing for low rent. In all cases, the government set the rent standards, and existing publicly owned housing that conformed to local-government regulations for low rent could have its rent fixed according to its own governing policies. However, the rent of housing from other sources was, in principle anyway, to be fixed on the basis of maintenance expenses and management fees, and would be raised according to the rising level of the minimum income. Moreover, lessees were to go through procedures of application, verification and approval, as well as to provide other documents, such as proof of family income and a certificate of housing conditions, to the competent government department in charge. When a family income surpassed the minimum level set for the year, families that lived in low-rent housing were to report to the competent department in charge of real estate administration and vacate the housing according to a schedule. If the housing could not be vacated as scheduled for justifiable reasons, the lease could be extended for a certain period of time, upon approval, but the competent department for real estate administration was also supposed to raise the rent accordingly.

3. Planning of Residential Areas and Housing Design: A Turn in a Demand-driven Direction

Establishment of the socialist market economy has strongly promoted growth in the real estate industry, and the commercialization of housing has become a fundamental part of housing reform. Moreover, compared to the 1980s, in the process of transforming the planned economy into a market economy, living standards and people's quality of life have been markedly improved. Nevertheless, at the same time there is an unprecedented disparity between rich and poor in China, and this disparity seems certain to produce an extensive range of material and spiritual lifestyles, resulting in diversified development of housing. When compared with the 1980s, the variety of housing today is not merely reflected in its forms and residential standards, but is an objective reflection of differing social lifestyles. Residential area planning and housing design have shifted from a supply-driven commodity to one that is now demand driven.

3.1. Policies for a Modernized Housing Industry: Establishing a Mature System of Housing Construction, Circulation and Consumption

After 20 years of housing construction, the living space per capita in urban areas of China rose from 3.6 square meters in 1978 to 8.8

square meters in 1997, with concomitant improvements in the quality of residential area planning, design, construction and management. However, the level of industrialization and labor productivity in housing construction was still rather low, and, under such circumstances, it was inevitable that the state would attempt to develop the housing industry in a comprehensive and completely modern manner. Indeed, in 1996, the Ministry of Construction issued its "Outlines for the Trial Work of Modernizing the Housing Industry" and the "Outlines for the Technological Development of the Pilot Projects for Modernizing the Housing Industry." Henceforth, the modernization of the housing industry referred to a process "with planning and design as the driving force, and related materials and components as the base, whereupon a standardized, industrialized and market-oriented housing construction system should be gradually established, guided by new technology and aimed at large-scale, socialized production." According to this definition, modernization of the housing industry should be based on the planning, design and construction of residential areas. Already, comprehensive development with coordinated construction had proven in practice to be an effective approach, with beneficial economic, social and environmental results. Second, the housing industry was to orient itself towards the market, and the industrialization of housing was to focus energetically on developing affordable housing as the key to resolving prevailing housing problems. Third, by relying on progress in technology, the industrialization of housing would be guaranteed. The backwardness of housing was to construction resulted mainly from low levels of technology, and existing forms of construction have caused too much waste. Furthermore, the functional and qualitative improvement of housing depend on the application of new technologies. Fourth, the industrialization of housing was to adhere to strategic objectives of sustainable development. Energy, land and ecological issues are vitally interrelated in human development, especially as the contradictions between environmental protection and development become more and more acute. Accordingly, the industrialization of housing should seek to address these problems from the very beginning. Finally, the primary contents of housing industrialization should include the establishment and improvement of the dwelling structure and component system, provision of an adequate system of technological guarantees, quality control and supervision, and an adequate form of functional appraisal.

The production objectives of the housing industry were as follows. During the last four or five years of the twentieth century, an area of 240 million square meters was to be constructed in urban areas every year, and 560 million square meters in rural areas. In the first decade of the twenty-first century, an area of housing of 330 million square meters is to be constructed in urban areas per year, with 500 million square meters in rural areas. With regard to quality, the objectives were that every family should have a commodious apartment, with complete functions and a good environment, reflective of sustainable development.

The state formulated "Projects for Industrializing the Construction of Comfortable Housing in Urban and Rural Areas for the Year 2000" as a concrete measure to develop the housing industry further. More specifically, the projects contained the following two components. First, there were six key scientific research issues involved: guiding principles for planning and design of comfortable housing; the use of technology to guarantee the quality of living environments; research and development of housing products and policies; research in saving energy; comprehensive use of technology in rural areas; and the actual planning, construction and appraisal of comfortable housing projects. Second, a total of 50 to 60 residential areas of comfortable housing were to be built as models, totaling 10 million square meters and, on the basis of this construction, modernization of the housing industry was to be propelled forward and a new generation of housing established. By 1999, the planning and design of 63 residential areas of comfortable housing had been adopted, and the construction of 17 areas had begun, covering a total area of 2 million square meters, of which 90,000 square meters had been completed.

The industrialization of housing has profound significance for housing circulation, consumption and production. In the extensive discussion of housing industry policies among experts in various circles, a viewpoint was put forth that "industrialization of housing" refers to a reform that widely introduces advanced technology and management and, therefore, it has the same meaning as "the modernization of housing industry." Housing, however, is a special commodity with properties different than those of common consumer goods (e.g., a long consumption period and high prices). Therefore, in the modernization of the housing industry, emphasis should not be placed on construction housing at the expense of circulation and consumption (Zuo Ling, 1999).

3.2. People-centered Living Environments:
Proceeding from Demand

When housing becomes an expensive individual consumer good, consumers naturally become very discriminating in terms of the housing itself and its environment. Modern life brings with it not only an abundant supply of material, but also brand-new concepts of life, accompanied by modern technology and culture.

3.2.1. The Rise of Estate Management

In 1986, there were three residential areas listed by the Ministry of Construction in the first group of its pilot urban residential areas. Among them, the Yanzishan neighborhood in Jinan, had won the title as one of the Ten New Sceneries of Jinan City. However, twelve years later, the area had changed significantly. The main road became a messy and noisy peddlers' market. The sign honoring the area erected in front of the management center of the area was still there, but was covered by clothes hung on it by the peddlers. The housing groups had many additional buildings attached, and all the balconies were enclosed with colorful glass and looked like dovecotes. What made this happen? Backward management was a decisive factor. After the founding of New China, a mode of administrative supervision was adopted in estate management, whereby the owner of title took responsibility for the management of an area. After a residential area was constructed, it was faced with many problems, including the maintenance and renovation of apartment buildings, the maintenance and renewal of accessory facilities, the maintenance and management of public places, the maintenance and improvement of fire equipment, the management of bicycles and vehicles, as well as maintaining public security, cleaning public areas and generally tending to the area's landscape. As might be imagined, this was rather a hard job for an owner to assume.

Estate management in China is a specialized, social business enterprise, mainly concerned with conducting maintenance and management of apartment buildings, public facilities and related places associated with urban real estate development, and is now largely a result of China's economic reform. In 1981, a company for specialized management of commercial housing for foreigners was established in Shenzhen and, from then on, as real estate developed, people gradually began to accept this function in their lives. However, until the state issued its "Measures for the Management of Newly Constructed Residential Areas in Cities" in 1994, estate management was not established in law, and this legitimization of estate management services was seen as a way of supplying tidy, comfortable, safe and elegant living environments for residents. Currently, the Mingyayuan Project in Guangzhou is the National Excellent Pilot Residential Area, where the quality of its estate management is the guarantee of its fine living environment. There, a semiclosed style of management was adopted, providing for three levels of paid service. The public services included cleaning public spaces inside and outside of buildings; disposing of rubbish; planting trees, flowers and grass; handling residents' complaints; and maintaining public order. Special and on-demand services included maintenance and management of fire-fighting and anti-theft equipment, ordered cleaning of rooms, sending for a doctor and taking residents' children to school or kindergarten. In recent years, when intelligent supervisory measures were applied in some expensive residential areas, new means and methods of estate management emerged. For example, the Ruijingxincun residential area of Xiamen was equipped with a video intercom system, a wireless anti-theft alarm system, and a remote system for metering water, gas and electricity. If a road lamp did not work or some device was missing, security guards would enter the information code into their hand-held monitors. This code would then be transmitted to the server of the computing center, and the personnel of the corresponding section would respond, greatly improving overall management efficiency.

3.2.2. A Breakthrough in the Planning of Residential Areas

Since the reform and opening-up policies, the space of residential areas has all been planned and organized around housing clusters as basic units. The concept of housing clusters stems from understanding relationships between neighbors. Some research into living environments shows that most resident activities occur within housing clusters and that frequent communication between neighbors contributes to a strong relationship, which is in turn beneficial to the general psychological welfare of residents and the management of residential areas.

In China, the law stipulates that "the neighborhood committee is a grass-roots non-governmental organization for residents to manage, educate and serve themselves," and "in accordance with the living conditions of the residents, the neighborhood committee is generally set up within 100–700 households based on the principle of management convenience." Accordingly, when a residential area is planned, the form of a housing group is naturally combined with the management method of a neighborhood committee. Generally, a housing cluster comprises 500 households and a residential area is made up of several housing clusters. In addition, the space is equally divided for each housing group by the roads within the area. Thus, several housing clusters surround a public open space, which, particularly in pilot schemes, generally occupies ten to twenty hectares of land and is suitable for division among four housing groups, prompting some people to say, jokingly, that this arrangement is like "four dishes and one soup."

With new modes of area management appearing continuously, especially with specialized estate-management companies adopting advanced management techniques, the intermediate level of management service can be reduced and a high level and efficiency of estate management can be realized. Under such circumstances, the former mode of housing clusters is not needed. Besides, it has proven impossible for a single planning mode to exist in circumstances of continuous development and, consequently, the planning of high-standard residential areas has broken through the functional and conceptual limits of the housing cluster, allowing the formation of outdoor space to play a more prominent role. More specifically, by not being restricted by the scale of a housing cluster, both the layout of buildings and the distribution of public spaces are freer, and can be deployed to make distinctive arrangements in conformity with the surrounding context. For instance, the Chunyuan neighborhood, in Kunming—a pilot project of the Ministry of Construction—put forth the idea of weakening the hold of the housing cluster but strengthening the concept of the courtyard, thus improving the area's living environment and public facilities (Fig. 9-1).

Beside the conceptual breakthrough in the use of the housing cluster, denser residential areas have appeared during the process of renewing and renovating housing in cities, resulting in high-density urban developments. These residential areas integrate living functions, public service facilities, transport facilities and infrastructure facilities into one unit. Within one building complex, for instance, there are often shops, recreation and

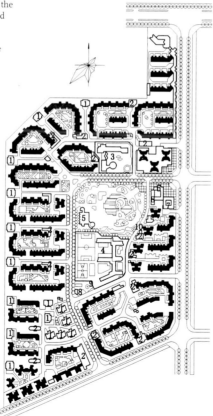

Fig. 9-1: Master plan of the Chunyuan neighborhood in Kunming

1   Detached Garden House
2   Bicycle Shed
3   Daycare/Kindergarten
4   Elementary School
5   Cultural Center
6   Office
7   Security
8   Electric Station
9   Water Tower
10 Gas Station

sports facilities, commercial centers and hospitals. This kind of residential area adopts an intensive type of arrangement and three-dimensional traffic management, while economizing on land and generally providing an excellent living environment for residents. Its spatial structure is completely different from that of traditional residential areas. The Fourth Xiaoyin Residential Area in Beijing, for example, the national model for a comfortable residential area, adopted this intensive type of planning and design. Supporting facilities are properly placed inside the complex, and thus most of the residents' daily needs can be satisfied without going outside. The residents and vehicles are separated through three-dimensional roadways and walkways and there are well-designed emergency routes for people and vehicles. Also, there was a three-dimensional, multi-level orientation taken toward landscape in order to "green" the area. And, within the apartments, comprehensive and rational wiring creates an excellent environment for different forms of computer equipment.

3.2.3. Construction of Community

Due to efforts made over the past few decades, China's housing construction has developed from a single-purpose approach to a multi-purpose perspective, and from the mere release from housing shortages to the pursuit of comfortable housing. Because of people's improving lifestyles, the residential area that only meets their physiological living needs is far from satisfactory. Moreover, when making a home purchase, people pursue their best interests, toward material and spiritual benefits. Therefore, policies worked out by the state for the development of comfortable houses and high-quality real estate place stress on creating a cultural community atmosphere that reflects harmony between people, as well as between man and nature. Consequently, citizens show great interest in the environment of the residential area as a whole during their home purchases, as well as the social strata of neighbors and the meaning of an area's architectural image. Following this approach, the Wanke Enterprise Group, a fairly successful enterprise in China, has developed the Wanke Urban Garden for rising wealthy white-collar workers and self-employed individuals, and has recorded good sales. The Soho Modern City in Beijing was built, from the very beginning, for well-educated customers of thirty to forty years in age. With a concept of the "single's agreement" to promote its modern and simple style, the Small Office Home Office (SOHO) apartments were designed to satisfy customers, providing the development with considerable success. By contrast, the Xingtao neighborhood puts stress on perfecting educational facilities, and the Xingtao School, in the residential area, is meticulously designed. In addition, the developer made a considerable investment to strengthen the school's teaching staff and, to date, the Xingtao neighborhood has been well received by consumers.

3.2.4. *Attaching Importance to the Ecological Environment*

The protection of environmental ecology is a global issue, and how to solve the apparent contradiction between construction and its demise has become important. Consequently, sustainable development is a principle that is widely applicable. Some issues, such as how fully and reasonably to utilize natural resources, and how to set up a harmonious relationship between man and nature, have been gradually advanced by architects and designers.

During the planning and design of the Beiluchun neighborhood, architects and planners conducted research about how to maintain the development of the ecology of the environment in a sustained way. Their purposes were as follows. First, they wanted to increase the purity of the atmosphere. Therefore, fuel and stoves for cooking and heating in the residential area would be placed under strict control, and the main roads in the city would be flanked by wide landscaped areas. Second, they wished to recycle waste water. Two sewage treatment stations were to be set up, handling waste water and rainwater, respectively. After being treated, the waste water was to be used to clean the roads, water the landscape and wash automobiles. Third, they wanted to recycle garbage within the residential area itself. Garbage-burning stoves, conforming to

Fig. 9-2: Master plan of the Beiluchun neighborhood in Beijing

advanced international standards, were to be used to control environmental pollution. Fourth, they were interested in the control of noise with the use of landscape elements and the establishment of grade-separated transportation facilities. Fifth, they wanted the area to be vegetated by trees, flowers and grass in a scientific manner, and emphasized the importance of growing trees for environmental protection. Finally, they wished to save energy by adopting new types of wall materials and energy-saving windows and by trying to use solar energy and geothermal power (Fig. 9-2).

Fig. 9-3: The Baishida neighborhood in Shenzhen

3.2.5. Solving the Problem of Car Parking in Residential Areas

More and more Chinese families now have cars, and the car has gradually become an important aspect of modern life, especially among people

Fig. 9-4: Parking building (foreground) of the Hongjing neighborhood in Zuhai

with high incomes living in expensive residential areas. Therefore, the fact that many residential areas have small parking lots, or have no parking at all, has become a prominent problem. Moreover, adding parking lots to residential areas not served by parking has proven difficult. Hence, more often than not, many cars are parked by the roadside and in vacant lots in front of houses, thus blocking traffic, polluting the environment, increasing noise and adversely affecting resident's daily lives. Comfortably off residential areas require that the number of parking bays accommodate 20 to 25 percent of the total number of households, for the first time in China. Now, there are various kinds of parking lots. Some are independent underground parking garages and others are underground or ground-level parking lots provided in direct connection with houses (Figs. 9-2 to 9-4). In the Baishida Garden in Shenzhen, for instance, there is a terrace between two houses. Under the terrace, residents can park their cars, and the top of the terrace is a place for outdoor activities. Furthermore, the well-designed skylight of the semi-underground parking lot provides scenery at the top of the terrace (Fig. 9-3). In 1999, the Beijing city government issued new regulations, specifying that in a newly designed residential area, the number of parking spaces for motor-driven vehicles should be equal to 30 to 50 percent of the total number of apartments and, for long-term design purposes, each household should have a parking space. Further, to avoid motor-driven vehicles occupying the green open space of residential areas, the number of ground-level parking spaces should not exceed 40 percent of the total number and the remainder should be in underground, semi-underground or multi-storey parking lots.

3.3. The Division of Social Strata and Enrichment of Residential Variety: An Inexorable Trend of the Market Economy

In order to resolve the contradiction of inadequate housing supply, strict restrictions were imposed on the standard of residential areas under the system of welfare-housing allotment. The standards of residential interior furnishings and equipment were also very low because of the limited level of state investment. In the 1980s, although an experiment in the commercialization of housing policy was carried out, the welfare housing allotment system still predominated and, as a result, residential standards were restricted by the state. With further diversification of the social economy and increasing pressure for housing reform, a multi-level housing supply system had taken shape by the mid- and late 1990s, with ready-built houses for sale and a predominance of affordable housing and comfortable housing projects. Recognizing different social strata, the state no longer imposed restrictions on the maximum floor space per apartment, although it continued to specify the minimum standard of floor area to guarantee reasonable housing. As a result, an unprecedented variety of houses with different living standards has emerged, with living spaces ranging from 40 square meters to more than 200 square meters. Different housing types have also appeared, such as high-rise houses, small high-rise housing (with approximately eight to ten storeys), multi-storey housing, low-rise high-density housing, terrace houses and villas. Beside traditional apartment plans—such as one bedroom and one living room, two bedrooms and one living room, and three bedrooms and one living room—houses with many living rooms and toilets have become more popular. Garages and servant rooms have also even become standard in some houses.

After the initial development and feverish stages of the
1980s and the early 1990s, the
real estate market became more
rational and specialized. Aimed
at diversified market demands
and different social strata, the
benefits of real estate development were not only directed
towards building houses and
seeking high density, but
human considerations also
became an increasingly important factor. Planning, construction, housing design and the

Fig. 9-5: Multi-storey housing with
independent entrances

construction of a residential culture were all aimed to show off individual characteristics in the marketing of real estate. For example,
Wanke Lily Garden broke the traditional concept of public stairs in
housing. Each individual unit contained two households covering
three storeys, and the upper unit had an independent staircase connected with the outside. The style resembled that of a villa, but with
the density of multi-storey housing (Fig. 9-5). Two-storey dwellings
were also available in some high-rise complexes, whose living
rooms occupied spacious areas suitable for high-income groups. As
a new innovation in the organization of indoor communications,
two passages were designed in some houses, mainly to guarantee
the autonomy of livingrooms. In effect, these configurations could
be regarded as an effort to perfect functional requirements under
the limited standards of a residential area (Fig. 9-6).

With a growing rate of household consumption, the exterior
style of housing was increasingly valued. As a result, houses were
named "Garden," "Manor," "Plaza" and "Lofty Housing Area." Various housing styles were designed, either stressing local cultural features or introducing the design styles and methods of foreign architecture. For example, many real estate development projects had a
preference for the so-called Continental European style, which had
no specific definition, and only referred to the classical Western
style in general, combining an exotic atmosphere with high-rise residential structures and forming a novel landscape for purchasers.
Most such houses manifested this Continental European style
through adopting the colors, column order, artificial molding and
roofs of Western classic architecture. The effects of imitation also
differed in numerous ways. Shenzhen's Baishida Garden and

Fig. 9-6: Plan of a double-circula-
tion house

Fig. 9-7: The Gubei neighborhood
in Shanghai

Fig. 9-8: The Mingdu Yuan
neighborhood in Shanghai

Fig. 9-9: The Donghai
neighborhood in Shenzhen

Shanghai's Gubei Housing Area remain typical examples (Figs. 9-3,
9-7 to 9-9).

Suzhou's Tongfangxiang Housing Area was a successful illustra-
tion acknowledging local characteristics. Efforts were made to maintain the style and features of Suzhou, a 2,500 year-old city. The
architectural style and detailing embodied the characteristics of its
domestic architecture—small and well-defined in volume, light and
graceful in shape, with white walls, black tiles and abundant space.
The scheme's outdoor courtyards resembled those of old Suzhou
gardens (Fig. 9-10).

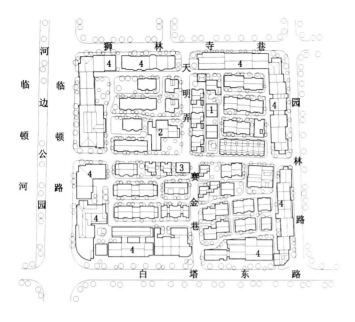

Fig. 9-10: Master plan of the
Tongfangxiang neighborhood in
Suzhou

1 Preserved Older Construction
2 Day care/Kindergarten
3 Electric Station
4 Public Facilities

3.4. Comfortable Housing Design

During the period, new standards were put forward for residential quality, in order to improve people's living standards and the state's policy of realizing its goal of providing comfortable housing. According to the state's policy of housing industrialization, in order to reach the standard of comfortable houses, five basic needs had to be satisfied. They were: excellent habitability, comfortableness, safety, durability and economy. Habitability included residential thermal properties, air quality, and an adequate acoustic and optical environment; comfortableness meant

effective house plans, adequate equipment, good design of kitchens and bathrooms, as well as visual effects to increase the apparent size of floor space. Safety included structural safety, fire prevention, precautions against burglars and anti-skidding on horizontal surfaces.

Durability referred to the residential structure and its durability, waterproofing and anticorrosion properties; finally, economy covered analysis and appraisal for establishing a viable cost. Compared with comfortable houses, some houses in the 1980s were too small in floor area to meet the need for separating public from private space, passive from active space, and providing the need for special space. The areas allotted to living rooms, kitchens, bathrooms and storerooms were also too small. The houses were technically backward, and poor in structural quality, wall materials and equipment. They were also low in their degree of standardization and the systematization of the equipment used, and other products were limited in their scales of production. Efforts were then made to improve techniques and to cut costs. Many efforts in housing design during the late 1980s and 1990s were therefore directed toward further study of the functional demands of housing and toward developing an appropriately packaged technology for the housing industry.

Different from the traditional sleep-type and subsistence-type houses, comfortable houses persisted in "taking mankind as their core" and making residences convenient, comfortable, harmonious and more closely connected in design with people's real living habits. Further attempts were made to design suites of rooms in various configurations, and there was a definite division between every two suites. Each suite had its own entrance and at least the basic complement of spaces, such as a bedroom, a livingroom, a kitchen, a bathroom and a storeroom. The space division of indoor functions became more meticulous as well as complete, and houses became more convenient for private use. In addition, the space provided for living, such as a diningroom and bedrooms, became larger. Each living area, though comparatively independent, shared common space with other rooms. The specific functional designation of rooms increased and, besides the usual bedrooms for guests and children's rooms, there were reading rooms, fitness rooms, working rooms and cloakrooms. To meet the needs of increasing domestic electrical appliances, efforts were made to design complete kitchens. Working balconies were also enlarged to make them more comfortable. Suggestions were put forward for the spatial arrangement of each functional activity in "A Guide to a Model Comfortable Housing Area." These included: separating public rooms from private areas, diningrooms from bedrooms, livingrooms from bedrooms, and clean rooms from those that would become dirty. Housing patterns also tended to become more rational. Fig. 9-11, for instance, vividly illustrates the analysis of components of the model of a "comfortable house."

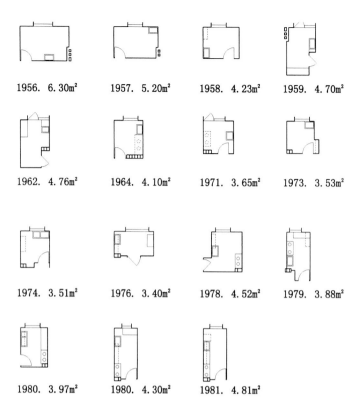

1956. 6.30m²   1957. 5.20m²   1958. 4.23m²   1959. 4.70m²

1962. 4.76m²   1964. 4.10m²   1971. 3.65m²   1973. 3.53m²

1974. 3.51m²   1976. 3.40m²   1978. 4.52m²   1979. 3.88m²

1980. 3.97m²   1980. 4.30m²   1981. 4.81m²

With the improvement of living standards, kitchens, bathrooms and toilets received more emphasis and became more colorful, rich and complicated in their furnishings, sometimes producing extensive technical and construction problems. Consequently, the level of pre-fabricated assembly of kitchens and bathrooms became a part of industrialization and the attempt to improve living quality. After all, the comfortable housing model demanded that they should not only satisfy functional needs, but also be commodious.

In a house in the mid-term of the 1950s and 1960s, a toilet with a pit and a kitchen with a coal stove were normal (Fig. 9-11). By contrast, the standard equipment in a kitchen of a comfortable house included a kitchen range, a cooking table, a sink, shelves, upper and lower cupboards, a garbage disposal and a refrigerator. In the bathroom there was a toilet, a bathtub, a shower, a washbasin, a wastometer, a mirror, a washing machine, an air-exhaust flue and mechanical exhaust equipment. In layout, they were divided into the functional areas of urination and defecation, shower, face washing and clothes washing. Two or even three bathrooms were available in a large suite of rooms in some dwellings.

In comfortable houses, the scientific and technological contents were to be improved to guarantee excellent habitability, comfort, safety, durability and economy, principles that had been stressed since the Ministry of Construction conducted their earlier experiments in urban housing. During the mid-term of the 1990s, the science and technology involved in housing development became key issues. The earlier demonstration and experimental housing projects were required to adopt new materials, products and technologies, while the comfortable houses at the end of the 1990s stressed the use of more packaged technologies. The development of housing science and technology mainly included new structures and wall materials, as well as heat preservation and insulation. It involved development of energy-saving windows and development of internal dividing wall products to meet the demands for the flexible separation in large rooms. Improvement in kitchens and toilets was also another important task, including applying new tubular products and developing new interface products to make pipelines invisible. Moreover, better elevator technologies for middle- and high-rise housing developments were and remain important. Besides these basic housing requirements, many needs must be satisfied in the information society of the twenty-first century, such as office work, education, entertainment, guest reception, physical exercise and parking.

Due to the broadening variety of needs, the level of intelligence involved in residential buildings will be improved increasingly. This includes the establishment of computer-automated management centers in residential areas with automatic calculation and collection for water, electricity, gas and heat. The closing down of residential areas by automatic monitoring of security, fire and harmful gas leakages are also all in line with this type of development. In addition, service-call systems, centralized management of key equipment and installation with remote supervisory control of its operational state, as well as computer networks connected to the city to share information and resources, are quite likely. All of these systems will be capable of rendering public services, automatic forms of medical treatment, recreation and business through network terminals, as well as providing electronic reading materials and publications over domestic computers. In short, integration of modern information systems will likely be carried out in housing areas to achieve the goal of improving environmental quality, offering effective management and reducing costs and the number of working days.

Notes

1. *China Reform and Development Report 1992–1993* (Chinese Economic Publishing House, 1994).
2. Speech of Chen Xuebin, Director of the State Council Reform Office, at the Symposium on China's Housing System, Xinhua News Agency, June 16, 1997.
3. Plan of the State Council for Implementing the "Live-in-Peace" Social Housing Project, January 20, 1995.
4. Opinions of the Ministry of Construction on the Implementation of the State "Live-in-Peace" Project, March 8, 1995.

Conclusion

by Peter G. Rowe

Since the onset of the Opium War in 1840, the road to modernization in China has been long, arduous and full of ups and downs. At
the beginning of the twenty-first century, the country finds itself in
the position of being moderately well-developed by most measures,
still relatively poor and saddled with outmoded economic and institutional practices, in spite of recent successes and a resurgence of
interest in urbanization. As narrated in this book, China has gone
through three relatively distinct periods of development. The first,
spanning from 1840 to 1949, was characterized by relatively sustained foreign contact and occupation, as well as a diminution of
influence in the prevailing feudal society. Modern industries were
established, a break was made with the centuries-old dynastic form
of rule, and modern cities began to emerge, most notably Shanghai
and several smaller cities in the north like Harbin, Qingdao and
Dalian. In a trajectory not too dissimilar from other countries,
industrialization begat urbanization and modern forms of real
estate development began to emerge. Housing progressed through
the incremental modification and adoption of traditional housing
types to a more modern way of life, and foreign contact and partial
occupation provided avenues for the introduction of new building
technologies and different styles of (mainly Western) housing. For
the most part the beneficiaries of this progress were well-off members of society, as the differentiation between upper and lower social
strata persisted and even became more exaggerated, while the middle class and their influence—so much a hallmark of modernization
elsewhere—remained small.

The second period, beginning with the People's Republic of
China in 1949 and spanning until 1978, was dominated by revolutionary social ideology in an attempt to make a complete transition
into communism. Most, if not all, of the socio-political and economic framework of the prior period was either suspended or obliterat-
ed, often with very grave consequences, in an apparent search for a
broader and, to many, a better socialist way of life. Foreign influence
was confined to the early stages, largely through the former Soviet
Union, with which China had a shared ideological perspective, after
which China charted its own course through the Great Leap Forward and the Cultural Revolution. Investment in housing suffered

appreciably under the guiding philosophy of "production first and livelihood second" and, as housing became a "ration article" of social welfare provided by the state in a time of almost steadily declining fortune, poverty and very poor shelter conditions became the rule rather than the exception. This was also a time of standardization and the almost exclusive construction of multi-storey dwellings in urban areas, and when both the standards and quality of construction, with few exceptions, were never allowed to vary from what could be afforded as the lowest common denominator.

The third period, in which China still finds itself, spans from 1978 to 2000 and was marked by sweeping economic and to some extent social reform, as well as an opening-up to the outside world. After numerous debates, adjustments and experiments, a market economy has returned to China, including real estate development, albeit in an evolving socialist form. Sharp rises in relative income for many, together with external events, like the Southeast Asian economic crises of 1997, have now pushed the state into adopting a posture of encouraging individual home ownership, together with a variety of financial and management mechanisms to ensure social fairness and rising quality in housing. Now, with widening gaps in personal income and housing opportunity, a diversity of housing has appeared once more in China, although, for reasons of land and other economic constraints, largely confined to multi-storey and high-rise buildings in burgeoning urban areas. From around 1985 onwards, apartment-style living, with a full complement of services and rooms reserved largely for specific functions, has appeared broadly in China for the first time, almost completing the evolution, as it were, of the modern dwelling. Today, China faces many of the same housing problems encountered elsewhere in the developed and developing world and with many similar market mechanisms and institutional practices in place, as well as turning its attention to a prodigious program of catch-up and to accommodating rapidly rising future increases in urban population. Nevertheless, like most if not all nation states, its future in housing also belongs in its past, and there one finds some very distinctive episodes of broader interest, as well as features that seem to have persisted in spite of China's at times chaotic and inconsistent pattern of modernization.

1. Welfare Versus Commodity

Certainly the most distinctive aspect of housing in China, at least during the past fifty years if not before, has been the extreme positions taken in the fundamental way in which housing was provided.

Throughout the world, many societies have struggled with the idea of housing as a commodity, which is developed and then bought and sold in the real estate marketplace, and the extent to which governments must intervene in order to ensure some modicum of equity and adequate accommodation for all. By now, the preponderance of conventional wisdom has it that the provision of housing is usually best left to the marketplace to produce and distribute efficiently, with in-kind or monetary subsidies for those who can ill afford it. This process certainly characterizes what has occurred in the developed countries of the Western world over the past fifty to one hundred years, and is largely seen as a successful model for others to follow, including, nowadays, China. It does not, however, mean that the state is uninvolved, and both opinion and practice have varied considerably with regard to the extent to which housing should be viewed as a fundamental entitlement, sometimes verging on a public good. Usually, governments have intervened strongly during times of economic depression, when private capital for the housing enterprise was scarce and demand was high, and taken a hands-off attitude when times were more favorable. Some, like the Netherlands and Singapore, for instance, have closely linked housing with urban policy, building at consistently high rates as urban population has expanded, and contracting the state's role when it has not. Others with generally strong economies, such as the United States and Japan, have taken a more laissez-faire attitude towards social distribution, although sometimes, as in the United States during the Great Depression, they have made housing a more central part of national economic policy for putting people back to work and stimulating internal demand, much as China has done recently. Nowhere, however, has the same state regime taken such an extreme set of views on housing provision and on such a scale as in China, moving essentially from the remnants of a free-market system of private ownership to absolute public ownership and social welfare provision and then back—albeit with more and better guarantees of social fairness—to a market-oriented system once again.

Quite apart from issues of the broad efficacy of socialist versus private enterprise provision, in which the latter surely seems to be the best for the most, at least outside of times of severe economic crises, China's extreme trajectory through fundamentally different modes of housing provision highlights the very different ways in which housing can be understood both as a good and as a component of a living environment. During the failed experiments of the Great Leap Forward and the Cultural Revolution, investment in housing was quite literally forced to sink as low as less than 1 percent of Gross National Product in favor of other higher priority forms of production like heavy industry. As a result of pressing housing shortages to begin with, as well as a lack of anything like adequate maintenance, housing supply declined drastically with regard to demand to the lowest point in living memory, resulting in an appallingly low 3.6 square meters of habitable space per person, most of it unappointed and of very low quality. Moreover, these conditions became so extreme that in order to compensate materially and psychologically, so to speak, inhabitants appear to have shifted the centrality of their expectations of housing in their daily lives to somewhere else, usually to much larger and often better-appointed environments outside. Terms like "ration article" and "sleep-type unit" crept into the language—hardly those one would associate readily with more conventional definitions of house as home, certainly, or of one's dwelling place occupying a significant position in one's life. More interesting, though, were the less extreme moments in China's socialist program, when still relatively meager housing standards did begin to take hold, but were clearly orchestrated together with other measures of communal environmental amenity outside of the dwelling unit itself. Reading between the lines, so to speak, one gets the impression that a duality something like "I live here but stay there" was a prominent feature of Chinese life at the time, or, perhaps more accurately, it was more than a duality in that distinctions between private, communal and public life were rendered less sharp than in other foreign locales where very different concepts like "home," "work" and "places of recreation" came into play. While certainly not condoning for a moment the often appalling conditions in which people stayed, the rather exaggerated multi-faceted definition of a dwelling environment that emerges is not entirely without merit in any critical reappraisal that might be made of other contemporary dwelling environments. For one thing, it avoids the almost automatic conventional conflation of all aspects of dwelling into one particular environment—the house. For another, it allows freer reign to consider more thoroughly the social-transactional spaces of daily life and how they might be shaped best. However, with the return of private ownership to China, the centrality of the house and its power to bring together many aspects of life has also returned. Indeed, as described in detail in the third part of this narrative, the modern dwelling with all its special functions, services and appointments is now being widely sought after. What the full impact of this rather sudden change will be on Chinese social, communal and public life is still difficult to answer in full. It seems certain, nevertheless, to create much sharper distinctions between the various conceptual compartments of life and the physical environments that might otherwise go with those distinctions.

Finally, another aspect worth noting in the swing towards housing as a form of welfare, and then as a commodity, was the point of emanation of the reforms involved. Unlike the West, for instance, they occurred first in rural areas, and were shaped by more or less successful experimentation that took place there. This was certainly the case with the People's Commune Movement, and also later on with initial market experiments during the earlier stages of the post-1978 reforms and opening to the outside world. In a country with the overwhelming majority of people living in the countryside and a strongly agrarian-based political ideology, such phenomena may also appear easily understandable. Nevertheless, it is striking when one thinks of most processes of modernization originating in urban areas and when the ultimate outcome is usually city life itself. Without making too much of the issue, it also illustrates the different circumstance of China with regard to modern housing, and how certain assumptions about predominant models of modernization *ergo* urbanization should be questioned.

2. Urbanization

Levels of urbanization in China have been and remain low, particularly relative to many developed and modernized countries elsewhere in the world. During the early socialist period, the proportion of the population living in urban areas dropped as low as 15 to 16 percent, rising to the present level of 30 to 35 percent, with the expectation of reaching 55 percent by the year 2030. this compares with a present level of 72 to 75 percent for the United States, a similar proportion for Japan and as high as 80 or 85 percent in places like Korea and Australia. Often, urbanization is equated with modernization and a strong shift away from agricultural production as a major source of employment and, according to this measure, China, though improving rapidly, is economically still relatively underdeveloped. There are, however, other mitigating circumstances behind this apparently low level of urbanization that obscure, to some extent, the degree of modernization. Throughout much of its relatively recent history, China has been self-consciously aware of the scarcity of available land—primarily confined in measures of productivity to its three large river basins—and sought to actively discourage urban encroachment. Today, a general policy of containing the outward extension of large cities, while encouraging the growth of smaller cities and discouraging the proliferation of small towns and hamlets, is in effect. Economically, a relatively high degree of industrialization has occurred in smaller settlements in the countryside at or near the origin of surplus labor, and networks of productive enterprises have been formed to produce a wide variety of manufactured goods and services. In effect, distinctive zones have materialized in the closely populated countryside, characterized by both intensive agricultural and non-agricultural production, with rapidly improving transportation between sub-centers within each zone. Many areas of the Changjiang Delta, west of Shanghai, for example, operate in this manner, and today the so-called township-village enterprises account for close to 30 percent of China's Gross Development Product. What the future will hold for this pattern of settlement and production is again difficult to predict. However, it does seem likely that agglomerations in the economic scale of many forms of production will push further in the direction of more fully fledged urbanization.

While remaining relatively unorganized, cities and towns in China have almost always been and remain very dense. Indeed, during the Qing Dynasty of the nineteenth century, China had several cities of a population in excess of one million inhabitants, larger and denser then comparable urban situations in the West. If anything, under prevailing current conditions of land scarcity and high urban development costs, urban densities are rising in many places. As described in this text, the past fifty years of housing construction have been dominated almost exclusively by multi-storey developments, and high-rise residential construction has been a fixture on the Chinese urban scene since at least the late 1930s. In fact, Shanghai today has more high-rise buildings than practically any other city on earth, most of them residential accommodations. There and in Hong Kong, where spot densities consistently reach as high as 2,000 people per hectare, the phenomenon often referred to as hyperdensity is emerging. Other than living close together—a condition with which the Chinese have already had lengthy experience—it is difficult to say what the full effects of hyperdensity might be on the urban residential experience. Certainly it does not necessarily mean a diminution of convenience and access, as amply demonstrated by Hong Kong's multi-level and multi-modal transportation system and dense array of non-residential establishments, and by substantial similar improvements now being made in Shanghai. Nor does it necessarily mean a diminution in light or open-space amenity, although the manner in which they are provided may vary significantly, at times, from at- or near-ground living conditions. A more direct engagement with large surrounding geographic features like rivers, mountains and harbors, for instance, seems likely, and open-space use of intermediate levels, often well above ground level, becomes practical if not necessary. It probably does mean, however, an overall perception and experience of urban and urban-residential space that verges on a difference in kind rather than simply one of degree. Verticality, for example, combining the sensations of constantly moving vertically through urban space, a predominant vertical cone of visual and associated perception, and rather consistent attention to the multi-layered aspect of urban environments, will undoubtedly effect and reshape commonplace experiences and familiarity with urban life. The elongated temporal parenthesis experienced by many high-rise dwellers before joining the maddening crowd below may also have a constituent effect on senses of community and privacy, especially when combined with so many other evident symbolic reminders of the sheer density of nearby precincts.

Another related aspect of emerging housing conditions in China is the sheer rate of urbanization and the rather immediate "strange new world" effect it will have on many rural immigrants. While very rapid urbanization has occurred elsewhere in the world at different times, for example in Chicago during the latter part of the nineteenth century, fully 500 million more urban dwellers are expected in China during the next thirty years. Moreover, many if not most have had practically no prior urban experience, given the persistence and strong enforcement of China's household registration system. Although the effect of this sudden change of living environment is also difficult to gauge fully, it will surely be palpable in the future majority's perception and appreciation of life and the manner in which they lay claim to issues on the national agenda. It was often said of Shanghai during its heyday in the 1930s that it was like no other place in China. This affect of "otherworldliness" now seems likely to spread both widely and rapidly and, when it becomes more fully familiar, the impact on Chinese society will likely be considerable. For example, a rise in the middle class—never a strong constituency in China—seems likely to exert a more considerable influence. Already it has begun to take hold in several urban settings and the early traces of civil society have begun to emerge. Moreover, this modern trend in social development, barring outside intervention or intervention from the top, seems likely to continue and intensify and, if nothing else, it will further reshape China's residential environment.

3. Standardization and Industrialization

Throughout various phases of its modern housing development, China has placed considerable emphasis on industrialization as a primary means of production. Moreover, this attention was not confined to the socialist period, when it might have been expected, but extended back in time to other episodes of mass housing construction in the trading port cities and in the emerging company towns in the north, where contact with new imported building materials and technologies was most direct. As elsewhere in the world, acute housing shortages and a scarcity of resources made the promise of greater "throughput" capacity and material efficiency, inherent in industrialization, very appealing. Indeed, it has enjoyed and continues to enjoy an almost unshakeable confidence within China's housing construction industry, in spite of significant disappointments and failures.

Nevertheless, the consistent style of industrialization has often been quite specific, particularly in comparison to other approaches practiced elsewhere in the world. Essentially it has involved *a priori* standardization of building components and dwelling unit layouts into relatively narrow and fixed reference designs, to which engineering and material considerations have been brought to bear in order to produce a fully manufactured and mass-produced product. At least this appears to have been a persistent aim, even though the actual experience with emulating other forms of manufacturing, such as heavy industry, often fell well short of its goal, amounting to low levels of technological development. This conceptual approach may also be contrasted rather sharply with other forms of housing industrialization, as for example in the United States, where far less emphasis has been placed on an endpoint of production and far more on the shape and variety of intermediate components, materials, construction techniques and process management. The difference conforms closely with Buckminister Fuller's distinction, made during the late 1930s, between what he termed "mass production" and "industrialization," where the latter referred to the conceptional realm of organizational principles whereby many different products could be produced, rather than the optimization of a specific set, aimed towards a lesser variety of possible outcomes. Considerable conformity has arisen from the American style of housing construction and at far lower densities although, given the instances of practical variety that have also emerged, this is probably a matter of cultural preferences in the form of modern housing than of particular technical processes.

Of greater significance in China, though, has been the fundamental functional insistence on standardization in lockstep with top-down administrative predetermined reactions to prevailing economic circumstances and social positions. Thus, housing often became the very mirror of society rather than something more muddled and confusing. When times were bad, housing standards, almost across the board, were contracted by fiat and, when times were prosperous, they were improved appreciably, with various fine-tuned adjustments being made in-between these two positions. All of this is probably very understandable in a country where citizens are constantly coping with and still cope with very poor, or relatively poor, economic conditions. Indeed, most of this book has focused on the process of housing modernization that has been largely conformed to the richer eastern coastal regions of China, where it has actually occurred, in contrast with the persistent poverty of the western and central regions, where it has had less of an impact. And, of course, housing standardization has its advantages by ensuring adequate living space, light and ventilation requirements for inhabitants. Nevertheless, such a dominant and singular version of standardization in basic function and layout can also produce inefficiencies in provision, when and where people's dwelling needs and acceptable preferences are more diversified and unexpectedly varied. Judging from elsewhere, investment in renovation and reuse of building *per se*, residential or otherwise, can often give fuller reign to these more vicarious demands and, consequently, housing takes on a less monolithic complexion across the face of a city. Again, the ultimate impact of this persistent history of standardization from above—and with it, the definition of housing—is difficult to assess fully. The variety of housing has certainly risen during the recent years of relative prosperity, sometimes even appearing as the pursuit of diversity for its own sake, rather than a concerted effort by people to house themselves in a fuller experiential and cultural manner. Novelty, after all, has its appeal in most forms of cultural development, and it remains to be seen how many Chinese, when given the opportunity, will seek to transcend matters of function and handed-down prescriptions for housing. In short, particular technological means of production and related functional measures of adequacy, if not a success, have conditioned understanding of what housing can be in China, and this cycle has fed on itself for a long time without interruption, producing a version of "what you can get is what you can see!"

4. Formal Trends and Foreign Influences

As reiterated several times in this book, the formal aspects of modern housing in China, with regard to matters of shape and appearance, have followed several reasonably distinct trends. Early on, during the semifeudal and semicolonial period of the nineteenth and early twentieth centuries, the single-storey residential compound and traditional courtyard form of Chinese housing was gradually transformed to accommodate evolving needs. Family size came down, thus requiring less space. Urbanization increased and, with both a scarcity of available land and purchasing power on the part of many urban inhabitants, household dwelling units also became smaller. This general trend could be observed in the Shikumen linong houses in Shanghai and the southeast, as well as in the northern-style courtyard housing. The introduction of foreign terrace houses into the same urban circumstances also had an influence on the evolution of the traditional form of housing, resulting in a new round of hybrid development combining features of both types in the form of two-, three- and sometimes four-storey linong or lane houses, with courtyards and small private gardens attached. Meanwhile, particularly during the period between 1910 and 1930, different types of foreign housing were also introduced, forming a second trend. These included semidetached and detached single-family housing—usually for the well-to-do in the concession districts of treaty port cities and in places like Harbin in the north, also under strong foreign influence—as well as multi-storey walk-up apartment buildings and, later on, high-rise dwellings. Overall, by the late 1930s, the urban residential landscape in China was dominated by clustered multi-storey housing, built primarily of masonry and ranging in architectural expression from Chinese gate, wall, roof and other decorative motifs to unabashedly modern. Often the architectural character of residences reflected prevailing tastes in the foreign country of influence, like the half-timbered and steeply-gabled roofs in German Qingdao, or neoclassicism in prominent areas of the French concession in Shanghai. As the People's Republic of China took over after 1949, multi-storey housing intensified under strong Soviet influence, producing row upon row of five- and seven-storey dwellings with various forms of vertical access. High-rise towers and apartment buildings were also introduced, in attempts to increase density and to improve land-use efficiency, with the result that today's urban residential landscape is still further dominated by multi-storey buildings, even though the variety and scale during recent years has increased appreciably.

Residential area planning also received its fair share of foreign influences, with the planning of what amounted to new communities, where foreign powers and international companies were free to experiment with the latest practices of the day. Subsequently, "garden city" principles, "neighborhood unit" concepts and even neo-classical town-planning layouts were tried out and employed to develop new sections of existing towns. Over time, debates arose over the use of perimeter-block apartment configurations, closely defining the underlying street network, and parallel housing cluster arrangements with open space in-between, the tide turning eventually in favor of the latter. Throughout much of this history an incipient or administratively imposed three-part consideration of residential planning issues was employed. The first level was for the residential area as a whole, often reaching a very large scale on the order of a district. The second was at the level of the neighborhood cluster and the third at the building and unit level. Of these, the neighborhood cluster was perhaps the most consistent, sometimes earning the nickname of "four dishes and one soup" because of its distinctive layout, although, as pointed out in the last chapter, recent administrative and management changes have potentially weakened the hold of this physical arrangement on people's lives.

Absorption of foreign influences in the typological development of modern Chinese urban housing also had a distinctive, although not unusual pattern. The first step usually involved copying foreign models directly. This was certainly often the case in the trading port concessions and in the cities to the north, where the new housing type was introduced by the foreigners themselves. It also occurred at the beginning of the People's Republic when the Soviet standard model was simply adopted. What followed was an incremental process by which the foreign model was adapted to prevailing Chinese dwelling conditions, resulting in successive transformations. The most self-conscious example of this process was the way in which room layouts, space standards and manners of entry and egress, as well as orientation, were gradually and yet systematically altered from the original Soviet model. Almost without exception, subsequent transformations of a particular housing type did not result in a new type altogether. The one exception was the linong housing, which seems to be anchored in both the western terrace house and the Chinese courtyard house traditions, but is a relatively distinctive housing type in its own right. In this case, the beginning of successive transformation appears to have started in the Chinese tradition, rather than the other way around. However, in this kind of discussion one also has to ask how many fundamentally different housing types can be imagined, *ceteris paribus*, to which the answer is probably not many and, therefore, the expectation of there being an entirely new residential landscape is rather unlikely. Comparatively, cross-sectional design development of housing and wide experimentation with different forms of dwelling-unit aggregation were not a strong part of the historical architectural evolution of housing in China. Nevertheless, the successful rise and persistent deployment of the modernist idea of housing blocks in a landscape setting—sometimes referred to as "slabs in the park"—was a distinctive aspect of Chinese residential area development. In spite of conspicuous failures of this idea elsewhere, it appears to have become well adapted to Chinese living conditions and made workable through a combination of social management, real use of the outdoor ground level space and, perhaps, the lack of any other clear alternatives. In sum, foreign influences appear to have been copied, then modified and finally indigenized as relatively recognizably Chinese. Moreover, this process is not dissimilar from the introduction of foreign technologies elsewhere, such as in Japan, even if the final results are less distinctive and less likely to form models for still others to copy and absorb. Throughout, as described in the text, a relatively small number of prototypes have formed the backbone of the general process of adaptation and transformation, even to the point of monotony, by the Chinese people's own admission. For the most part, they have been clustered forms of multi-storey housing arising out of both the Chinese tradition and foreign importations, the Soviet standard model of apartment dwelling and its variants and, more recently, the by-now common international practice of high-rise building.

5. Future Developments

What the future will hold for Chinese housing remains uncertain. In many ways China still stands at the beginning of a truly modern era of development. Nevertheless, there are several aspects that augur well for the future. First, high residential densities could serve China positively with regard to further community development, environmental sustainability, and rational land use in the tradeoffs that are inevitably there between arable and urbanized land. Further, this could be reinforced by the relatively fine grain of mixed-use and interdigitation of a variety of non-residential uses, which is a widely present aspect of China's urbanization. In practically all situations, high density could bring substantial economies of scale and technical efficiencies in recycling, transportation and public service delivery. Moreover, high density seems to be absolutely required if further substantial declines in cultivated land are to be avoided.

Second, and as a corollary to the issue of density, the strong linkage between housing and urban policy in general will be of paramount importance in the future, as China seeks to adequately accommodate a further 500 million urban dwellers and rehabilitate the urban living conditions of those already located in cities. On the face of it, although high sustained rates of production will be required, this does not seem fundamentally to be a problem of housing production *per se*, but rather one of coordination with other urban functions and the provision of sufficient flexibility in urban district configuration, so as not to have to start all over again once the more stable level of urbanization has been reached. Currently, the rate of new urban housing construction is around 240 million square meters per annum, with an additional 560 million square meters in rural areas, and is expected to rise soon to 330 million square meters of urban housing and 500 million square meters of rural housing per annum during the decade 2000–2010. Arithmetically, if sustained, this would allow the projected new urban population to be accommodated at close to twenty square meters per person—well above the present national average—and with a further swing of overall housing production in favor of urban areas, necessary rehabilitation and replacement might also be accomplished. Furthermore, the overall rate of housing production, by similar measures, would amount to around 10 dwelling units per 1,000 population and, although high by international standards over such a long duration, does not seem to be out of the question. Both the Netherlands and Singapore accomplished reasonable sustained rates of 15 dwelling units and above, per 1,000 population, during recent times, although in Singapore's case probably with some dislocation in the national economy. The highest annual rate of production in the United States was 11.2 dwelling units per 1,000 population in 1972, although there the baseline of already well-established housing stock was very much higher and the need far less than in China. Nevertheless, in spite of the favorable arithmetic, in more than doubling its present urban population of around 370 million in the comparatively short period of 30 years, China is confronting an enormous and unprecedented task, raising all sorts of questions about sustained wherewithal, economic stability, institutional evolvement, further market expansion and rational coordination with other policies. Furthermore, the widening gap between those who can afford housing and those who cannot—let alone the overall need to substantially raise the quality of urban housing in so many quarters—also should give pause to those predicting a successful outcome. Here, continual application and further development of the embryonic social security system now in place will be required. At least for much of the future under consideration here, market housing cannot be the only answer.

Turning to the matter of a rapidly evolving urban-residential culture, the differences between now and then are also likely to be significant, involving China, along the way, with a distinctive orientation. As noted earlier, a relatively ingrained tolerance and even exploitation of looser distinctions between conventional conceptual categories of urban dwelling and the physical components in which they might be normally housed could continue to shape this different cultural outlook. Further, hyperdensity and its effects on the experience and appreciation of urban living could lend another element to this evolving cultural attitude, together with the effects of estrangement, and then familiarity, on so many with little prior urban experience. In addition, the concentration of significant elements of an emerging middle class, along with the accoutrements of civil society, will be a new experience for China. Finally, age-old distinctions between urbanism and the countryside, abetted by this sudden estrangement on the one hand, but also ameliorated by a heightened sense of environmental interdependency on the other, could also shape the future urban culture. Again, cultural development of almost any kind is difficult to predict, and the potentially radical effects that such a turn of events might have on a nation that is only now rapidly modernizing and has primarily lived before in rural circumstances, could be substantial, leading to unforeseen impacts on future urban housing. In these regards alone, modern urban housing in China is still in its infancy.

Bibliography

Part One:

Bao Muping & Shen Xinrong. "The Modern Plan for Manchuria Railway Construction Company Housing in Shenyang in the 1930s." In *Collected Thesis of the 5th Seminar on Modern Architectural History of China*, Wang Tan & Zhang Fuhe, eds. Beijing: China Construction Industry Publishing House, 1998.

Bureau of Social Affairs, the City Government of Greater Shanghai. *Standard of Living of Shanghai Laborers*. Shanghai: Shanghai China Publishing House, 1934.

Chen Bochao, ed. *A General Survey of China's Modern Architecture, Shenyang Volume*. Beijing: China Construction Industry Publishing House, 1995.

Civic Affairs Bureau of Nanjing. *Report of Working Affairs Bureau.* 1937.

Ding Richu. *Economic History of Modern Shanghai (Vol. 1, 1843–1894)*. Shanghai: Shanghai People's Publishing House, 1994.

Dong Jianhong, ed. *Development History of Chinese Cities*. Taibei: Mingwen Publishing House, 1984.

Gao Zhonglin. *Modern Architecture in Tianjin*. Tianjin: Tianjin Science and Technology Publishing House, 1990.

Guo Husheng, ed. *A General Survey of China's Modern Architecture, Xiamen Volume*. Beijing: China Construction Industry Publishing House, 1993.

Guo Shihao, ed. *The Workers' Conditions of the Kailuan Coal Mine in Old China*. Beijing: People's Publishing House, 1985.

Hou Youbin, ed. *A General Survey of China's Modern Architecture, Harbin Volume*. Beijing: China Construction Industry Publishing House, 1992.

Hu Sheng. *From The Opium War to May 4th Movement*. Beijing: Red Flag Publishing House, 1990.

Hu Shuzhi, ed. *A General Survey of China's Modern Architecture, Xiamen Volume*. Beijing: China Construction Industry Publishing House, 1992.

Huang Jiantong & Li Pei. "The Villages for Common People in Shanghai." In *Selected Historical Accounts of Past Events of Shanghai*, vol. 63. Shanghai: Shanghai People's Publishing House, 1989.

Li Chuanyi, ed. *A General Survey of China's Modern Architecture, Wuhan Volume*. Beijing: China Construction Industry Publishing House, 1992.

Liu Songfu. "China Eastern Railway Houses for Workers in Harbin." In *Collected Thesis of the 3rd Seminar on Modern Architectural History of China*. Wang Tan, ed. Beijing: China Construction Industry Publishing House, 1991.

Liu Xianjue, ed. *A General Survey of China's Modern Architecture, Nanjing Volume*. Beijing: China Construction Industry Publishing House, 1992.

Luo Shuwei. *The Modern History of Tianjin City*. Beijing: China Social Science Publishing House, 1993.

Luo Suwen. *Great Shanghai-Shikumen: Ordinary Families*. Shanghai: Shanghai People's Publishing House, 1991.

Luo Zhiru. *Shanghai in the Statistics Table*. Nanjing: National Research Institute of Social Science, 1932.

Ma Xiuzhi, ed. *A General Survey of China's Modern Architecture, Guangzhou Volume*. Beijing: China Construction Industry Publishing House, 1992.

Nanjing City Government, *The Past and Future of the Workers' Housing in Nanjing*. (government materials), 1935.

Pi Mingxiu, *The Modern History of Wuhan City*. Beijing: China Social Science Publishing House, 1993.

Qi Dayun & Ren Antai. *A Hundred Years of Ups and Downs—The Path of Development of National Industry and Commerce in Modern China*. Beijing: China Radio and Television Publishing House, 1991.

Qiao Hong. *Annals of Urban Construction in Tianjin*. Beijing: China Science and Technology Publishing House, 1994.

Qiao Zhiqiang, ed. *The Modern History of Chinese Society*. Beijing: People's Publishing House, 1992.

Sha Yongjie, Lu Wei & Ji Yan, "The Development of Urban Housing in Modern Dalian." In *Collected Thesis of the 5th Seminar on Modern Architectural History of China*. Wang Tan & Zhang Fuhe, eds. Beijing: China Construction Industry Publishing House, 1998.

Shen Hua, ed. *Shanghai Linong Houses*. Beijing: China Construction Industry Publishing House, 1993.

Sui Qingxi, ed. *A General Survey of China's Modern Architecture, Dalian Volume*. Beijing: China Construction Industry Publishing House, 1995.

Tang Zhenchang, ed. *The History of Shanghai*. Shanghai: Shanghai People's Publishing House, 1989.

Tchou, M. Thomas. *Outlines of Report on Housing and Social Conditions Among Industrial Workers in Shanghai*. Shanghai: The Industrial Department, National Committee, Y.M.C.A. of China, 1926.

Tu Shipin. *Grand View of Shanghai*. Siming: China Book and Journal Company, 1948.

Urban Economy Research Group in the department of Economy of Shanghai Social Science Academy. *The Evolution of Slums in Shanghai*. Shanghai: Shanghai People's Publishing House, 1962.

Wang Shaozhou. *Urban Architecture of Modern Shanghai*. Nanjing: Jiangsu Science and Technology Publishing House, 1989.

Wang Shaozhou & Chen Zhimin. *Linong Architecture*. Shanghai: Shanghai Science and Technology Publishing House, 1987.

Wang Tan, ed. *Collected Thesis of the 3rd Seminar on Modern Architectural History of China*. Beijing: China Construction Industry Publishing House, 1991.

Wang Tan & Zhang Fuhe, eds. *Collected Thesis of the 5th Seminar on Modern Architectural History of China*. Beijing: China Construction Industry Publishing House, 1998.

Summary of Plan for Constructing Shack Dwelling Areas. 1937.

Wu Jiang. *Architectural History of A Hundred Years in Shanghai*. Shanghai: Tongji Publishing House, 1997.

Wu Wenhui. *An Investigation on Nanjing's Families Living in Shacks*. Nanjing: Department of Sociology at Central University, 1935.

Xu Feipeng, ed. *A General Survey of China's Modern Architecture, Qingdao Volume*. Beijing: China Construction Industry Publishing House, 1992.

Xue Yongli. "Evolution of Slum Areas in Shanghai." In *Real Estate Business in Old Shanghai*. (Selected Historical Accounts of Past Events of Shanghai, vol.64). Shanghai: Shanghai People's Publishing House, 1990.

Yang Bingde. *China's Modern Cities and Architecture*. Beijing: China Construction Industry Publishing House, 1993.

Yang Songlin, ed. *A General Survey of China's Modern Architecture, Chongqing Volume*. Beijing: China Construction Industry Publishing House, 1993.

Zhang Song. "An Analysis of the Character of Modern Shanghai." In *Collected Thesis of the 4th Seminar on Modern Architectural History of China*. Wang Tan & Zhang Fuhe, eds. Beijing: China Construction Industry Publishing House, 1993.

Zhang Zhongli. *Research on Modern Shanghai City*. Shanghai: Shanghai People's Publishing House, 1992.

Zhu Bangxing, Hu Linge & Xu Sheng. *Industries and Employees in Shanghai*. Shanghai: Shanghai People's Publishing House, 1980.

Zhu Jiancheng. *"Rising of Real Estate Business in Old Shanghai."* Real estate Business in Old Shanghai (Selected Historical Accounts of Past Events of Shanghai, vol.64). Shanghai: Shanghai People's Publishing House, 1990.

Zhu Maocheng. *A Survey of the Conditions of Workers and Their Housing.* Shanghai: National Workers' Union of China Christian Youth Society Publishing House, 1926.

Zou Yiren. *Studies on Population Change in Old Shanghai.* Shanghai: Shanghai People's Publishing House, 1980.

Part Two:

"Carrying Out the Policy of Putting Emphasis on City Construction." *People's Daily.* August 11, 1954.

"Decision on Several Issues about Enhancing the Construction Work of New Industrial Areas and New Industrial Cities." May 8, 1956.

The Office of Industrial and Civil Construction of Institute of Building Science. "Development Trend of Housing Structures." *Journal of Architecture* 1 (1960): 32-35.

"On the Nature and Policies of Urban House Property and Rent." *People's Daily.* Xinhua letter box. April 25, 1949.

"Opposing Waste in Housing Construction." *People's Daily.* March 28, 1955.

"Some Opinions on Strengthening Basic Construction Management." Endorsed by the State Council, June 1973.

"Strengthening the Construction of New Industrial Areas." *People's Daily.* August 13, 1954.

"Under the Mao Zedong Banner." *Red Flag.* July 18, 1958.

Bi Baode. *Studies on China's Real-estate Market.* Beijing: Chinese People's University Press, 1994.

Bo Yibo. "Opposing Extravagance and Waste, Guaranteeing the Quick, Better and Economical Completion of Capital Construction Projects." June 30, 1955.

Cai Derong. *Research on Housing System Reform in China's Cities and Towns.* Beijing: China Financial and Economic Publishing House, 1987.

Central Committee of CCP. "Decision of the Central Party Committee on practicing strict economy." July 4, 1955.

Chen Guangting. "Urban Housing Issues in Contemporary China." In *Challenges in Urban Housing in China.* Beijing: Beijing Science and Technology Publishing House, 1994.

Chen Jiao. "Socialist Realism is a Correct Method in Socialist Architectural Creation." *Journal of Architecture* 5 (1982): 43–48.

Chen Zhaoyong. "Design of the People's Commune of Beiguan District in Shenyang." *Journal of Architecture* 11 (1958): 31–33.

Deng Qing. "Transformation of Urban Social Structure and the Housing Problem." Doctoral dissertation of Beijing University, 1995. Unpublished.

Design Bureau of the Ministry of Construction and Engineering of the Central Party Committee. "Standard design work for the past three years." Material from the national standard design conference of the Design Bureau of the Ministry of Construction and Engineering of the Central Party Committee. February 12, 1954.

Ding Baoxun. "On the Standard Design of the Second Phase of the 55-6 Housing Development." *Journal of Architecture* 2 (1955): 24.

Dong Jianhong. "Several Issues of Urban Construction During the First Five-Year Plan Period." *Journal of Architecture* 3 (1955).

Editorial Committee of the Construction History of Beijing. *Beijing's Urban Construction Since the Founding of the People's Republic of China.* Beijing, 1985. Internal publication.

Editorial Department of Editorial Committee of the Urban Development History of Beijing. *Materials about Beijing's Urban Development Since the Founding of the People's Republic of China, VI.* 1993.

Guo Shutian, Liu Chunbin et al. *China That Has Lost Its Balance.* Hebei People's Publishing House, 1990.

Hu Shide. "Progress and Prospects in Industrialization of Housing Construction in Beijing." Beijing: Science and Information Centre of China Architectural Center, 1993.

Hua Lanhong. "The Design of Xinfucun Residential Area in Beijing." *Journal of Architecture* 3 (1957): 16–35.

Institute of Architectural Design under the Institute of Building Science, State Construction Commission "Appraisal of Four Building Systems of Housing." *Journal of Architecture* 2 (1979): 4–5, 20.

Ji Ping. "Discussions on the Layout of Residential Buildings." *Journal of Architecture* 2 (1956): 9.

Jin Oubu. "Architectural Design Must Reflect the Great Need of the Development of People's Commune in Cities." *Journal of Architecture* 11 (1958): 13.

Li Fuchun. "Practice Strict Economy and Strive to Complete the Construction of Socialism." Vice-Premier's Report at the Conference of High-ranking Cadres. June 13, 1955.

Li Yongguang. "Some Problems and Discussions Concerning Current Standard Design of Housing." *Journal of Architecture* 2 (1956): 9.

Li Jianhua. "Designs of the Buildings Built With 'the Materials Other Than the Four Materials' in Harbin." *Architectural Design* 4 (1958): 7–9.

Liubin Tuoniefu. "The Planning and Construction in Urban Residential Areas." *Journal of Architecture* 1 (1958): 10–15.

J. Maikefakuer and Fei Zhengqing. *Cambridge History of the People's Republic of China, 1949–1965.* Beijing: China Social Sciences Publishing House, 1990.

Lu Qixian. "Experimental Projects of Assembling Large Scale Block Masonry System Housing." *Journal of Architecture* 9 (1958): 1–3.

Lu Qixian, Shen Zhaopeng and Jin Chen. "The Design of the No.1 Scheme of Standard Apartment Building in Beijing." *Journal of Architecture* 3 (1958): 29–32.

Min Yulin. "Planning and Design for Large-scale Construction of Low-rise Urban Housing." Post-graduate thesis of Architecture Department of Tsinghua University. 1955. Unpublished.

"Notice on Strengthening the Management of Urban Maintenance Expenses." Issued by the State Planning Commission, the State Construction Commission and the Ministry of Finance. December 22, 1973.

State Statistics Bureau. *Statistics Yearbook of China, 1984.* Beijing: China Statistics Publishing House, 1984.

Sun Jian. *The Economic History of the People's Republic of China (from 1949 to the early 1990s).* Beijing: The Publishing House of the People's University of China, 1992.

Sun Qinghua. *Housing Reform and the Psychology of Housing.* Beijing: China Construction Industry Publishing House, 1991.

Tomokiyo Takakatu. "The Function of the Living Room and the Development of Apartments with a Living Room," transl Lin Jianping. *Journal of Architecture* 8 (1995): 41–44.

Wang Dingzeng. "Studies on the Design and Quality Standard of Residential Areas in Shanghai." *Journal of Architecture* 7 (1959): 13–36, 39.

———. "The Planning and Design of Caoyang Xincun Residential Area in Shanghai." *Journal of Architecture* 2 (1956): 3–6.

Wang Dingzeng & Qian Xuezhong. "Some Opinions on the Building of High-rise Housing in Shanghai." *Journal of Architecture* 4 (1980): 34–41.

Wang Hua. "Discussions on the Planning and Design of Residential Areas." *Journal of Architecture* 5 (1956): 23–29.

Wang Huabin. "Improving the Level of Design in Residential Buildings." *Journal of Architecture* 2 (1962): 14–22.

Wang Jiye. *China's Contradiction of the Dual Economic Structure and the Strategic Choice of Industrialization.* Beijing: China Planning Publishing House, 1996.

Wang Shouju. "Research into the Design of Apartments with Livingrooms (Ting)." *Journal of Architecture* 4 (1978): 27.

Wang Sijun, ed. *The Study of the Regional Development of China's Urbanization.* Beijing: Publishing House of Higher Education, 1996.

Wang Xiaoming. *Chronicle of Events (1949–1986), Construction and Management of Modern Urban Housing in China.* Wuhan: Wuhan Engineering University Press, 1988.

Wang Ye & Chen Qingzhuang. "Studies on Several Problems in the Planning and Design of Residential areas in Shanghai." *Journal of Architecture* 6 (1960): 21–30.

Yang Tingbao. "Report on the Fourth Congress of International Architects' Association." *Journal of Architecture* 2 (1955): 69–82.

Zhang Bingchen, Chen Jiyuan & Zhou Xixing, eds. *China's Path Toward Urbanization.* Harbin: Heilongjiang People's Publishing House, 1991.

Zhao Dexin, ed. *A History of Economy of the People's Republic of China, 1949–1966.* Henan: Henan People's Publishing House, 1988.

Zheng Shounan, Zhang Ming. "Introduction of the 1964 Experimental Project of the Large Wall Panel System Housing in Shanghai." *Journal of Architecture* 8 (1964): 1–3.

Zhou Jinxiang. "Standard Design in Architecture." In *Architectural Yearbook of China, 1984–1985.* Beijing: China Construction Industry Publishing House, 1985.

Zhou Yixing. *Urban Geography.* Beijing: Commercial Press, 1997.

Zhu Yaxin. "Housing Development and the Design of Small Size Apartments." *Journal of Architecture* 2 (1962): 26.

Xu Tianfeng. "The Design of the Socialist Big Family Building in Hongshunli in Tianjing." *Journal of Architecture* 10 (1958): 34–35.

Part Three:

Bai Demao. "A Review on the Awarded Schemes in Beijing Tayuan Neighborhood Planning Competition." *Journal of Architecture* 5 (1981): 7.

———. "A New Temptation In Neighborhood Planning." *Journal of Architecture* 5 (1981): 7.

Bai Demao & Shou Zhenhua. "The Continuity of Urban Space—Fuqiang Xili Neighborhood, Beijing." *Journal of Architecture* 10 (1988): 43–47.

Bao Jiasheng. "SAR Housing Planning and Design." *Journal of Architecture* 2 (1985): 62–66.

Cao Hongtao & Chu Chuanheng. *Urban Construction of Contemporary China.* Beijing: China Social Sciences Publishing House, 1990.

Chen Huaning. "Temptations of High-rise High-density Housing Design." *Journal of Architecture* 1 (1985): 30–32.

China Architecture Standardization Design Institute. "A Selected Collection of New Concept Schemes of Brick-Concrete Structure Housing." Internal publication, 1984.

China Planning Research Institute. *Residential Area Planning.* Beijing: China Construction Industry Publishing House, 1984.

Deng Qing. "Transformation of Urban Structure and the Housing Problem." Ph.D Dissertation of Beijing University. 1995. Unpublished.

Fu Xiurong. "Landscape, Form, Technology—the Design of Haijing High-rise Apartment in Huaqiaochen, Shenzhen." *Journal of Architecture* 8 (1994): 29–33.

Gu Zhongtao. "Yandang High-rise Residential Building, Shanghai." *Journal of Architecture* 3 (1986): 52–53.

Housing Research Institute of Beijing Architectural Design Institute. "Xibahe High-rise Residential Building, Beijing." *Journal of Architecture* 11 (1989): 15.

Hu Dejun. "My Opinion on the Design of the New Concept Project." *Journal of Architecture* 2 (1984): 10.

Huang Hui. "Catch up the New Era—Inspiration of the Human Habitat Research Seminar, 1994." *Journal of Architecture* 4 (1995): 6–9.

Jing Tihua. *The Economy of China—Growth and Fluctuation*. Beijing: Beijing Publishing House, 1994.

Lei Mutai. "Discussion on Duplex Residential Building Design." *Journal of Architecture* 3 (1986): 56–57.

Lu Youjie. *Live-in-Peace Social Housing Project: The System of Social Security Commodity Housing*. Beijing: China Construction Publishing House, 1996.

Lü Junhua. "Design of Terraced Garden Housing System." *Journal of Architecture* 12 (1984): 15–17.

Ma Yunyu. "Case Study of Resident Designed Housing." *Journal of Architecture* 11 (1993): 39–43.

Ma Yunyu & Qi Yu. "A Review of a High-rise Residential Tower." *Journal of Architecture* 11 (1997): 17.

Miao Leru. *Public Reserve Funds and Housing Consumption Credit*. Beijing: China Goods and Materials Press, 1996.

Shanxi Architectural Design Institute. *Urban Housing Design*. Beijing: China Architectural Publishing House, 1983.

Shen Jiren. "Review of Neighborhood Planning in Recent Years in Beijing." *Journal of Architecture* 2 (1983): 9–17.

Wang Feng. "Introduction of a 20-storey Residential Building at Zhongshannanhu, Shanghai." *Journal of Architecture* 3 (1986): 54–55.

Yang Lu & Wang Yukun. *The Housing Reform: Theoretical Introspection and Realistic Selection*. Tianjin: Tianjin People's Publishing House, 1992.

Yao Jinling. "A Group of High-standard Apartments for Returned Overseas Chinese—Design of Aijian Apartments." *Journal of Architecture* 1 (1985): 25–27.

Ye Weijun. *Tentative Research on the Chinese Way of Urbanization—China Urban Infrastructure Construction*. Beijing: China Zhanwang Press, 1988.

Ye Rutang. "Status Quo and Development of Housing in China." *China Construction* 7 (1987): 3.

Ye Yonglie. *The Battle of the Housing Market*. Fudan: Fudan University Press, 1997.

Yue Mincheng. "Challenge of Modern Family Life in Urban Housing Design." *Journal of Architecture* 9 (1985): 54–56.

Zhang Feifei. "Standardization and Diversification of Housing Design in Tianjin." *Journal of Architecture* 6 (1982): 9–15.

Zhang Kaiji. "Improve Housing Design to Save Construction Land." *Journal of Architecture* 6 (1978): 22–23.

Zhang Kaiji. "Multiple-floor or High-rise: Controversy on High-density Housing Construction." *Journal of Architecture* 11 (1990): 2–5.

Zheng Naigui & Hu Huiyuan. "Our Opinion on High-rise Residential Buildings." *Journal of Architecture* 3 (1981): 40–42.

Zhu Jianda. *Contemporary Residential Area Planning in the World*. Beijing: China Construction Industry Publishing House, 1984.

Zhu Jianhong. "The First Step to Success: Report on the Establishment of Public Reserve Funds for Housing in Shanghai." *People's Daily*. June 20, 1995.